£2.50

D1824669

SOCCER
in the dock

A History of British Football Scandals 1900 to 1965

SOCCER
in the dock
A History of British Football Scandals 1900 to 1965

SIMON INGLIS

Willow Books
Collins
8 Grafton Street, London W1
1985

Willow Books
William Collins Sons & Co Ltd
London . Glasgow . Sydney . Auckland
Toronto . Johannesburg

First published 1985
All rights reserved
© Simon Inglis 1985

British Library Cataloguing in Publication Data

Inglis, Simon
Soccer in the dock.
1. Soccer − Great Britain − History − 20th century
I. Title
796.334′0941   GV944.G7

ISBN 0 00 218162 2

Set in Melior
by Ace Filmsetting Ltd, Frome, Somerset
Printed and bound in Great Britain by
Robert Hartnoll Ltd, Bodmin, Cornwall

Contents

	Acknowledgements	vi
	Introduction	vii
1	Soccer in the Dock	1
2	Edwardians Exposed	8
3	'Knocker' in the Dock	31
4	Dear Sir, I Must Protest	56
5	Getting the Right Result	63
6	Arthur Kingscott and the Rebounding Ball	80
7	'A Little Bit of Folly in the World'	93
8	The Last Straw	116
9	Dear Sir, I Must Protest Again . . .	140
10	'Please Sir, Can We Have Our Club Back?'	156
11	Power to the People	176
12	Could it Happen Now?	209
	Bibliography	212

Acknowledgements

Many people have helped in the compilation of this book, not least the countless journalists who, over the years, have withstood considerable opposition to expose bribery, corruption and foul play within football. Wherever possible I have tried to acknowledge their researches and their newspapers within the text.

To enable me to find all the references I needed I am deeply indebted to the staff at the British Museum's newspaper library in Colindale, London. The local libraries in Camden, Leeds, Manchester and Middlesbrough have also been helpful.

I should like to point out that the Football League, the Football Association and the Professional Footballers' Association co-operated with me fully in my research, allowing me free and unhindered access to their files and records. Considering the sensitive nature of some of the material their co-operation was very much appreciated.

I thank also the following for their background information, advice and statistics; David Barber (FA), Cliff Butler (Manchester United), Alex Chaplin, Ken Chisholm, Jack Ditchburn, Tommy Graham (William Hill Organisation), David Green, John Harding, Jimmy Hill, Alan Hindley, Geoffrey Kingscott, John Litster, Cliff Lloyd, James Middlesmass, John Roberts (*Daily Mail*), Sir Stanley Rous, Len Shackleton, Jack Steedman (Clydebank FC) and not least the former footballers and their relatives who have all passed on information freely.

For giving me the encouragement to complete the manuscript in a manner befitting the computer age I thank my 'user-friendly' brother, Jonathan Inglis, and for her toleration, support and help during the past year my heartfelt thanks as ever to Jackie Spreckley.

Finally, I am extremely grateful to Edward Grayson, author of *Sport and the Law*, for his vetting of the manuscript and his many words of widsom and experience. I only hope that this book adds some weight to his admirable endeavours.

Introduction

'**E**VERYONE knows things go on. Everyone that is, except the English. They are so honest, they expect honesty of all others.'

So said the former Dutch and World Cup international referee Leo Horn, speaking to *The Sunday Times* in June 1973. And compared with so many other footballing nations the English, and all the British, are remarkably free from taints of corruption. Indeed, when we consider the bribery scandals which have affected football in Italy, Spain, Belgium and Hungary since 1970 the British scene seems almost angelic. Furthermore, when we have found guilty men in British football their punishments have usually been considerably more severe than those imposed abroad.

But we should never be complacent. There is always a danger that if we sweep the unfavourable snippets of our soccer history under a carpet of respectability we, and future generations, will forget just how susceptible and fragile our national sport can be. The words of C. B. Fry are no less relevant today than they were in 1911, when he said, 'In football it is widely acknowledged that if both sides agree to cheat, cheating is fair.'

Soccer in the Dock therefore is a history of some of the scandals, legal wrangles and, I hasten to add, the more whimsical controversies affecting British football between 1900 and 1965. The 'dock' may be that of a court of law, it may be that of an FA or Football League commission of enquiry.

Sometimes there have been criminal intentions, often there have been allegations of the most serious nature, but always, always, always there has been the major problem of finding evidence. Not just rumours or anonymous letters, but concrete evidence, good enough for a judge. Throughout our history there are examples of players and officials providing information one minute then refusing to acknowledge or put it in writing the next. 'If you repeat this conversation I shall deny it ever took place' has, unfortunately, been all too common a cry.

For several years before 1915, however, it was widely believed that as far as football's internal system of justice was concerned, evidence hardly mattered at all. In 1884 the FA passed a rule which was its way of circumventing such an obstacle. The rule said:

'The Committee . . . may call upon the clubs or individuals charged with offending against the rules, to prove to the satisfaction of the Committee that the offence has not been committed, and failing such satisfactory proof the clubs or individuals shall be adjudged guilty of the offence . . . The Committee shall have power to call upon any club or player to produce any books, letters or documents of any kind that the Committee may desire.'

In other words, a player or a club was 'guilty until proved innocent', and what is more, the burden of proof rested upon the defendant. This was, of course, contrary to the most ancient tenet of English law – that a man is innocent until proved guilty – but for reasons which I hope will become clear, no one in the game ever saw fit to challenge this one, iniquitous rule (fortunately, the FA dropped it after the First World War).

Herein lies a central theme of *Soccer in the Dock*. The Football League is a member of the Football Association. Its rules are secondary to the parent body. Rules passed by both the FA and the Football League are internal rules only and are forever subject to the higher law of the land. In reading this book it is important not to blur this distinction between FA and Football League rules on one level, and the law on another.

So, the FA may discipline a player for perhaps an obscene gesture or remark to the crowd, but unless members of the public or the police decide to take action against the player, the law would not intervene (the same goes for tennis players at Wimbledon). Similarly, if the FA passes a rule which appears to be challengeable under the law, it does not necessarily mean someone in the game is going to make that challenge. In 1900 for example a rule was passed by the English FA (but not in Scotland) which restricted a footballer's income to a specified maximum. Another rule, passed in 1891, said that a player could receive a maximum signing-on bonus of only £10.

These rules were quite without precedent or equal in any other sphere of English life, yet they survived until 1961 and 1958 respectively, simply because until the late 1950s not only was opposition to them so weak and fragmented, but also the idea of taking football's ruling bodies to court seemed somehow anathema. 'Sport' and 'the law' just did not mix, and so in most cases while the game's administrators jealously guarded their own control, free of judicial interference, any complainants held back for fear of rocking the boat.

Their reticence was understandable. In March 1912 the Players' Union all but made itself bankrupt by unsuccessfully challenging Aston Villa (but really the FA) over the retain and transfer system. It needed courage, money and extremely good legal advice to take on the might of the game's administrators, however just the cause.

On the other hand, there was always a tendency to blame only the FA or the Football League for long-resented restrictions, but as I hope to illustrate in *Soccer in the Dock*, it was often individual club chairmen who voted for these rules at annual meetings, against the advice of the administrators, and then promptly went home and broke those same rules time after time. Commenting on the 1884 rule I referred to above concerning evidence, the noted League official Charles Sutcliffe wrote, 'It is not easy to justify, and it is a matter of serious surprise to me that the clubs ever consented to it.'

In such cases however, hypocrisy rather than any criminal offence was the outcome. When two Sunderland directors were banned in 1957 for making 'illegal' payments to players, they were contravening League regulations, not breaking the law.

Of course, there have been cases when clubs or players have broken regulations and the law at the same time. For example, 'fixing' the result of a game for betting purposes is not only against FA rules but might also be construed as conspiring to defraud a bookmaker. Yet because of their almost obsessive desire to prevent football's name from being dragged through the courts, football administrators in the past have not always alerted the police or the Director of Public Prosecutions. Perhaps they felt – rightly in many instances – that their own punishments were enough. On many other occasions the police have been informed, only for them to drop the case through lack of evidence.

Thus, among several inequalities which litter this history, we find in 1963 one footballer banned for life by the FA for accepting a bribe, while in 1964 another player committing the same offence is not only banned but imprisoned as well.

Soccer in the Dock is also an account of changing attitudes. The 'dock' is sometimes therefore one of my own making, in which the game itself becomes the defendant.

There are several famous football scandals I have not examined in this book, mainly because they have been well recorded elsewhere. Among these I would include the expulsion of Leeds City in 1919 (see *Herbert Chapman, Football Emperor* by Stephen Studd, London, Peter Owen 1981, and *Huddersfield Town 72 Years On* by George S. Binns, H.T.A.F.C. 1984) and Arsenal's highly controversial 'promotion' to Division One in 1919 (see, not surprisingly, *And the Spurs Go Marching On . . .* by Phil Soar, Hamlyn 1982 and *Forward Arsenal!* by Bernard Joy, London 1952).

There are other scandals which are much better known but I feel have little to do with football. Among these I would include just about every scandal involving the personal lives of managers and players. To those who were hoping to read about the lives and loves of Best, Allison,

Docherty *et al* I apologize in advance.

There are other subjects, such as drug-taking among players, the players' battle for decent wages and freedom of contract, and alleged corruption at boardroom level in the past twenty years which demand more space than would have been possible here, and I have deliberately ended my study with the bribery scandals exposed by the *People* in 1963–64. The various financial trials and tribulations of clubs like Port Vale, Peterborough, Derby, Wolves, Bristol City and Southend are therefore not examined. Nor is the Eastham case of 1963.

Readers will note my heavy reliance on newspaper sources, and in part *Soccer in the Dock* is as much a passing review of football journalism as of the game itself. Although actual football reporters were responsible for only a few of these stories – they tended to leave the controversial bits to news men – we owe a great debt to certain newspapers for their investigative work in exposing some of the real ills in our game. To *The Times* we owe much for its constant supply of provocative and often sanctimonious editorials and letters.

Finally, we must not forget those judges, bishops, Lord Mayors and Members of Parliament whom we encounter along the way; vital characters in any half-decent British scandal, footballing or otherwise.

There will be people within the game who might question my motives in writing this book and ask, what is the point of reappraising these forgotten scandals and court cases? My aim is most certainly not to blacken the good name of British football. *Soccer in the Dock* is a history – a history of one small, but important part of the national sport. It is not a comment upon the contemporary game.

History can teach us many things, but if this book can achieve anything it will be to remind us that however delightful and glorious those bygone years of football may seem, there were many victims, many fallen men and many injustices perpetrated along the way. I hope also to show that despite the inequalities, the corruption and the hypocrisy which has coloured certain events in the past, football has survived remarkably strongly.

Part of the game's strength, I hope, is the ability to understand its own history, and especially those darker moments, so that with care and vigilance they will not be repeated.

London
March 1985

1
Soccer in the Dock

ON 5 January 1912 the chairman of Southern League Norwich City, Mr Pyke, received a letter with a Blackburn postmark. This was hardly a surprise because eight days later City were due to play mighty Blackburn Rovers of the First Division in a FA Cup match. Perhaps the letter contained some tickets or details of the arrangements.

But it was nothing of the sort. The letter was signed, apparently, by the Blackburn Rovers goalkeeper Alfred Robinson. Mr Pyke read in amazement:

Dear Chairman of Directors,

I know you will be greatly surprised on receiving this letter from me, but after seriously considering my position I decided to make you an offer regarding your Cup tie with the Rovers at Blackburn, so I am making this offer providing my conditions are strictly carried out:–

(1) that I will make two or three slips which will enable your forwards to score and make it a draw if possible

(2) as it is not necessary to let the players know anything, advise your centre-forward to keep well up, and I will do my utmost to enable you to share in a replay without causing any suspicion whatsoever

(3) that I must not be interviewed by anyone whatever

(4) that your final reply must be sent to me as addressed by Saturday morning, when I will call for it, as we are probably going to Blackpool after our match with Middlesbrough on Saturday, January 6

(5) I will undertake to benefit your club financially on your promise to send me a £5 note with your reply and a further sum of £15 on January 15, providing you are satisfied that I have done as promised, and the match is a draw

(6) I think my offer reasonable, therefore I cannot entertain any other conditions whatever. You have no need to be afraid of being found out, and I ask you to destroy this letter after the match.

If I don't prove myself as I have promised, ask to see me, also Mr Middleton (the Rovers secretary), as soon as the match is over, and I will be responsible for your £5 to be returned at once.

The Norwich chairman was flabbergasted. Here was the goalkeeper of one of the leading sides in the First Division – Rovers won the Championship that season – offering to throw an important Cup tie for £5 in advance and £15 later. Only two years before there had been a similar letter, sent to Burnley, also purportedly from a player offering to throw a Cup match. A subsequent enquiry proved the letter to have been a fake, but the culprit was never caught. Was this 'Alfred Robinson' letter a fake also?

Mr Pyke immediately wrote to Ewood Park, where Mr Middleton quickly confirmed that the Rovers goalkeeper had indeed written no such letter. The mention of Rovers going to Blackpool after the Middlesbrough match was a clever device to persuade Pyke that the correspondent was privy to the players' movements, but Middleton remembered that the trip had been mentioned in local newspapers.

So the police were consulted and on the advice of the Blackburn Chief Constable a trap was laid. Mr Pyke sent a postcard to 'Alfred Robinson' at the Head Post Office, Blackburn, informing him that a registered letter would follow, containing an enclosure.

Plain clothes policemen then began a vigil at the post office, to see if their man would turn up. For a few days they were disappointed – perhaps the guilty man had become suspicious, perhaps it was all a hoax – but on the Saturday morning of the Cup tie with Norwich a man did call at the post office and ask for a letter for Alfred Robinson. He was definitely not the Blackburn goalkeeper, or any professional footballer, judging from his poor and tattered dress. Immediately the letter was handed over, PC Rigby of Blackburn Constabulary confronted him with the charge.

'Quite right', came the forlorn reply. 'I admit it.'

That afternoon the Cup match went according to form, Rovers winning 4-1 (they actually went on to the semi-final, only to lose to West Bromwich Albion), and the public knew nothing of the 'Alfred Robinson' letter until it was revealed in the newspapers on Monday morning.

Richard McNeall was twenty-seven, a locked-out cotton weaver of Stephen Street, Mill Hill, who was struggling to feed himself and his wife. The letter to Pyke had seemed like an easy way of getting funds in a hurry. He admitted to having sent a similar letter to Burnley a couple of years earlier, and was sentenced to two months' imprisonment.

A sorry tale, but only one of several unfortunate cases involving football in the decades before and after the First World War. It was not that there were more dishonest folk about in that era as the fact that football, in its infancy as a major industry, was ripe for exploitation, both from within and without.

The football authorities were only just beginning to come to terms with commercialism, while players and officials were themselves often rough and ready in their attitude towards the game. Of course there are bad elements in every industry, but the growth in football had been so rapid that, almost invariably, there were opportunities aplenty for the sharp-witted to prosper. Here then are just a few stories which illustrate the manifold ways in which unscrupulous individuals used the game for their own ends.

Betting was at the root of much of this corruption. Take for example John Harlock and Solomon Isaacs of Forest Gate, Essex; two former insurance agents of previously impeccable character, caught by the betting bug and turned to ruin.

In Autumn 1910 they wrote to the famous Bradford trophy manufacturers, Messrs Fattorini and Sons – who were months later to design and create the present FA Cup – and on behalf of two clubs from Leyton and Romford ordered eighty-three gold and silver medals. Such orders were quite common, so why should Fattorini's be suspicious? Every club wanted medals in those days and new league and cup competitions were starting up all the time.

Of course neither club existed, the bill was unpaid and both men obtained an easy £64 by pawning the medals. In December they also received prison sentences of three months each.

McNeall and this unfortunate pair were just two examples of football-related crimes before 1914. After the First World War there were others, equally simple.

In Newcastle for example, on Good Friday 1926 and Boxing Day 1927, United fans emerging from St James' Park were able to buy a printed sheet which gave all the afternoon's football results – so much quicker than the normal channels available on public holidays, when no football finals were printed. But as unwitting purchasers soon discovered on Good Friday, only one of the thirty-seven results given was correct, and that was purely coincidental. Robert Harrison, the vendor, had simply invented and printed all the results hours before.

Similarly, in Ebbw Vale in 1923, local sports journalists became aware of a man selling results sheets before their own Saturday final editions could come out. Suspecting that the only possible source of such a fast service was their own Exchange Telegraph and Press Association information they decided to lay a trap to catch the suspected mole within their midst. A false result was circulated in the newspaper office, and sure enough it appeared unaltered on the rival's printed sheet. A local man, twenty-three-year-old L. Berni was ordered to stop 'pilfering football results'.

Souvenirs and programmes provided a wondrous free-for-all for unscrupulous traders, since few official club shops existed until long after the Second World War. Highbury in particular suffered from unofficial programme sellers during the early 1930s, and there were always opportunities for forging tickets. A London man, Cecil Hall, even went to the lengths of writing to all the provincial League clubs in 1922, signing himself as Charles Clegg of the FA.

Hall instructed the clubs to send cash within twenty-four hours if they wanted Cup Final tickets. Incredibly, even though he did not use the FA's official address, some clubs fell for the ruse. Others did not, and Hall was eventually arrested. (He was not as devious as another man who, in modern times, advertised in the national press: 'Cup Final seats at £15 each'. Purchasers were shocked to be sent in return a small canvas stool from Woolworths, worth £3, with the words 'Cup Final' written on the seat.)

The range of opportunities for exploiting a public hungry for football and all its trappings was (and is) wide indeed. But these mis-demeanours were petty compared with the activities going on within the game. As FA enquiries into affairs at several clubs, particularly Manchester City and Middlesbrough between 1904 and 1911 showed (see Chapter Two), there were many instances of players and clubs breaking football's own, self-imposed rules.

If a club broke FA rules, however, it did not necessarily follow that a criminal offence had occurred. The law was not concerned if a player received over the maximum wage or if more than the maximum £10 signing-on bonus had been paid. But although the FA's restrictions on earnings went counter to much of the prevailing economic theory of the pre-war period – the idea of a wage ceiling was anathema to the late Victorian and Edwardian ideal of a free market economy – the FA had one major trump card: in order to play professionally a player had to be a member of the FA, and to be a member of the FA he had to abide by its rules.

Thus, whenever a player, official or any member of the FA was suspected of offering a bribe or of complicity in an arranged match, the case was dealt with under the FA's jurisdicition (as we shall see in the Billy Meredith affair in Chapter Two).

But there were several cases in the early history of the game when attempts to bribe players were made by people outside the game. Whenever this happened the matter was always referred to the police – after 1906 under the Prevention of Corruption Act – and the FA played no part in meting out justice.

In Scotland in 1924, for example, a major scandal erupted when two former professionals, one an international, were sentenced to sixty days hard labour for attempting to influence the result of a Second Division game between Bo'Ness and Lochgelly. John Browning, the former Scotland, Celtic, Chelsea, Dumbarton and Vale of Leven player was accused with Archibald Kyle, once of Rangers, Blackburn Rovers and Clyde, of going to the home of Bo'Ness player Peter Brown to offer him an inducement 'for failing to exercise his skill'.

A couple of days later they met Brown and another player, Thomas Anderson, who both appeared to take the offer seriously. In fact the Bo'Ness men had informed their manager and policemen were listening in to the conversation from a concealed position. Browning and Kyle arranged to meet the players at Glasgow's Queen Street station after the game and, in a nearby pub in Dundas Street, as £30 in notes was handed over, the police moved in.

This was a terrible blow to Scottish football, for both Browning and Kyle had only recently been famous names. Although it was soon established that they were only acting as front-men and that someone, almost certainly a bookmaker, had sent £200 in a plain envelope to Browning's bank in Alexandria, near Dumbarton, neither man would reveal their backers.

Two years later a traveller from Falkirk was sentenced to three months' imprisonment for attempting to bribe the Stenhousemuir goalkeeper J. Shortt. Donald Douglas was accused of approaching Shortt as he alighted from the Glasgow train at Larbert railway station, on his way to the home game against Broxburn United.

'I don't suppose you want to win the League,' Douglas was reported to have said.

'We're doing our best anyhow,' replied Shortt.

'There is £50 for you if you lose today's game,' said Douglas. As the court report put it, Shortt then told the man to 'go to a warm place'.

Douglas claimed in his defence that he had told Shortt another club was interested in signing him, and there would be a £50 bonus, but the court did not believe him and he was found guilty. For the record, Stenhousemuir won 6-2.

In February 1932 another former Scottish professional was accused of a bribery attempt. Gavin Hamilton, the ex-captain of Montrose, was charged with offering £40-50 to Montrose left-back David Mooney to fix the home match against Edinburgh City on 5 December 1931. Mooney told the Glasgow Sheriff Court that Hamilton had told him 'to lie down', and that if goals did not come quickly enough he should give away a penalty. Mooney's brother overheard the conversation and they both reported it. Hamilton received a sixty-day prison sentence.

England also had its share of bribery cases, but one in 1919 had an unusual twist in that the accused man had allegedly been paying players to win, rather than lose. Henry Thatcher, also known as G. Wilson, a bookmaker from East Dulwich, had offered two Millwall players,

Douglas Thomson and Richard Griffiths, £1 down with £3 to follow if Millwall beat Brentford.

'We are always out to win,' Griffiths had replied resentfully. Thatcher told them he had put £50 on Millwall to win at odds of 5-4, so the winnings would hardly have been great, and though both players refused to accept the inducement Thatcher insisted and thrust £1 notes in their pockets as he left.

Millwall won the game, but by then the manager had been told. Now under police instructions Thomson was told to arrange a meeting with Thatcher at the ABC shop adjacent to Westminster underground station. There, Thatcher asked Thomson to bring the Millwall goalkeeper and captain in on the act, with a promise of £15 each if Millwall won their next game. Again, a £1 note was tucked into Thomson's pocket.

The story, when told in Bow Street court, seemed most improbable, but Thomson was a Canadian with a good war record and no apparent interest or connection with betting. Thatcher therefore was given a three month sentence, but he appealed successfully and this was commuted to a £50 fine plus £100 costs. By paying players to win, Thatcher said, 'I did not realize I was doing anything seriously wrong.'

More convoluted were the proceedings which followed an attempt in 1913 to bribe the England and West Bromwich Albion captain and full-back Jesse Pennington, by a man variously known as Frederick Pater and Sam Johnstone. In the latter guise this middle-aged but distinguished looking man had entered Pennington's shop on the day before Albion's home match against Everton and offered him a bribe. This was tantamount to asking a vicar to blaspheme at the altar. Pennington's character was of the purest and strictest kind, yet the Albion man kept his cool and asked the visitor to put his offer in writing.

'November 28 – I, Sam Johnstone,' wrote the man, 'agree to present to Jesse Pennington £55 on the termination of the match played at West Bromwich on November 29 if the result is a draw or a loss – Sam Johnstone, 34, Cleveland Mansions, Brixton, London.'

The £55 was supposed to constitute £5 per man for the Albion team. Pennington immediately referred the matter to his chairman, Mr Bassett, and as in all the other cases we have seen, together with the police they set a trap. Meanwhile none of the other players were told and the match went ahead. By a complete coincidence it ended in a draw, and watched by the police Pennington went up to Johnstone, who was standing in the crowd, and asked him for the money. DetectiveBarker was on hand to make the arrest.

But the sixty-seven-year-old Johnstone, alias Pater, nearly got away with his crime on a legal technicality. When he was put in front of the

Smethwick Police Court a few days later his defence successfully argued that the proceedings had not been properly conducted. Under the Prevention of Corruption Act the consent of the Solicitor-General was needed to begin an action and this had not been obtained. Johnstone was therefore allowed to leave the court.

Outside, however, he was immediately rearrested, but, to everyone's amazement, under the name of Pascoe Bioletti. He seemed most anxious that this newly-revealed identity be kept secret, apparently because he was an actor. The charge against him was repeated, but another was added; that he had also tried to bribe the Birmingham captain Francis Womak.

A week later Bioletti alias Johnstone alias Pater was back in Smethwick Police Court, where it was revealed that he was the father of Wiliam Alfred Bioletti of Hove, Sussex, who carried on an extensive football coupon betting business based in Geneva, under the name of White Fisher. On Bioletti's person was found a book of football guessing coupons for a £5000 sweepstake on the FA Cup, organized by White Fisher.

The case eventually came to trial on 18 February 1914, at Staffordshire Assizes. Justice Lush presided and despite the defence's plea that Bioletti had already been acquitted of the same offences once before and could therefore not be put in peril again, sentence was passed – five months imprisonment in the second division. An apposite term for such a footballing offence.

But what of the cases of corruption within football clubs themselves which were investigated only within the confines of the FA and Football League and never reached the law courts?

The Edwardian era was full of them.

2
Edwardians Exposed

O NLY one issue remained unresolved on the final Saturday of the 1899–1900 season. Bury had won the Cup the week before, Aston Villa were assured of the Championship. The Wednesday and Bolton were already promoted to Division One and Glossop North End were definitely relegated to Division Two. But who would join Glossop?

Burnley were the favourites, and they travelled to Nottingham Forest on 28 April 1900 knowing that only a win would save them. That particular Saturday was also the day of the annual Forest sports competition, and with the Burnley team delayed until fifteen minutes after the scheduled kick off, the crowd at the City Ground had to wait until 5.30 p.m. for the vital game to begin.

When it ended Forest were comfortable 4-0 winners, and Burnely were relegated for the second time in the twelve-year history of the Football League. But the matter did not end there.

A few days later the Forest secretary, Mr Hallam, wrote to Frederick Wall at the FA to complain about the activities of the Burnley captain and goalkeeper, Jack Hillman, before the game. When the players entered the field, wrote Hallam, Hillman said to McPherson, the Forest captain: 'Look here, take this match easy today and we stand you £2 a man.'

McPherson replied, 'No, it is more than I dare do, and we are paid to play and go straight,' to which Hillman allegedly responded, 'Alright, I will see you at half-time.'

During the interval, when Burnley were 2-0 down, Hillman approached McPherson again. 'Look here,' he was supposed to have said, 'we will make that £5 each,' to which McPherson replied, 'No, if you want to do anything of that sort you had better see our committee.'

And so our tale of twentieth century soccer scandals truly begins on Wednesday, 9 May 1900, at the Old Boar's Head Hotel in Manchester, where a joint FA and Football League commission of enquiry met to investigate Mr Hallam's very grave allegations.

It was to be the first of many such enquiries into the errant behaviour of professional footballers, administrators and officials, and in some ways can also be interpreted as one sign that the end of football's own, golden Victorian era was over.

Shortly after the joint commission meeting in Manchester, though not because of it, the FA passed at its annual meeting a regulation limiting the wages of a professional footballer to a maximum of £4 a week. The League had tried to pass a similar rule as early as 1893, without success, but now that the FA had introduced it the League was able to implement the rule for the beginning of the 1901–02 season. How the late Queen Victoria, who died in January 1901 would have lamented this artificial limitation on her subjects' earnings, and rightly so, because for the next sixty years this one iniquitous but fiercely-defended rule was at the root of a dozen or more major soccer scandals in England and Wales.

Jack Hillman's concern had been to avoid relegation and therefore the threat of lower wages. Maximum wage or no, there was, at that time, no minimum wage either. Known to his fellow players as 'Happy Jack', Devon-born Hillman had started his career at Burnley before moving to Everton and then Dundee, where, during the 1897–98 season he was suspended by the club for allegedly 'not trying', although it was suspected that the real reason was because Dundee were bankrupt and could not afford his wages.

Hillman was a real character; at six foot and sixteen stone he was second only to his contemporary custodian, Billy 'Fatty' Foulke at Sheffield United. According to *The Manchester City Story* by Andrew Ward (Breedon Books 1984) he once made a bet to keep goal in a charity match using only one hand. His team won 1-0 and Hillman won his wager. Burnley brought him back to Lancashire for £130 and a year later Hillman gained his one and only England cap in England's 13-2 victory over Ireland at the newly-opened Roker Park.

But now in Manchester, charged with attempted bribery, Hillman found himself facing the wrath of some of the very men who selected him for that international; men such as Charles Clegg, the chairman of the FA, Frederick Wall, the secretary, J. J. Bentley of Manchester United (who, from 1892–1900, had been editor of *Athletic News*) and Charles Alcock, a former secretary of the FA and originator of the English (now FA) Cup. We should note some of these names well.

Clegg, an experienced lawyer, a director of both senior Sheffield clubs and a former Sheffield and England amateur footballer, tended to be the chief inquisitor. A tall and well built man then, he was known to have reduced many a professional to a perspiring wreck under questioning. But he was also a very moral, religious man and a fair judge who commanded wide respect.

Under close examination Jack Hillman admitted that he had used the words attributed to him by Mr Hallam, but he insisted 'It was all chaff', partly inspired by the fact that Forest themselves had been the subject of suspicion only a few weeks before. Forest had lost 8-0 to struggling

West Bromwich Albion, having beaten them 6-1 at Nottingham earlier in the season. Hillman claimed he had only asked McPherson jokingly for the same kind of favour.

The joke was not appreciated, however, because a week later at the Albion Hotel in Manchester the FA decided to ban Jack Hillman for one season. But for his previous good conduct, it was announced, Hillman would have been banned for life. Even so the Burnley goalkeeper stood to lose a promised benefit of £300, a year's wages, and the possibility of his future career in football (though as we shall see his career survived, albeit not without further controversial moments).

Burnley and their supporters meanwhile were outraged at Hillman's sentence and angry with Forest's behaviour. As the *Burnley Gazette* commented sarcastically, 'Notts Forest, with a recollection of their 8-0 defeat at West Bromwich so fresh in the public mind, would surely figure as worthy exponents of the purity gospel in football!'

If Hillman's approach was serious, and later events strongly suggest that if so he might well have been acting on the instructions of his manager or chairman, it did indicate to the FA that professional football needed to be closely monitored if it was not to become a pre-arranged farce, with money buying results and honours.

But bribery attempts were insignificant compared with the trouble created by the imposition of the maximum wage. Indeed, so irksome was the problem that in 1910 the FA handed over the regulation of wages to the Football League, soon after a players' strike had threatened in 1909.

At least seven clubs were investigated and punished for financial irregularities in the period between 1901 and 1911. They were Queen's Park Rangers, Sunderland, Manchester City, Glossop, Coventry City, Manchester United and Middlesbrough. Many other clubs were thought to have been guilty but escaped punishment.

For example, Fred Rinder, a prominent figure in the League and chairman of Aston Villa, was once asked to explain the term 'presents to players' which appeared alongside the sum of £320 in the club books. Brazenly, and with a smile, he said they were merely 'a few little trinkets'. Thus Villa escaped investigation into what looked suspiciously like illegal bonuses. Other clubs gave their players bogus jobs, such as working in the ticket office, or in one instance, as James Catton ('Tityrus' of *Athletic News*) recalled, as a professional checker of all the club's advertising posters. One professional recalled having to travel miles every week to his chairman's works, where he was listed as an employee, simply in order to collect his weekly 'wage'.

League clubs who refused to pay illegal wages were almost certainly, in the First Division at least, few and far between. Their most valuable talent, second only to skill on the pitch, was in laundering the accounts. As Billy Meredith, the Welsh outside right who played first class soccer from 1894–1924 once wrote, 'Of course clubs are not punished for breaking laws. They are punished for being found out.'

Meredith knew this only too painfully, because he played for Manchester City, one of the two clubs which seemed incapable of keeping secrets from the authorities. The other was Middlesbrough. Between them the two clubs were responsible for most of the major footballing scandals to erupt in the Edwardian era, as Tityrus once commented in *Athletic News*: 'Manchester City and Middlesbrough are like the poor. We always have them with us. It seems we cannot escape from them.'

But before we examine their various misdemeanours, we should study some of the other cases of the period to establish an idea of how strict – or arbitrary, some might say – the football authorities were.

Sunderland, for example, were fined £250 in October 1904 for paying bonuses, contrary to FA regulations. All the players were questioned and all but one admitted receiving extra payments. The directors and the club secretary, rather than the players, were suspended for periods ranging from one to three seasons.

One of the longest surviving and probably one of the most ignored rules in football held that players should receive a maximum signing-on fee of only £10. This amount was set by the League in 1891 and incredibly, it was not changed until 1958. Even in Edwardian Britain £10 was a pittance, if not an insult to a player who might well, if transferred, have to move his home and family for little more than the promise of a year's employment.

But although many players asked for more than £10 and received it, perhaps as money added on to their weekly wage, in the form of free accommodation or maybe even a partnership in a local business, not every club was prepared to break the rule. In 1908, for example, Everton reported to the FA a young Leicester Fosse player, R. F. Turner, who demanded in return for his signature the sum of £100. Since this was the first case recorded, the FA let Turner off lightly with a fine, but players were warned that any future breaches might lead to permanent suspension (Turner's wedding a year later was to have an unusual after-effect, as we see in Chapter Three).

George Parsonage of Fulham was by no means the only player not to heed that warning, but he was the only one we know to have been caught. The safest procedure, apparently, was to make sure first of all that the buying club did pay illegal bonuses (the players' grapevine would confirm this) and if so, to phrase one's enquiries in such a way as to avoid a straight demand for money.

Parsonage was wanted by Chesterfield, though he was not keen to move. The usual offer of a £10 signing-on fee was made, to which Parsonage replied, on his own admission, 'Make it fifty and I'll sign.' Chesterfield reported him, Parsonage claimed it was a joke, and once again the FA failed to laugh. George Parsonage received the harshest penalty within the FA's power – he was banned from football for life, deprived in an instant of his livelihood by one ill-considered remark – and despite a petition of 4000 signatures in his support the FA refused to alter their draconian stance.

Consider therefore the mood of the professional footballer in Edwardian England; employed by directors who mostly knew little of the game, limited in his earnings by a distant body of amateurs, performing weekly in front of thousands of people and yet subject apparently to the most arbitrary form of justice. Parsonage was allowed no legal representation at his hearing and was granted no appeal.

Thus was created the mould which was to govern the often awkward triangular relationship between the player, his club and the FA for the next six decades. In return for the 'privilege' of playing professionally the footballer could be shunted around the nation at the whim of his bosses, compensated for his inconvenience (or desperation for another job) by a mere £10, or, as often happened under the 'retain and transfer' system, prevented from seeking a move because his present club paid him the maximum wage and just felt like hanging on to him for whatever reason (this was broadly the cause of the Kingaby v Aston Villa case in 1912). Had it not been for illegal extras, many players might have been forced to give up, while those clubs who resisted breaking the rules often found it hard to sign up the best players.

For the authorities, determined that rich clubs should not buy a monopoly of talent, it was a never-ending and thankless task to keep the system in order, and it can be no coincidence that once the FA handed the responsibility of wage control over to the Football League the number of investigations dropped. After all, the League's Management Committee knew very well what was going on simply because it was often composed of club chairmen who were themselves breaking the rules. (After the First World War, apart from the somewhat harsh treatment meted out to Leeds City – expelled in 1919 for illegal payments – only minor punishments were handed out for wage irregularities until 1957, when Sunderland took the full force of the FA's pent-up anger with a £5000 fine, as we shall see in Chapter Eight.)

Manchester City's problems began in 1904, just after they had won the FA Cup. Briefly stated, City had been paying the players more than £4 a week, plus bonuses for wins and draws, which were also illegal at the time. 'What was the secret of success of the Manchester City team?' wrote Billy Meredith in 1919. 'In my opinion, the fact that the club put aside the rule that no player should receive more than £4 a week.' Meredith, a leading figure in the Players' Union, openly admitted that from 1902 he had been paid £6 a week and in the Cup-winning season 1903–04 had received an extra £53 in bonuses. 'The team delivered the goods and the club paid for the goods delivered, and both sides were satisfied,' he wrote.

But Manchester City were only partially found out, and that was because of an investigation into the affairs of Second Division Glossop, who had already been in trouble twice; in 1903 when their chairman and trainer were suspended for a year for having illegally approached a Newcastle Swifts player, and in January 1904 when their secretary received a similar punishment for making payments to an amateur. For their third offence, wholesale mismanagement and deception, they were fined £250, four directors were suspended for three seasons, the secretary was censured and six players were suspended for three months. Five of them had to change their status from amateur to professional (it was often possible to earn more as an amateur by receiving expenses).

While the FA examined Glossop's accounts they came across other suspicious information concerning the transfer of two players to Manchester City, Irvine Thornley and Frank Norgrove. As a result of a further lengthy enquiry, in October 1904 City were also fined £250, their Hyde Road ground was ordered to be shut for two home games, five directors were suspended, four for nearly three seasons, one for life, and Irvine Thornley was suspended for the rest of the season. But the FA had not been able to find or prove the payment of illegal wages or bonuses . . . yet.

A fair gauge of local reaction to City's punishment in 1904 came from *Athletic News*, a Manchester newspaper which invariably gave voice to the Football League's view rather than that of the FA, which was perceived, rightly or wrongly, as a Southern body dominated by amateurs.

City proclaimed their innocence and complained that they had not been given a fair chance to defend themselves. *Athletic News* blamed the affair squarely on the FA.

'The mistake was ever to pass such absurd rules,' it commented. Would Parliament ever pass a law forbidding any English worker from receiving more than £4 a week? It was the height of folly to meddle with wages. It was also unfair, said the newspaper, to punish the City fans by closing Hyde Road. They had committed no crime.

It should be added that at the same time the FA passed a rule forbidding players to wear shorts which did not cover the knee when standing upright. Perhaps the wittiest and most acerbic football writer of the period, 'Argus Junior' wrote in the *Birmingham Sports Argus* ('a journal of all manly pastimes') that the only reason for these rules which 'tampered with money and knickbockers' was 'so that the FA can justify its existence'.

Meanwhile Manchester City were, with difficulty, seeking out men of sufficient calibre who might wish to join their depleted board of directors, while one of the suspended directors, John Chapman, stood as a Conservative candidate in the local Ardwick Ward elections. In a fit of irrational fervour *Athletic News* urged all sports lovers to vote for him as a show of support for the club, though the electors saw differently and chose the Labour candidate instead.

City's next confrontation with the authorities was totally unexpected. For the most detailed account of the affair see John Harding's excellent biography of Billy Meredith, *Football Wizard* (Breedon Books, 1985). Suffice it to say here that the scandal arose out of investigations into two Manchester City games at the end of the 1904–05 season, when the club was challenging for the First Division title. Both games, at Goodison Park and Villa Park, had been marred by violence, the latter being particularly serious because it was alleged that Alex 'Sandy' Turnbull of Manchester City had been attacked by Villa players in the tunnel after the game.

For weeks afterwards the respective sporting newspapers of Liverpool, Manchester and Birmingham gave their own versions of the events, each one refuting the other's evidence. The Liverpool press accused City's Frank Booth of provoking his namesake, Tom Booth, in the Everton team, while Manchester commentators said that Everton's Booth had flattened his opponent quite brutally off the ball. The *Birmingham Sports Argus* accused Turnbull of striking Villa's mild-mannered captain Alec Leake, while the *Bolton Football Field* claimed that Leake had thrown mud at Turnbull, before hitting him when the referee was not looking.

Nevertheless, to neutral observers it certainly seemed strange that two normally good-tempered players, Tom Booth of Everton and Alec Leake of Villa, should have been involved in violent scenes against the same team. For over three months the footballing public awaited the FA's judgement. Would Villa Park be closed for a month because of stone-throwing incidents after the game? Would both Booths, Turnbull and Leake be suspended? Would Manchester City be fined once again? Most of all the newspapers asked, why were such apparently isolated cases of violence taking up so much of the FA's time and energy?

By mid-July the reason became apparent. A charge more serious than ever anticipated had been levelled against one of the clubs implicated, and a special commission had been appointed. Even so, no one in the country, however close to the game, could have expected the FA to reach the incredible conclusion it reached on Friday, 4 August 1905.

Overshadowing all the uproar over violent incidents was the announcement that Billy Meredith, Manchester City's captain and Welsh international outside right was to be suspended for one season for attempting to bribe the Aston Villa captain Alec Leake with £10. The FA elaborated no further, and Meredith, who had not figured in any of the violent scenes at either of the games, was suddenly and unexpectedly the subject of the greatest scandal British football had ever known.

The shattering nature of this disclosure can barely be appreciated today without assessing Meredith's reputation and standing in the football world at that time. The 'Prince of Dribblers' enjoyed an acclaim hardly less than subsequent idols such as Stanley Matthews or George Best, and his integrity and honour was no less regarded than that of Bobby Charlton. In short, he was one of the major footballing heroes of his time. But was he guilty?

'I am entirely innocent and am suffering for others,' was Meredith's first reaction.

Meanwhile, hardly surprisingly, the incidents for which the enquiry was originally set up were almost forgotten, but the FA did act on these too. The referees of the games at Goodison Park and Villa Park, Mr J. T. Howcroft and Mr R. T. Johns respectively, were both suspended for one month. Howcroft (who we meet again in Chapter Six) was criticized for 'his extraordinary feebleness in a critical match'. This was quite a blow for Jack Howcroft, a normally strict referee who was well known for having once stopped a match at West Ham in order to address some rowdies who questioned one of his decisions. His career survived however, and he went on to referee the 1920 Cup Final.

Tom Booth of Everton and Sandy Turnbull of Manchester City were suspended for one month by the commission, yet Alec Leake was not even mentioned, even though it had been plainly stated that Turnbull had been assaulted by Villa players after the game.

Small wonder therefore that in the eyes of many neutrals the FA appeared to bear a grudge against Manchester City, a nouveau riche club with no traditions. Villa, in contrast, were solidly reliable, brimming with honours and very much part of the football establishment. Some commentators noted caustically that Leake was an England international while the other players were not. Meredith meanwhile complained, 'Had I been anyone but a Welshman I should have been better dealt with.' But Harricus of *Athletic News* said the FA's methods had seemed 'un-English, most autocratic and arbitrary'.

One thing was certain, the football world had been thrown into confusion, and this was no better illustrated than by the comments of the normally decisive and authorititive Tityrus. In one tortuous sentence he leaned towards this conclusion:

> 'It is impossible to believe that a trained and experienced lawyer, a man accustomed to weigh the value of evidence, to compare discrepancies and estimate the worth of corroboration and circumstantial details like Mr J. C. Clegg, a man in whom the football world has such unbounded confidence, could make up his mind, in conjunction with his fellow commissioners, to suspend Meredith unless he was convinced beyond all probable shadow of doubt as to his guilt.'

But in his next few sentences Tityrus went on to suggest why there were 'so many reasons for Meredith not to have acted in this manner, apart altogether from his natural instincts as a man'. As 'a thoroughly respectable person' known for 'his careful life and thrift' Meredith would surely never jeopardise his forthcoming benefit for a £10 bribe. Of all the commentators, if Tityrus was undecided, the public must have been positively baffled.

Yet how simply all this speculation could have been avoided had the FA not always conducted its hearings in private. Argus Junior was particularly annoyed that the FA had made 'a pathetic claim' that there would not have been enough room for all the reporters. Without question this secrecy heightened an already general suspicion that FA justice was somehow improperly conducted.

Even when the FA did announce its verdicts there was rarely any explanation. This was infuriating to the public, and like a red rag to a bull for the press, who launched into a wave of rumour and supposition whenever a commission of enquiry met. The *Daily Dispatch* reported on the Meredith case that the whole nation was outraged by the lack of details, which enshrouded the affair in a 'Russian darkness'.

Though few could believe that Meredith was guilty – why, for example, had Leake not reported the incident straight after the match? – subsequent events were to prove that the FA had indeed been acting on solid information. It transpired that they had been tipped off by a noted Birmingham gentleman who happened to overhear Leake talking about Meredith's approach, which Leake had regarded as a futile and foolish gesture not worth reporting.

Had the matter rested there, albeit in a state of uncertainty, Manchester City with Meredith back in the fold a year later might well have gone on to greater glories. Instead, the twelve months of his suspension were dogged by friction between player and club, as Meredith persistently claimed wages and support while Manchester City grew increasingly nervous and irritated by their former star player. The outcome of this stormy relationship was that Meredith, either from desperation or spite, began disclosing titbits of information concerning illegal payments at Hyde Road. He even claimed that City had promised to pay him to keep quiet. For their part City were being closely watched by an FA auditor, Tom Hindle, who told the club in February 1906 to report Meredith to the FA for his improper conduct.

Regrettably, it all became rather sordid. City placed Meredith on the transfer list because of his insulting behaviour, while the FA decided to appoint another commission to investigate the club's affairs. In front of this new commission, which included Charles Clegg, Charles Crump and Daniel Woolfall, Meredith admitted everything – his guilt at Villa Park and his acceptance of illegal wages and bonuses. So the unthinkable really had occurred. Billy Meredith, idol of thousands, had offered a bribe.

Meredith also claimed that it was the City manager, Tom Maley, who had instructed him to offer Alec Leake £10 to lose the match, because the directors had promised the team a bonus of £100 if they won the League or at least finished level on points with Newcastle.

Meredith showed the commission a letter from Tom Maley, dated 4 August 1905 (the day of the FA's twelve-month ban on Meredith) promising to support the player during his suspension but advising him to say nothing to the press and keep away from Hyde Road as long as Tom Hindle was about. Meredith claimed that this letter proved that the club recognized how he had suffered as a scapegoat for their actions. The letter was his confirmation that City would pay his wages throughout his suspension. Maley would later assert that the letter was merely that of a sympathetic friend who was sure that the public would remember Meredith kindly when his benefit next came around.

So Billy Meredith was now guilty on three counts; offering a bribe, accepting illegal payments and perhaps worst of all, informing on his old team-mates and the club which had paid him for eleven years. But the public, not knowing this, had a long wait for the outcome. 'The wheels of the FA grind slowly, but they grind exceeding fine,' commented *Athletic News*, which was by now well geared up to this kind of affair.

If the previous judgement had been a shock, the next one, delivered on Thursday, 30 May 1906, was positively catastrophic for Manchester City. As a result of Meredith's information, and subsequent admissions by the staff, an astonishing total of seventeen current and former Manchester City players were fined a combined sum of £900. They were also suspended until 1 January 1907 and, worst of all for City, forbidden to play for the club ever again. In addition, two directors were suspended for a year, and a former chairman, W. Forrest, and the present manager Tom Maley were banned from football *sine die*. The club was also fined £250.

A more crushing blow to any single club has never been dealt by the FA. In one, sweeping judgement they wiped out an entire first team squad, including most of the Cup-winning team, and robbed the game of one of the most charismatic managers of the period.

'And now,' said *Athletic News*, 'Manchester enjoys the unenviable distinction of owning more suspended directors than any town in Great Britain . . . but all of them ran risks against the law, and they have to suffer for their wrong doing . . . the rules may be deemed absurd, but the majority of the clubs have placed them on the statute book.'

Not only that, on the very same afternoon that City's punishment was announced, at a meeting in the Holborn Restaurant, London, a majority of clubs and associations reaffirmed the League's commitment to the existing FA rules by rejecting a motion forwarded by Aston Villa and seconded by Everton to abolish the maximum wage. A proposal by Liverpool to legalize bonus payments was also voted down. Thus the very rules which led to Manchester City's downfall remained intact, by democratic choice.

But there was some sympathy for City in that, under Hindle's watchful eye, their players had actually been paid according to the regulations between 1905–06. The suspensions were instead for payments made by the previous board of directors during the 1904–05 season, a period when the newly-suspended chairman, John Allison, had been far away in Australia.

There was little sympathy for Meredith. The club's minute book recorded how as early as September 1905 the board warned him about 'the continued annoyance and insult caused by (his) attitude and speech'. One director, John Allison, had even proposed taking private proceedings against the errant star. According to John Harding's biography however, even after the crushing FA sentence of June 1906, 'Meredith was unrepentant. He remained fully convinced that he had been betrayed and that the directors had let him take all the blame.'

Athletic News criticized him bitterly, saying that he was lucky to have been given a second chance to continue his career at all. He had shown 'no sense of gratitude for all the managers who, over the years, remunerated him so that he became comparatively rich'. Meredith's only form of defence was a letter to the newspaper stating how much money he stood to lose from his total of eighteen months' suspension.

He might also have lost the respect of his fellow professionals, especially those at Manchester City who were now suspended largely as a result of his behaviour, but in fact Meredith's standing in the game suffered to a remarkably small degree, partly because he was such a popular entertainer and partly because after 1906 he worked hard to improve the status of his fellow professionals, as a prominent member of the Players' Union. John Harding suggests that this latter commitment might have been motivated by a complex psychological blend of penance combined with a deep-rooted desire for justice.

Back at Hyde Road meanwhile there were plenty of problems to sort out; directors to be found and players to be signed. A new manager was appointed, Harry Newbould from Derby County, whose former profession was appropriately enough that of accountant. On the playing staff City had only eleven men still available, and they desperately needed quality players to start the new season. Chelsea offered one of their players who was recovering from injury, but some clubs, knowing City's desperation and relative wealth, hiked up their prices for available men. Leicester charged City the relatively high fee of £600 for their goalkeeper.

City's most welcome tonic came from Manchester United's chairman, J. J. Bentley, who was by now also President of the League (but no longer editor of *Athletic News*). In addition to expediting City's various transfer deals during the summer, Bentley went so far as to redirect one Brighton player who was due to sign for United to Hyde Road instead. But the United chairman could afford to be generous, because he had already managed to secure Meredith's registration for when the player's second period of suspension expired on 1 January 1907. Although the Welsh winger was by then thirty-two years old, United were happy to pay £500 for his signature, plus the £100 FA fine Meredith incurred.

But what of Tom Maley and the other suspended players?

Known affectionately as 'All-of-a-sudden-Tom' because of his rapid-fire delivery. Maley's *sine die* ban was particularly hard because his brothers, Willy at Celtic and Alec at Hibernian, were both still managers. In a valedictory speech in Manchester, Maley said that if all the First Division clubs were investigated, not four would come out 'scatheless'. But he assured other clubs that he would not become an informer yet, though when the time was right he would make an open attack on those 'at present laughing up their sleeves while looking on so benignly and complacently'. (These might so easily have been the sentiments of Herbert Chapman when he was suspended in 1919 as a result of similar irregularities at Leeds City. Most people close to the game then knew that the majority of the guilty men had gone unpunished.)

Maley denied any part in the attempt to bribe Alec Leake. It was the idea of three players, he said. As to the illegal payments, he could not deny making them. They were a regular and orderly part of the club's business as he found it on his arrival in 1902. With this, the educated and popular man left Hyde Road and went back to his native Scotland to become a schoolmaster in Cleland, Lanarkshire. Only when the FA softened their stance in 1908 and withdrew the *sine die* ban did Maley return to England, first as manager of Bradford Park Avenue and finally, for a short spell at Southport.

Apart from Meredith most of the other suspended players had to wait some time before their futures were decided. One of them, Davidson, was with Airdrie, but the Scottish FA decided to ignore his English suspension.

A couple of other players, W. J. Lyons and Will 'Doc' Holmes, had been with new clubs for at least a season since receiving the illegal payments at Hyde Road, and their new clubs, Preston North End and Clapton Orient, were furious at having to lose their services because of another club's malpractice. Of the fourteen others still at Hyde Road, three who had been reserve players in 1904–05 appealed on the grounds that even with bonuses their 1904–05 wages had not totalled the maximum £208. None of their appeals succeeded. Nor did a petition signed in October by 4128 City fans begging the FA to reconsider.

This was a relief to all the club scouts who were by now eagerly awaiting the suspensions to end on 1 January, when there promised to be the biggest sale of footballing talent ever witnessed in Britain. 'How these football flies did settle round the Manchester preserve.' commented *Athletic News*.

The bargaining began at Hyde Road on 1 December 1906 after the local derby with United. 'Never in the history of the game was there such an auction of famous players,' reported the *Manchester Evening Chronicle* (subsequent accounts were to locate the auction at the Queen's Hotel in Manchester, but the main business was conducted in the club offices).

The FA had decided to give clubs permission to approach the suspended players before New Year's Day, and there were representatives from at least eight League clubs hoping to do business. Herbert Burgess, the diminutive but tough England left back, known as 'the Mighty Atom', was the main attraction, with a fee of £1000 being mooted.

By 8 December six clubs were after Burgess, though City had actually promised Everton the first option. Rumours spread that he had signed for Celtic, while scouts from Newcastle, Leeds and Bradford sought him out in Manchester. Everton still wanted Burgess however, and continued to believe that City would keep to their agreement, which stemmed from the free transfer of an Everton player to Hyde Road. But no one could find the man, and it was only a day or so later that Manchester United announced that they had signed Burgess on 5 December and had been hiding him ever since at a secret address in the city.

Everton and Celtic were furious, City pocketed about £750 and a few weeks later had to explain themselves to the League. It turned out that their agreement with Everton would not have earned City a transfer fee, so they made a quick sale instead.

The other transfers were less dramatic. Alex 'Sandy' Turnbull, the Scottish comedian of the City team who figured prominently in the controversial tussle with Leake, joined Meredith and Burgess at Manchester United. (Turnbull's career was to end in controversial fashion several years later, as we shall see in Chapter Three.) Jimmy Bannister, Meredith's favourite inside-forward partner from Hyde Road, also joined United, who had just been promoted to the First Division. With these signings playing a prominent part, two years later United won the League.

Bury signed up McMahon and Frank 'Tabby' Booth, the latter becoming the first player to return to City when the FA granted their amnesty in 1908. The reserve goalkeeper Edmondson was sold to Bolton for £250, while Arsenal took Hynds, and George Livingstone (who later returned to play for Manchester United) went to Ibrox Park and thus became only the second man ever to have played for both Celtic and Rangers.

Of the remaining suspended players we shall mention only one – City's first choice goalkeeper who we met earlier in this chapter – 'Happy Jack' Hillman. After his year-long suspension at Burnley in 1900 Hillman signed for City and played a major part in the Cup-winning and successful promotion side between 1901 and 1905. Now aged thirty-five, Hillman was one of the last of the City players to be signed up, together with Sammy Frost, by Southern League Millwall Athletic. His career ended shortly afterwards with an elbow injury which left one arm permanently crooked.

Altogether the auction realized a sum of around £2600, almost exactly what it cost City to rebuild their side. But money alone was no compensation for City's loss of a great team, and they had to suffer further when a strengthened United became the top team in Manchester. But the cruellest irony of this whole episode was the method and conditions under which the suspended players were each signed up. As Billy Meredith was later to write, 'The League met and the representatives of each club voted in favour of the punishment . . . and while their representatives were passing this pious resolution most of them had other representatives busy trying to persuade the "villains whose punishment had been so well deserved" to sign on for them under conditions very much better, in most cases, than the ones we had been ruled by at Hyde Road.'

No one was more qualified to confirm this than Meredith. He had been signed by Manchester United on terms way above the legal maximum – and who was the man who sanctioned those terms? None other than J. J. Bentley, President of the Football League. No wonder Meredith was bitter.

Before we leave Manchester, let us just take a quick look at the debuts of Meredith, Burgess, Bannister and Turnbull for their new club Manchester United, at Clayton on 1 January 1907.

Meredith had not played competitively for twenty months, since that fateful game at Villa Park in April 1905. For any player such a long lay-off would have been a handicap, but for a thirty-two-year-old it might have been disastrous. The weather was miserable, the air foul, as was so often the case at Clayton, but there were 40,000 fans present, many of them chanting the names of their new heroes from across the city. Meredith and his former City team-mates were said to have been quite overwhelmed by the reception and the messages of goodwill from all over the world.

As the teams warmed up, Meredith looking a touch overweight, he and Sandy Turnbull were seen to be shaking hands warmly with the opposing team. It was Aston Villa.

If Manchester City were guilty of calculated breaches of regulations, Middlesbrough seemed to transgress as much through mismanagement as sheer ambition. Indeed, so chaotic and secretive were much of their affairs that by the end of the Edwardian era they could count themselves lucky to have retained their membership of the League.

Having been elected in 1899 Middlesbrough reached the First Division in 1902, and a year later opened one of the finest grounds in the country, Ayresome Park. But the £10,000 expenditure stretched the club so much that a few years later it was struggling with reduced gates, heavy losses and at one stage not one away win in two years.

It was at that point, in February 1905, that Middlesbrough shocked the football world by paying a record £1000 to Sunderland for their goalscorer Alf Common. At the time the average transfer fee was around £300 to £500, but Middlesbrough were desperately near the bottom of the division and badly needed a player of Common's proven goalscoring ability.

The transfer met two kinds of opposition. Firstly, a consensus within the League supported the view that buying one's way out of trouble was somehow unsporting, and hardly tolerable from such a new League member. Middlesbrough, it was said, should have bought ten players at £100 each rather than pay an inflated amount for one, although the main objection was probably based on fear that the level of transfer fees would immediately rise beyond control. (Chelsea, also newcomers to the League, tried to buy their way out of trouble in 1910, although unlike Middlesbrough they failed. Thus for the 1910–11 season the 16 March deadline for transfers was introduced. It survives until today, the deadline now being 5.00 p.m. on the fourth Thursday of March.)

The second source of opposition to Common's transfer was more awesome in power. It was the chairman of the FA, Charles Clegg, who was already bitterly opposed to any form of transfer payments. He had tried to pass a rule abolishing them in 1894, without success, and he would try again in 1899 and 1908.

But Clegg had a much more pragmatic objection, and that was because his own club, Sheffield United, had only months before sold Alf Common to Sunderland. Common had told United that he was so desperate to return to his native Sunderland, where he had a business to tend, that he would give up football rather than stay at Bramall Lane. Reluctant to hold on to an unhappy player, which they could have done so easily as long as they offered him the maximum wage, United sold Common for a very reasonable fee of £375.

So when, barely seven months later, Middlesbrough purchased him from Sunderland for the massive fee of £1000, before the season was even at an end (a rare occurrence then) Sheffield United and their chairman Clegg were naturally enraged. They would never have sold him had they known such a quick profit was in the offing, or, at least they would have sold him to a club other than Sunderland who were prepared to pay more than £375.

To make matters worse, when Common returned to Bramall Lane a few weeks after his controversial transfer, he scored Middlesbrough's winning goal. Middlesbrough were not therefore among Charles Clegg's favourite football teams.

For the shareholders of Middlesbrough there was another problem. Delighted though they were with Common, who steered the club to safety with his fine example of scoring prowess, they wanted to know where the £1000 transfer fee came from. Indeed the shareholders had become so worried with the general running of the club that they had gone to the trouble of appointing a sub-committee to work closely with the board of directors, to help rather than interfere, to advise rather than snoop.

'But the directors,' wrote Tityrus in *Athletic News*, 'adopting the attitude of a King to a Black Beetle, treated the shareholders with scorn, and refused to take them into their confidence.'

This proved to be a great mistake, for at the end of the 1904–05 season the club's annual balance sheet was late in arriving. The directors blamed the auditor, the auditor objected, and in a fit of pique he told the committee of shareholders exactly why the accounts were not complete. In short, there were so many matters of discrepancy, he said, including obviously illegal payments to players, that he felt unable to sign them. Horrified at what the auditor had told him, one of the shareholders informed the FA.

So it was that having conducted separate investigations into Glossop, Sunderland and now Manchester City for a second time, the FA then turned its attention to Middlesbrough. The club was, wrote Tityrus, 'at the present time dwelling in Queer Street'.

Amid widespread rumours, the first commission meeting took place at York on 21 July 1905, by which time no doubt Charles Clegg was beginning to feel heartily sick of all these apparently dishonest professional clubs (he was a staunch advocate of amateurism).

But how could it be otherwise, asked Tityrus, 'so long as clubs send to London representatives who vote with one hand for the retention of the £4 per week maximum for players, and with the other hand they are breaking the rule all the time'.

As Arthur Appleton relates in his history of North-Eastern football *Hotbed of Soccer* (Rupert Hart-Davis, 1960) Middlesbrough's directors hardly aided their cause by co-operating as little as possible, so that the enquiry dragged on into the following season. Finally, on 17 November 1905, the directors admitted making illegal payments worth some £400 over the previous two seasons and creating fictitious accounts to conceal their actions.

Inevitably the FA fined them £250, apparently the going rate at that time, but in return for their reticence a total of eleven out of the twelve Middlesbrough directors were suspended until 1 January 1908, and one of the players, Teddy Gittins, was fined £10 for making false statements. The shareholders were given until 1 January 1906 to appoint a new board.

Perhaps the most notable example was set by John Robson, the former Middlesbrough secretary/manager, then at Crystal Palace, who went unpunished simply because he had very shrewdly demanded from the Middlesbrough board a written agreement which absolved him of any responsibility in the payment of illegal monies. If only Tom Maley and several managers since had followed Robson's example . . .

Middlesbrough's punishment hardly shook the footballing world, but then in the aftermath of the Meredith bribery verdict their wrongdoings seemed slight in comparison. Nevertheless, anxious that its local club should not be tainted as a black sheep the *North-Eastern*

Daily Gazette commented '. . . the judgement of the special commission does not carry with it the moral censure outsiders might be disposed to attach to it. It is part of a struggle against unnatural conditions.'

The club's first task was to find a new board, under the chairmanship of the sole surviving director, the impressive sounding Lieutenant-Colonel Thomas Gibson Poole. Poole, who derived his rank from the First North Riding Volunteer Artillery, was an extremely successful watchmaker and jeweller with branches all over the region. A prominent freemason, he was also an active and rising local politician, having joined the town council as a Conservative in 1896.

When Poole took control of the club he found £20 in the bank, a week's wages owed to the players and the FA's £250 fine unpaid. There was so little money that in January 1906 the club was actually suspended temporarily until Poole sent the FA a personal cheque for the fine.

Despite their punishment, Middlesbrough continued in their former ways – making illegal payments and trying to buy their way out of trouble as they struggled once more against relegation. It has even been said, though it is impossible to verify, that some of the other First Division members so disapproved of Middlesbrough's behaviour that they deliberately took matches easy against the club's fellow strugglers, Bury. That this may have been so is illustrated only by the fact that Middlesbrough's next tangle with the FA came about as the direct result of incriminating remarks made by a well-known trainer. Afterwards, this outspoken individual claimed he had only been joking. How many times we have heard such belated retractions?

Certainly the FA took his comments to heart, because in May a second investigation began into Middlesbrough's affairs. The issue in question this time was the transfers of Bloomer from Sunderland, Wilcox from Birmingham and the aptly named W. F. Brawn from Aston Villa (he was 6ft 1in and weighed thirteen stone five). This time however, the enquiry proceeded very quickly. Representatives from Sunderland, Aston Villa and Birmingham were interviewed, followed by the Middlesbrough manager Alex Mackie and his chairman Gibson Poole. Mackie must have felt particularly vulnerable because he had already been suspended for three months on another matter.

Again the FA found the club's books to be a mess, although the only infringement they could find was an illegal signing-on bonus paid to Bloomer, for which Middlesbrough were fined a token £50 on 1 June 1906 (the same day Manchester City learned of their massive punishment). More serious for the club was a decision to send, at Middlesbrough's expense, two members of the League Management Committee to inspect the books at least twice before April 1907. Now, surely, they would have to behave.

The first visit in November 1906 suggested no reform whatsoever. The books were as chaotic as ever, with one set of accounts being presented in a neat, orderly manner – obviously for show only – and the others, supposedly detailing gate receipts and expenses, being a complete mess. Gibson Poole, it appeared, was mixing up club money with his own and at the time of the report reputedly owed Middlesbrough £500.

Once more the FA took action. Steve Bloomer was suspended for fourteen days, Alex Mackie was permanently suspended – though this hardly mattered because by then he had already decided to leave the game, perhaps in disgust – but for some reason Gibson Poole went unpunished. He did not even receive a censure.

Middlesbrough continued to struggle on the pitch, before escaping relegation that season with a late burst. They did much better in 1907–08 and kept it up the following year, but 1909–10 saw them near the bottom again, and in April 1910 Gibson Poole found himself facing yet another investigation.

This time the charges were serious. It was alleged that Middlesbrough's home match against Newcastle United on 9 April 1910 had been fixed between the players to give Middlesbrough a much-needed win (they escaped relegation by a couple of points). No proof was found, but the investigation was just one more black mark for the club in the eyes of the authorities. As it happened, the FA did not have long to wait for a return to Ayresome Park. Two further complaints brought Middlesbrough nearer to the painful, bitter end of their Edwardian nightmare.

The first was an alleged illegal approach by the new manager Andy Walker to a couple of players at his former club, Airdrieonians (by coincidence, one of them was R. Davidson, formerly one of Manchester City's seventeen suspended players). Walker was found guilty of 'poaching' on each count and became the first League manager to be suspended for such a misdemeanour, thirty days being his sentence. The club was also fined a total of £150.

This was in January 1911. At the same time a second, more serious complaint against Middlesbrough was being investigated. At the start of the 1910–11 season Middlesbrough had been near the top of the First Division and in very good form, so when neighbours Sunderland, at the time unbeaten and top of the League, were due to visit on December 3, a large crowd and a fascinating match was in prospect.

But on that particular Saturday Gibson Poole's mind was not so much on football as on the forthcoming parliamentary elections.

Since becoming chairman of the club, Poole's own political star had risen quite considerably. He had been mayor of the town for two terms, the last of which had only just expired, and on the Monday after the Sunderland match he was making his first attempt to get into Parliament, in a two-horse race against the sitting Liberal MP Penry Williams.

Politics and sport were not completely separate in Poole's mind, however. During the preceding week the chairman sent some of the Middlesbrough players out canvassing for him, while all of them were said to have signed a manifesto on his behalf (they probably had no choice). Strange as it may seem to relate, such was the intensity of local rivalry, both political and sporting, that the Liberals were actually calling for a Sunderland victory at Ayresome Park!

As he took his seat at the game Gibson Poole was reported to have had a standing ovation from the 30,000 crowd, and he must have been even more popular when the hard-fought game finished with Middlesbrough victors by one goal to nil.

But unknown to the spectators – and the voters among them – there had allegedly been an attempt to rig the match. Charles Thomson, the Sunderland captain, reported to his trainer that Andy Walker had approached him just before the game. The Middlesbrough manager, claimed Thomson, had said that he wanted to win the game for the sake of Gibson Poole, who thought a victory might enhance his prospects at the election. The reward was to be £10 for Thomson plus £2 each for the rest of the Sunderland team.

This was turned down flatly, and the Sunderland players did their best to win the game. In the end, despite Middlesbrough's victory, Poole did not gain an advantage in the Monday polls. In fact the Liberal candidate increased his majority of the previous election from 2914 to 3745. The Middlesbrough chairman went back to local politics and never fought a general election again.

On December 16, a fortnight after the game, the Sunderland directors alerted the FA to Walker's attempted bribe. We do not know why they waited so long, but we do know that Poole was immediately informed of Sunderland's complaint by the FA secretary Frederick Wall. Later Poole was to claim that this letter was the first he had ever heard of the matter.

The Middlesbrough chairman's first act was to contact his opposite number at Roker Park, Fred Taylor, and tell him he would call a board meeting at Ayresome Park that very evening. But there was no board meeting, and the other Middlesbrough directors knew nothing of the allegations or the incident until the night before a specially appointed commission met in Manchester on 6 January 1911.

Four men formed the commission; Charles Clegg, who was already investigating Walker's illegal approaches to the two Airdrie players and must have been thoroughly worn out by Middlesbrough at this stage; John McKenna, newly-elected President of the Football League; John Lewis, the respected former referee and Dan Woolfall, a former photographer who was now a powerful influence in the FA and was wont to describe his occupation as 'Clerk to the Commissioners of Taxes for the Hundred of Blackburn'.

Middlesbrough's standing with these men could hardly have been lower. Apart from the recent illegal approaches, Middlesbrough had at the time the worst record of disciplinary problems of any current League club, even Manchester City, whose errors seemed long ago. The Middlesbrough board did not help matters by leaving the unfortunate Walker to face the bribery commission on his own – an ill omen this, as Alec Mackie would have testified.

Three Sunderland players, Charlie Thomson, Guy Jarvie and James Gemmell were questioned, along with the club trainer Billy Williams. Each confirmed that before the game Walker had told Jarvie that he wished to see Thomson. Gemmell witnessed the ensuing interview, but did not hear it. Thomson had reported the bribery offer to his trainer immediately after it was made.

The commission decided to meet again the following week, but this time with the Middlesbrough directors in attendance. Walker insisted on his and Gibson Poole's innocence, but it was a difficult plea to make when the other directors had so obviously been kept in ignorance of the affair for such a long time.

On 16 January 1911 the FA gave its judgement. It was satisfied that despite Middlesbrough's denials a bribe attempt had been made, and as a result Andy Walker and Gibson Poole were both permanently suspended from football and football management.

The town of Middlesbrough was deeply shocked. Poole, a freemason, churchman and Conservative councillor, had dominated the club so so long and in such a controversial fashion that years of pent-up criticism were released. This was a political, not a football scandal, it was widely said, and yet the popular Walker was being made to suffer for his master's bidding. Supporters reacted immediately by gathering a 12,500 signature petition begging the FA to reconsider the ban on Walker, but it had no effect. The FA and the Football League were in truth heartily sick of conducting enquiries into Middlesbrough's affairs, so any sympathy was thinly spread.

Gibson Poole made a prompt reply to the allegations by trying to suggest that Walker had acted independently. 'If such an offer was made in my interests, as is suggested by the FA', he said hours after the judgement, 'it was entirely without my knowledge or consent. I knew nothing of the affair until receipt of the letter from the FA. There has been positively no evidence before the Committee to connect me in any way with the charge, and I do not intend to permit my name to be sullied in this manner. I propose to take legal advice and if possible seek a remedy in a court of law.'

Walker also kept up his denial of the charge and swore an affidavit to that effect. He claimed he had been 'cruelly wronged by this decision'. Alex Mackie had said much the same in November 1906.

But would a player of Thomson's reputation have simply concocted such a story and organized witnesses, including his club chairman, to corroborate? And if Walker and Poole had been innocent, why had Poole kept the affair from his fellow directors for so long? Surely they would have been publicly outraged at such an allegation. Furthermore, had Walker really acted without his chairman's knowledge it might have been expected that Poole, on receiving the FA's letter, would have conducted an internal enquiry at the club, and, if Walker had been found guilty, sacked him immediately. But there was no such enquiry, nor any other suggested source for the £30 offered as a bribe. Walker himself was unlikely to have afforded such a sum on his own.

Finally, if the FA's judgement was false, why did a man of Poole's wealth and public standing take no legal action to redress the undoubted slur that had been cast upon his name? He appealed to the FA, but that was all.

If there was any crumb of comfort to be drawn from this sorry tale, it was, said *Athletic News*, the fact that the bribery attempt had had nothing to do with football. It was purely and simply a cheap, political ploy.

Inevitably others saw it differently, as just another sign of degeneracy within the game. Again *Athletic News* was quick to put the record straight, accusing the press of being infected 'with the yellow journalism of America'. The unofficial 'voice of football' then listed all the various and worthy professions practised by directors of football clubs, telling of their sacrifices made in the love of sport. Never let it be forgotten, proclaimed *Athletic News*, that Thomson 'never hesitated about his duty . . .' and that 'the men of Sunderland realized their responsibility to a national sport . . .'

'If Middlesbrough desired to buy this match . . . the object in view was not to improve their position in the League, not to save the club from relegation, and not to specially serve the interests of the Middlesbrough club – but rather to enhance the personal popularity of Colonel Poole . . . The football club was used as an agency – but that has nothing whatever to do with football.'

Poole's sudden removal from the scene – he never did take legal action – might have been thought to signal the end of Middlesbrough's problems. In fact there was more trouble to come, but thankfully it was the last.

A few months later, in May 1911, four officials from the League, Messrs McKenna, Sutcliffe, Lewis and the secretary Tom Charnley sat up most of one night going through Middlesbrough's books, interviewing the club auditor, then in the morning quizzing the board of directors (you may recall that the year before the FA had handed all responsibility for such financial matters over to the League). Colonel Poole and Andy Walker, anxious to regain favour, came in to assist the League officials willingly.

On May 29 Middlesbrough received their last serious punishment in this troubled era, a £300 fine for flagrantly tampering with the club's books. It was discovered that minutes and wages had not been recorded properly, that certain players had not personally signed their annual agreements and that Andy Walker had been paid since his suspension.

Those directors who had been kept in the dark by Gibson Poole after the Sunderland match now found themselves facing the ire of the FA. Every single one of them was suspended. At the same time Poole and Walker had their appeals for clemency rejected.

Athletic News could only 'marvel that Middlesbrough have not been expelled from the League', a sentiment repeated by John McKenna at the club's AGM in June 1911. The Football League had had enough of Middlesbrough. Any more bad practices, he warned, and they would be out. But they stayed in, and after 1911 Charles Clegg and the League never had cause to investigate their affairs again.

As to Lieutenant-Colonel Thomas Gibson Poole, he survived the scandal with his reputation almost intact. Continued public service, his admirable recruiting powers during the Great War and his undoubted generosity in 1931 when he donated his large house to the borough for a public sanatorium, all contributed to his rising popular acclaim. Freedom of the borough was followed in 1927 by a third term as mayor, and on New Year's Day 1935 the former Middlesbrough chairman received his highest honour, a knighthood from George the Fifth.

When Gibson Poole died on 18 June 1937 – only eight days before the man he tormented, Charles Clegg – the newspapers carried long lists of all his achievements, honours, posts and responsibilities. Nowhere was it mentioned that he had once been active in the game of football.

Middlesbrough Football Club did however send a wreath to the funeral at Linthorpe Cemetery a few days later. We can only hope that the expense was fully accounted for.

3
'Knocker' in the Dock

'**A** plot to cheat the public', commented *Athletic News*, 'to sell to the faithful followers of football a sham instead of the genuine article, to rob bookmakers by criminal fraud, and to conspire for the suppression of the truth . . .'

'The most extraordinary match I have ever officiated in', said the referee, John Sharpe.

'The most uninteresting game ever seen on the ground which is shortly to be honoured with the (Cup) Final tie', said the *Sporting Chronicle*.

So went three opinions of the same game, and a remarkable one it was by all accounts, played between Manchester United and Liverpool at Old Trafford on Good Friday, 2 April 1915. It was so bad that even the United secretary/manager John Robson left in disgust before the final whistle.

His revulsion was well-founded. The result was rigged, it was obviously rigged, and it led to one of the longest enquiries ever held in British football history, followed by two court cases which exposed the scandal in a more detailed fashion than had ever been known before and was not to be known again until the major football scandal of the mid-1960s (see Chapter Eleven).

At the centre of these events was the Manchester United inside forward Enoch James West, known to his friends and supporters as 'Knocker'. He was not the only player implicated, nor was he particularly the prime mover, but for reasons which perhaps only he understood, West decided to challenge the punishment he received from the FA – not once, but twice – and in so doing open up the details of the case to the public's eager gaze.

But before we look at the unfortunate events of that April afternoon we should go back a little further to before the First World War.

In the decade or so before 1914 the football authorities had to deal with a whole catalogue of misdemeanours, almost all of them related to financial irregularities. These cases, such as at Manchester City and Middlesbrough (see Chapter Two) involved only the breaking of FA or Football League regulations. More serious was the matter of rigging match results.

There were two leading motives behind attempts to 'fix' matches.

The first and most common reason, as our history will show, was in order to achieve a certain League placing. These rigged games always took place near the end of the season and perhaps helped guarantee promotion or a 'talent money' placing, or maybe helped a club avoid relegation. The latter was Jack Hillman's apparent motive. In all these cases, since no outside body or agent had been directly involved, the FA never took the matter beyond their own disciplinary framework.

The second reason for rigging a result was in order to gain financially from betting, but because this involved a deliberate attempt to defraud a bookmaker or coupon company, it was considered a criminal offence. This was the case with the Manchester United v Liverpool game.

There were, however, two other matches involving Liverpool which had already fallen heavily under suspicion at the FA. The first, a drawn match against Newcastle in 1911, provoked an enquiry after which the players were exonerated.

The second, between Liverpool and Chelsea on 24 March 1913, was investigated more seriously, principally because the integrity of the match had been questioned by no less a figure than Henry Norris, the chairman of Arsenal and a noted public figure in West London (Norris was a controversial character himself. He orchestrated and financed Arsenal's move from South London to Highbury, and ended his involvement with football in 1927 after being suspended by the FA for financial irregularities).

Norris had gone to this match by chance (Chelsea, third from bottom, beat mid-table Liverpool 2-1) and a few days later he wrote in a West London newspaper '. . . had the Liverpool team, as a whole, desired to win the match they could have done so quite readily'. He expressed his sorrow for 'the genuine triers in the Liverpool team' and the Liverpool directors.

One of those directors was 'Honest' John McKenna, President of the Football League, and he was so disturbed by his friend Norris's comments that he ordered an enquiry. It came to nothing, Liverpool's poor performance being attributed to their heavy programme of three games in four days, and Norris admitted to having been indiscreet in his comments. His own team, Woolwich Arsenal, were, it should be said, bottom of the First Division at that time.

Inevitably, both these enquiries were still fresh in the public's memory when the Manchester United v Liverpool game took place, especially among Liverpool supporters. Some of them may have noticed afterwards that, coincidentally, when United faced Liverpool on 2 April 1915 they, like Chelsea in 1913, were also third from bottom in the First Division, while Liverpool were again comparatively safe in fourteenth place (out of twenty teams). United's rivals at the foot of the table, Chelsea, Notts County and Bolton were all in winning form, so United were strongly favoured to go down with Tottenham.

At the time of the Good Friday game the Football League was in a state of considerable turmoil. Many influential people felt that all professional football should be halted so that players could concentrate on the War effort, while it was also considered that playing for profit at a time of great sacrifice in the trenches was somehow distasteful. On the other hand, watching football did provide a vital escape for hard-pressed munition workers and servicemen.

Having decided to carry on when the War broke out at the start of the 1914–15 season, by Easter 1915 this policy was becoming increasingly difficult for the League to justify. For months *Athletic News* carried on its front pages snippets of speeches exhorting footballers to join up, and every man who did was warmly praised. Meanwhile, as the trench war in France intensified, the Russians were fighting their way into Hungary and the British Government was considering measures to limit the licensing hours in an effort to step up War production.

In such an atmosphere the players were well aware that the Easter games were probably going to be among their last as full-time professionals, at least as long as the War dragged on. Even if most of them did not reckon on being killed in action, many players must have sensed that by the time the War might end they would be too old to resume playing. A few players also figured that as their wages were almost certainly going to cease imminently, if there were any bonuses or illegal extras to be made, now was the time.

And so to Good Friday.

Liverpool were to field seven of the team which had played in the previous year's Cup Final against Burnley, including two men, Ephraim Longworth and Donald McKinlay, who had also played in that controversial match against Chelsea. Longworth was the first Liverpool player to have captained England (Kevin Keegan was the second). On the left wing was Jackie Sheldon, well known to the Manchester United fans as part of their championship winning team of 1911.

Three of Sheldon's old team-mates from that successful side were in the United line up for Good Friday; James Hodge, Billy Meredith – still an effective performer at the age of 41 – and at inside left, Enoch 'Knocker' West.

West was a successful goalscorer known for his 'cannon-ball shot'. Born in the village of Hucknall Torkard, Nottinghamshire, in 1886, he started his career at Sheffield United, where at the age of fifteen he was reputedly the youngest player ever to sign professional forms. From

Bramall Lane, West moved for a fee of £5 to Nottingham Forest, where he achieved his best ever season in 1907–08 by becoming the First Division's leading scorer with twenty-seven goals.

A year later on 21 April 1909 West was one of three Forest players to score hat-tricks in a First Division record-equalling victory of 12-0 over Leicester Fosse (West Bromwich Albion had beaten Darwen 12-0 on 4 April 1892). In view of the fact that this extraordinary result ensured Forest's place in the First Division an enquiry was made, but instead of finding any foul play a Football League commission discovered that the Leicester players, long resigned to relegation themselves, had been somewhat worse for wear after a two-night binge following the wedding of one of their former team-mates, R. F. Turner, of Everton (the youngster fined a year earlier by the FA after asking for more than the maximum signing-on fee).

After scoring nearly 100 goals for Forest, in 1910 at the age of twenty-four West signed for Manchester United, who were then on their way to their second League Championship, but only on the condition that West give up his other great passion, cricket. At one stage however, he did go on the groundstaff at Old Trafford cricket ground. United paid Forest £450, and in West's first season he finished as top scorer with nineteen goals. In the following four seasons he was top scorer again three times. Pleased with his form, United agreed terms with West of £4 10s a week in 1913, rising to the maximum permitted wage of £5 a week in 1914. United also promised him a minimum benefit of £500 for the 1915–1916 season. He was, according to Geoffrey Green, 'one of the most prolific goalscorers in the immediate pre-World War One period'.

Good Friday 1915 began at Old Trafford with a special visit from two FA representatives, Frederick Wall, the secretary and Arthur Kingscott (both of whom we meet as adversaries in Chapter Six). They had come to check on the arrangements for the 1915 Cup Final, scheduled for Old Trafford on April 24, but by the time Manchester United and Liverpool kicked off in heavy rain, the FA men had left the ground, which was just as well for them. The match was not only highly suspicious, it was abysmal to watch.

The 15,000 mostly drenched spectators saw United take a one-goal lead through George Anderson, United's promising, Manchester born centre-forward who they bought from Bury for £50 in 1911, but after the goal play really deteriorated, with Liverpool's forwards appearing to offer no threat whatsoever.

In the second half, as the weather brightened, United were awarded a penalty. Normally it would have been taken by Anderson, but for reasons unknown to the crowd this time the United captain, Irish international Patrick O'Connell, stepped up and placed his attempt wide . . . very wide.

By now, as the linesman Fred Hargreaves was to testify later in court, the crowd suspected the game was fixed and 'said so in unmistakable Lancashire fashion'. Jeers and booing sounded from all over the ground as Hargreaves and the referee, John Sharpe of Lichfield, discussed their suspicions in a brief moment after the penalty incident. But they allowed the game to resume, and Anderson scored once more for United.

As subsequently established, 2-0 had been the pre-arranged scoreline – which makes the penalty miss at 1-0 rather hard to understand – and the rest of the second half was, in the words of the *Sporting Chronicle*, 'too poor too describe'. Their correspondent added that it was not the War which was killing football, it was football which was killing itself, with matches like this.

There was, however, one chance for Liverpool to pull a goal back late in the game, when their centre-forward Fred Pagnam, who had apparently refused to play a part in the arrangement, hit the bar. He was immediately torn off a strip by one of his Liverpool colleagues.

West's performance was noted particularly by the *Daily Dispatch*'s correspondent. In the first half, wrote 'Veteran', West seemed to be suffering from ankle problems and looked slow and ponderous. He had two good chances which he shot wide, but otherwise '. . . West was chiefly employed in the second half in kicking the ball as far out of play as he could'. Giving evidence later, the referee endorsed this view. He said West had kicked the ball on to the grandstand roof rather than towards the Liverpool goal.

After the game, although there must have been considerable suspicion, little was reported in the newspapers for some days. This was partly owing to the gravity of any likely allegations, partly because the Easter weekend was full of shock results, and partly because on the day after United's game v Liverpool there was an even greater controversy at Middlesbrough, where the visitors were the First Division leaders Oldham Athletic. Oldham, making their best-ever challenge for the Championship, surprisingly found themselves 4-1 down with fifty-five minutes gone. At that point their bald veteran full back, William Cook, fouled a Middlesbrough player and was sent off. It is now well recorded how Cook refused to leave the field and so caused the match to be abandoned, the only time this has ever occurred in League history.

By Monday, therefore, the main talking point was not Good Friday's debacle at Old Trafford but Cook's inexplicable behaviour at Ayresome Park. Weeks later the League decided to let the 4-1 score stand, and Cook, an intelligent, likeable player who also played cricket for Lancashire, was banned for twelve months by the FA (and Oldham lost out in the Championship to Everton).

While Cook captured most of the attention for a while, Manchester United carried on losing; 2-0 at Newcastle on the Saturday, 5-0 at Bradford Park Avenue on Easter Monday and 1-0 at Oldham on Tuesday. According to the *Sporting Chronicle* however, at Bradford West had been United's best performer, but United were now bottom of the First Division and apparently doomed.

Off the pitch meanwhile people were beginning to swap notes about the Good Friday game. The *Sporting Chronicle* commented eight days after the game that United's 2-0 victory had led football followers to '. . . suppositions that left them cold with stupefaction. There is almost as much about this Manchester v Liverpool match as there was about the Liverpool v Chelsea match of a year or two ago, but in this case there was no gentleman like Mr H. G. Norris to make the gravest charges in print.

'Of course, some people may be unduly suspicious in the Spring, but unsavoury comments are made and the repetition of these observations, if not checked, is not likely to do the game any good, when football needs every friend that can be found.'

Henry Norris might not have been at the game, but there were others prepared to take action. A week later the *Sporting Chronicle* printed a coupon signed by 'The Football King'. It was issued on behalf of a betting firm and offered a £50 reward to anyone supplying information concerning allegations that 'a certain First League match played in Manchester during Easter weekend was "squared" '. The coupon went on to say that several footballers placed bets for substantial amounts on the match resulting in a 2-0 win.

By April 24 it was known that the Football League had appointed a commission to look into complaints about 'a certain match'. Among the members were two former Northern referees, Charles Sutcliffe and John Lewis (Lewis was a regular contributor to *Athletic News*).

The League's Management Committee also gave its full backing to 'The Football King' and asked that any information be sent on to the League headquarters at Preston. It was also suggested that if 'The Football King' publicly stated the match in question, and printed his name and address, the players involved might then sue him for libel and bring the whole affair out into an open court. The anonymous 'King' did not respond.

Manchester United meanwhile carried on the fight against relegation. They managed their first victory since Good Friday by beating fellow strugglers Chelsea 5-1 on April 20, the same day that Frederick Wall made the long-expected announcement that after the 1914–15 season there would be no more full-time professional football until the War had ended. A week later United just managed to haul themselves to safety with a 1-0 win over Aston Villa in their final game.

But the strain was not over for some of the players. Already three players had been questioned by the commission; Jackie Sheldon of Liverpool, Robert Beale, Manchester United's goalkeeper, and Arthur Whalley, who was on United's books but had not played on Good Friday.

On April 23, the day before the Cup Final at Old Trafford, more players were interviewed, and it became clear that unlike the Liverpool v Chelsea enquiry this time the investigations were not so straightforward. The commission's task was made harder by the fact that several of the players involved in the Good Friday game had now joined the army, while others from Manchester United, such as West, Anderson and O'Connell had gone into War supplies work at the neighbouring Ford Motor Works in Trafford Park. None of the players were receiving any wages from the club.

On May 10 at the Grand Hotel, Manchester, the Football League's three-man enquiry held its first official meeting, and for the next few months very little was said about the matter. *Athletic News* refused to comment further because the matter was, it considered, sub judice, but it did say that rumours abounded and that correspondence continued to pour into its offices. The *News* also reported that the commission was travelling all over the country collecting evidence and that the public must be prepared to wait patiently for a verdict.

Summer arrived. There had been no further reaction from 'The Football King', and while the War dragged on and more men went to their deaths, the commission of enquiry seemed to be taking forever. Then August came around, and once more there was talk of football, albeit on a regional basis and with the players performing for expenses only. Of those former professionals known to be in Manchester, West, Anderson and Meredith, who were among the many players questioned by the commission during the summer, were still available and apparently willing to play.

The commission meanwhile was beginning to give tentative hints, although it revealed little not already suspected by the public. Yes, there had been a conspiracy, but no, it would not name the match. All the League would confirm was that the game in question did have a bearing on the First Division relegation issue and that the affair was serious enough to pass on information to the FA. But that was all. Why was it taking so long? *Athletic News* confined its comments to echoing the words of the commission. 'If there are black sheep in the flock it is necessary to remove them.'

A few weeks later in September the Wartime regional leagues got under way, with Manchester United and Liverpool competing in the Lancashire section and the standard of play winning much praise from onlookers. Not surprisingly it was said that footballers seemed to play much better when they earned their main income elsewhere. 'Knocker' West certainly appeared to be in good form, according to reports of those early games in September 1915.

But he and the other players involved on Good Friday were still playing under a cloud. By September 20 even *Athletic News* was becoming restless. The failure of the commission to deliver its verdict was, said the newspaper, 'enough to try the patience of Job'. Were the authorities taking a season's rest, it asked.

Then on October 15 the commission met again, at the Mosley Hotel, Manchester, this time questioning Sheldon of Liverpool and Alex 'Sandy' Turnbull of Manchester United, both of whom had recently joined up. Turnbull had faced the authorities ten years earlier as a Manchester City player (see Chapter Two) and although he did not play in the Good Friday game he was possibly West's closest friend. West was also present at the hearing and was seen briefly.

But still there was no report.

'A state secret was never so jealously guarded', commented *Athletic News* on November 1. Yet so grave was the matter, it added, that 'we should be thankful to those who are probing this mystery to its depths'. Ironically, elsewhere in that issue was a report of a game at Anfield between Liverpool and Manchester United which United won 2-0. 'Knocker' West scored one of the goals.

On November 12 the commission met once again, in Liverpool this time, with the secretary of the FA, Frederick Wall, in attendance. Nine members of the Liverpool team were questioned. On November 26 it was the turn of the United players, at the Grand Hotel, Manchester. Meredith, Turnbull, O'Connell, West, Anderson and Woodcock were present, together with Howard of Manchester City and Messrs H. Hardman and J. J. Bentley, both directors of Manchester United (Bentley was also President of the Football League at the time).

It was now known for certain that the charges went beyond arranging a match to save United from relegation. There was another, more serious charge, of conspiracy to defraud bookmakers – a criminal offence. In view of this shocking disclosure the League was quick to publicly exonerate either club from complicity in the alleged crime. Liverpool and United, it was announced, were doing all they could to support the League in this difficult investigation.

Two weeks passed, until at last the report seemed ready for release, and on Thursday, 16 December 1915, the commission announced from

Manchester that it would be giving its verdict on the commission's report at four o'clock the next day. But as the press gathered in eager anticipation there was yet more disappointment as it was explained that there had been a disagreement among the commission members and that the report would therefore have to be delayed.

Yet surely the commission must have agreed on the principles of the case by now? Perhaps they were just quibbling about which of the players was to be punished and how. For the public this delay was frustrating enough. For the players it must have been sheer agony.

Six more days passed. It was now almost nine months since Good Friday. Finally, just before the second Christmas of the War, on Thursday afternoon, 23 December, the FA issued its final verdict, in the longest and most detailed statement it had ever released in such circumstances. It was also one of the most disturbing.

These were the FA's findings:

Manchester United v Liverpool, 2 April 1915

The Commissions appointed first by the Football League, and afterwards by the Football Association, have fully investigated the rumours and allegations largely circulated in several districts during and immediately after the above match, to the effect that the result was pre-arranged for the purpose of betting and winning money thereby. A mass of information was received.

The allegation of squaring the match carried with it a charge of conspiracy by some of the players, and as a result of long and searching investigations we are satisfied that a number of them were party to an arrangement to do so, and joined together to obtain money by betting on the actual result of the match.

It is proved that a considerable sum of money changed hands by betting on the match, and that some of the players profited thereby.

Every opportunity has been given to the players to tell the truth, but although they were warned that we were in possession of the facts some have persistently refused to do so, thus revealing a conspiracy to keep back the truth.

It is almost incredible that players dependent on the game for their livelihood should have resorted to such base tactics. By their action they have sought to undermine the whole fabric of the game and distort its honesty and fairness.

We are bound to view such offences in a serious light. The honesty and uprightness of the game must be preserved at all costs, and although we sympathize greatly with the clubs, who are bound to suffer seriously, we feel we have no alternative but to impose the punishments of which the players have been warned over and over again would be imposed.

We are satisfied that the allegations have been proved against the following:–

J. Sheldon, R. R. Purcell, T. Miller and T. Fairfoul (Liverpool).

A. Turnbull, A. Whalley and E. J. West (Manchester United).

L. Cook (Chester).

and they are therefore permanently suspended from taking part in football or football management, and shall not be allowed to enter any football ground in future.

There are grave suspicions that others are also involved, but as the penalty is severe we have restricted our findings to those as to whose offence there is no reasonable doubt.

F. Howard (Manchester City) is suspended until the expiration of twelve months after the registration of professional players has been resumed by the Football Association, for the unsatisfactory and contradictory manner in which he gave evidence before the Commission.

There has never been the slightest allegation against the clubs or their officials. It is, therefore, unnecessary to exonerate them from blame or complicity, and we are indebted to them for much assistance in our investigations.

Had there been no War, had the League been in full operation, had Christmas not been so close, this major football scandal would have commanded considerably more interest than it did. As it was, the newspapers did not give the FA's decision the sensational headlines one might have expected under normal circumstances. *Athletic News* was of course the exception. Half of its front page on 27 December was devoted to the scandal.

No longer inhibited by matters sub judice, the *News* released much hitherto unknown information. Apparently the commission had been greatly aided by several bookmakers who had been suspicious of a number of people, including players, making bets on the Good Friday game. They were doubly wary because so many had put money not only on United winning but on the 2-0 scoreline specifically. This was very unusual, even in the days when betting on one match only was still possible, but odds of seven and eight to one had been secured nevertheless.

Some people may not approve of the betting business, said *Athletic News*, but the majority of bookmakers were honourable and 'as much entitled to the protection of the law as other men'. Indeed without the corroboration of the bookmakers the commission could have not have found the vital proof it needed. It transpired that although most of the bookmakers knew very soon that they had been 'rooked', most paid up. Only a handful 'refused to disgorge'.

Athletic News also reported that at one stage of the enquiry there had been a complete deadlock, presumably during the summer, but, 'At this juncture there was a sudden revelation from one quarter, and proof was piled on proof.' The nature and source of this revelation were not revealed, but subsequent events suggested that it might have been one of the players finally cracking under the strain of deceit.

Such a devastating judgement was bound to have a serious effect on the morale of the game and in particular both clubs. Liverpool were especially hit with the loss of four players whose combined value on the transfer market was estimated at £2000 (at a time when the transfer record for a single player was £2500). Jackie Sheldon they had bought from Manchester United, where no doubt he had cemented friendships with players like West, Whalley and Turnbull. Bob Purcell had cost Liverpool £250 from Queen's Park in 1911, not in transfer fees but in a fine they incurred for allegedly poaching him. Tommy Miller came to Anfield via Motherwell, Third Lanark and Hamilton Academicals and Tom Fairfoul was another buy from Scotland.

But why had only one member of Manchester United's Good Friday team been punished? Surely 'Knocker' West could not have rigged the game for United on his own? Here was the weakest point in the commission's report. It stated that there was insufficient evidence to convict other players, yet Howard of Manchester City was suspended for 'his evasive and irreconcilable answers to plain questions'. It seemed hard to believe that Howard was the only one to behave in such a manner.

On the other hand, it would have been defamatory to print the names of those suspected but not convicted. As *Athletic News* said, 'In England there is no such verdict as "Not Proven". Those who are indicted are either "Guilty" or "Not Guilty". The public must assume that the others who played are all honest men . . .' But this was easier said than done, and for the ten United and seven Liverpool players in that unwelcome position, the cloud of suspicion hanging over them would undoubtedly take some time to disperse. For sure several of those players, if not the majority, were honest, because as the *News* commented, 'the conspirators were most anxious that the ball should not go to some of their fellows, who would, there is reason to believe, have spoiled the pre-arranged score of 2-0'.

Athletic News was, however, harsh in its criticism of the players convicted. They might have argued that with football obviously coming to an end they faced a summer without wages, but as the newspaper pointed out, '. . . many other people have lost their earning capacity during this war, but they have not lost their honesty'.

Apart from gaining financially there was no suggestion that the conspirators had had any intention of 'squaring' the match in order to improve United's League position, yet the very fact that the arranged victory helped United to stay in the First Division meant that Chelsea, who finished a point below United and were therefore relegated, felt understandably aggrieved.

This was perhaps the thorniest problem facing the League. United and Liverpool had both been cleared of complicity in the scandal so should not have suffered as a result. Chelsea, on the other hand, had suffered innocently.

'This is a subject which could be arranged with a little remodelling, for Chelsea are entitled to sympathetic consideration', commented *Athletic News*. The implication seemed to be that either Chelsea might stay up and only one club be promoted – though Preston, runners-up in the Second Division, would surely not have tolerated that – or, as eventually did happen in 1919, the First Division be expanded to allow Chelsea to remain as members. (The 1915 scandal certainly had little bearing on the subsequent controversy in 1919, when Tottenham were disgracefully sent down from the newly-expanded First Division in favour of Arsenal, who finished only fifth in the Second Division. See the Introduction for further references to this affair.)

There was a more immediate consequence of the commission's report. On Christmas Day, Sandy Turnbull and Arthur Whalley were due to play for the Second Football Battalion team against Birmingham. Permission to play them was strongly refused. Similarly, Howard and West had been picked to play for City and United in the local Christmas derby. They too were dropped instantly.

As if this were not hard enough on United, in the same week that West was banned the club announced a loss of £3732 for 1914–15, compared with a profit of nearly £2000 in the previous season. At the same time United's players received slightly increased wages. All this, added to the fact that men like West would have been about to receive lucrative benefits, made the illegitimate attempt to make a few extra pounds on Good Friday appear even more loathsome.

But with far greater horrors occurring daily on the battlefields of Europe and the nation's sympathy barely drawn towards a few allegedly greedy footballers, all the authorities could do was reassure the public that football had cleansed itself, and that this sordid kind of event was in fact a rarity. The League officials, via *Athletic News*, thus gave this dubious form of assurance:

'When we consider that League football has been a vogue for

twenty-six years, the number of matches which have aroused suspicion is extremely small. We have no hesitation in saying that 99 out of every 100 games are honest contests.'

Had the statement used the figures 999 out of every 1000, the League's insistence might have apeared more comforting, whereas the thought of even one per cent of League matches being suspect was in reality almost as shocking as the scandal itself. We can only hope that the League's arithmetic was at fault, especially because these were the figures repeated in various statements made whenever a new scandal emerged over the course of the next twenty years.

One man found himself cruelly torn by the commission's findings. John McKenna was not only the President of the League but also chairman of Liverpool. He did not dispute the judgement, nor did he question the punishments. He was instead personally hurt that for so many months Liverpool had chosen for the team such 'callous' men, whom, '. . . had we known their connection with this affair would never have been afforded the slightest sympathy. We would have had no dealings with them in any shape', said McKenna.

He was also disappointed with the other Liverpool players. 'I am sorry that the other players who were engaged in the match did not assert their individual views at the time and stamp out the foul plot.'

As we were to discover later, some of them had tried, but it had been easier said than done.

Christmas 1915 came and went, and the footballing world was left to discuss the questions which inevitably followed such a scandal. The most important one was, had the authorities closed the file or were other players the subject of further investigations? In London, the main talking point was Chelsea's right to stay in the First Division. Would the League order the Good Friday game to be replayed? Again *Athletic News* begged for patience. 'The mills of the FA grind slowly, but they grind exceedingly small. Retribution is often slow.'

But this time the mills ground exceedingly fast, and only a week later in January 1916 the League announced that the result at Old Trafford would stand and therefore the final League placings would be unchanged. There would be no more investigations, either. There was a War on, and the matter was now closed.

Unjust though this many have seemed, in practice it would have been impossible to replay the game. The players were long since scattered around the country, both in and out of uniform. Fortunately for the League, Chelsea accepted this ruling in a sporting fashion and decided not to appeal (though perhaps they had already been quietly assured of a place in the proposed expansion of the First Division).

Thus it really did seem as if the worst scandal ever to affect English League football was now well and truly over.

'Knocker' West carried on at the Ford works, his close friend Sandy Turnbull, Jackie Sheldon and others carried on their army training, while George Anderson was briefly in the news when he left England to play for Belfast United in January 1916, coincidentally the same month that conscription was first introduced in Britain. Manchester United, who still held Anderson's registration, were so angry with his conduct they suspended him *sine die*, but it was not the last we would hear of him.

Nor of 'Knocker' West.

West, it would appear, was extremely unhappy about his permanent suspension and refused to let the matter rest, however apparently convincing the evidence against him. Until 1917, however, we only had the commission's word that this evidence was so damning. No further details were divulged beyond that which had been stated in December 1915.

But the fact that West was the only one from the United team against Liverpool to have been punished meant that he must have undoubtedly suffered a disproportionate amount of opprobrium, perhaps at his workplace, perhaps in the Old Trafford district where he still lived in Railway Road, only yards from the football ground. He was also still young enough to play first-class football.

Whatever his reasoning, one thing is certain. West was so angry that, against the advice of his solicitors and at great personal cost, he went to extraordinary lengths over the next four years to clear his name. Never before had the FA been challenged successfully in a court of law. Would Enoch 'Knocker' West be the first to succeed?

West's return to the public eye came, appropriately, before a Wartime game between Manchester United and Liverpool at Old Trafford. The former player stood outside the ground – he was banned from entering – and handed out small handbills, printed to look like the original 'Football King' advertisements of 1915. Like the anonymous 'King' West offered a £50 reward, payable to any nominated Red Cross Fund, if anyone could prove that he had made a bet or won any money from the Good Friday match in 1915. What a curious, perhaps even tragic figure West must have appeared on that wartime afternoon.

Not surprisingly, no one came forward with any proof, and one wonders if anyone still cared. The War was now entering a difficult phase. German air raids had started over London, and in April 1917 West's pal Sandy Turnbull became one of 150,000 British casualties at the battle of Arras when he was blown up by a shell as he defended a rearguard action.

But West persisted, so much so that on 5 July 1917 he went to court in the first action of what was destined to be a long struggle. His aim was twofold; to claim damages for alleged libel against the FA and Messrs E. Hulton and Co. Ltd, whom he accused of libelling him in various articles written in the *Sporting Chronicle*, *Athletic News* and *Daily Dispatch* in December 1915, and secondly to seek from the presiding Justice Ridley 'an injunction restraining the FA from putting into force a resolution suspending him from taking part in football or football management' – in other words he wanted the FA ban to be dropped (in the same way that in 1979 Don Revie sought to overturn the FA's ten-year ban on him managing a club in England).

So, if the public had remembered only a few details of the affair from 1915, as a result of West's court action in 1917 they were due to find out a great deal more, because unlike FA proceedings, the Kings Bench Division was open to the public and the press.

Enoch James West, 31, the court heard, was at the time employed as a mechanic at the Ford Motor Works. He had applied to join the army but was turned down because of his occupation. The court was told the basic details of the Good Friday encounter at Old Trafford and reminded that the rules of the FA prohibited players from betting on matches or entering football competitions.

FA Rule number 47 was also explained. This was the rule referred to in the Introduction, by which the FA placed the onus upon the player to prove himself innocent of any charge levelled against him. It had been passed in 1884 but would be dropped shortly after the West case (although it is impossible to say whether the trial had any influence upon the decision to change the rules).

The court then heard how, at the commission's first meeting on 10 May 1915, at the Grand Hotel, Manchester, all the players, West included, were asked if they could throw any light on the Good Friday rumours. West had said that he knew nothing.

On 15 October during another meeting, at the Mosley Hotel, Manchester, West was asked his first direct questions. They were, had he ever written to a Mr Clarke of Hucknall Torkard, Nottinghamshire, where West was born? West had replied in the negative. The commission then asked if West would be surprised to discover that it actually had in its possession a letter written by him to Clarke. West replied that he knew perfectly well no such letter existed.

At another commission meeting, on November 26, also at the Grand Hotel, Charles Sutcliffe announced that he knew for sure that the game was squared. West, together with several other players present, again repeated his ignorance of the affair.

West now told the court that apart from those two questions about the letter, he was unaware of being suspected of taking part in a conspiracy. He had been asked no further direct questions. If this were true, then perhaps West was justified in his present court action. Maybe the commission had been unfair towards him?

It certainly seemed that way when West then told the court that he had obtained a copy of the commission's record of his evidence before them, and had been unable to find one word said or written against himself. West had therefore contacted his solicitors, who advised him to seek another hearing before the FA. The FA refused this however, and that was when, at his own expense, West had issued the handbill at Old Trafford.

Speaking as West's counsel, Cyril Atkinson KC told the court that the official reports of the enquiry contained many different names of players, 'and it really looked as if there was a tossing up as to who to put in and who not to put in'. Atkinson told the jury that they had to consider the following questions.

Was it true that West was a party to the match 'fixing'?

Did he swindle the bookmaker?

Did he bet on the result?

Did he play dishonestly in order to bring about that result?

The court now turned its attention to the last question. West claimed that he had played in a forward role during the first half, but after the break his captain, O'Connell, had instructed him to play back. West had bandaged ankles which hurt, but he carried on and 'played the proper defensive game having regard to the critical position of his club'. He heard no complaint about his play until he read the press reports (his former manager was to refute this later in court).

West stayed in the witness box to be cross-examined by Mr Rawlinson KC, MP, acting for the FA. This is how the *Daily Dispatch* recorded the exchange:

Rawlinson – Did you on Thursday, April 1, see Anderson, your centre-forward, whom I am going to call, and tell him that you had written to Nottingham to get £10 put on the match ending 2-0 at (odds of) 7-1, and did you add 'They won't get any evidence against me'?

West – No.

Rawlinson – Did you think the match was squared?

West – Not to my knowledge.

Rawlinson – What do you think?

West – Well, the papers made such a show of it, it makes one think.

Rawlinson – What do you think?

West – I don't know what to think. If people admit that the match was squared I can't think any other.

Rawlinson – Were the crowd shouting at you 'Play the game'?

West – I do not know. I never take any notice of what the crowds say. If a player takes notice of them it causes him to lose his grip of the game.

West did agree that after the game there was considerable talk of a fix, and he agreed with Mr Rawlinson that it was peculiar that there should have been so much heavy betting on the 2-0 scoreline in Hucknall Torkard, where West was born, but according to some reports there had been heavy betting in several other parts of the country too, said West.

It was then the turn of Mr Rigby Swift KC, counsel for Hulton Newspapers, to cross-examine West. There were, he said, three articles for which West had claimed libel damages. The first was from the *Daily Dispatch* of 29 December 1915, and it simply repeated the words of the FA's original statement. The second, from the *Sporting Chronicle* of the same day, said, 'It has been proved that this actual result has been arranged between some of the twenty-two players, and that these men who converted what should have been a genuine contest into a circus performance made bets with bookmakers.'

The third news report came from the *Athletic News* of December 27. It read, 'A plot to cheat the public and to rob bookmakers by criminal fraud, and to conspire for the suppression of truth, has been revealed. We have great sympathy with some of those who participated in this hippodrome hocus-pocus and this nefarious contrivance to rob bookmakers.'

Rigby-Swift turned to West. 'Assume that the match was squared', he told him, 'and that you had something to do with it, is there a word in the articles that you can complain of?'

'No,' replied West.

At this point the judge remarked that if the facts of the articles were true then it was 'fair comment on a matter of public interest'. One wonders, did Justice Ridley and others in court believe West was only adding to his own downfall by going through with this case?

More questions followed from both sides. Yes, West was aware of the penalties for betting. Yes, he knew he would stand to lose his benefit if ever he was disciplined.

Patrick O'Connell was next in the witness box. The former Sheffield Wednesday, Hull and Manchester United captain was now, coincidentally, a foreman at the factory where West worked.

He, too, denied any knowledge of an attempt to square the match. He had told the commission that West had played as well as he usually did and had not intentionally kicked the ball out of play. West had 'hugged' the ball, but that was his normal style. O'Connell also denied deliberately missing the penalty. 'I have missed dozens in my time', he remarked, to much amusement. Nor had he heard the crowd shout 'Play up you rotters!'

So far most of the evidence seemed to give West the benefit of the doubt, but the arrival of Jackie Sheldon in the witness box soon changed that. Sheldon was Liverpool's outside-right in the game at Old Trafford. Now in the army, perhaps he felt he had nothing more to lose.

Sheldon confessed to the court that it was he who had fixed the result with players in his own team. But his next remarks must have caused an even greater stir. On the Monday before the game, said Sheldon, he went to Manchester and met Sandy Turnbull, Arthur Whalley and Enoch West, his former team-mates at Old Trafford, in The Dog and Partridge pub. There it was agreed that the result on Good Friday would be fixed at 2-0 to United. On Thursday night this was confirmed. United would score one goal in each half.

Once those goals had been scored, said Sheldon, West had fallen back and repeatedly kicked the ball into touch. It was clear to the crowd what was going on because the United players kept passing the ball to West, on the left, rather than Billy Meredith on the right. Meredith had not been a party to the arrangement. Sheldon also claimed that several players knew about the fix and made their own bets. Some had offered him £3 each to join in the betting.

With Sheldon's testimony the case took on an entirely different complexion, and there must have been an added tension in the court as three more eye-witnesses were called to give their differing impressions of the game. Two were suspicious, one was not.

As the court adjourned for the day, did West regret his decision to take the matter so far, or was he doubly determined to clear his name, especially after what Sheldon had said of his alleged involvement? The footballing public awaited the next day's proceedings with awakened interest. Never before had such a scandal been so widely prised apart and reported in so many of its details. If nothing else, it provided a splendid diversion from the War.

First in the witness box on July 6 was George Anderson, described in court as a cotton manufacturer and former professional footballer. His sojourn in Belfast had presumably been a short one. Anderson said that on the day before Good Friday 1915 he had met West and two other men at the Great Central Station in Manchester. Sheldon had joined them and in a nearby pub one of the men asked, 'Is it still 2-0'?

West, claimed Anderson, had said 'Oh yes, I have just written to Nottingham for £70 to £10.' Sheldon told them he had also placed a bet, and Anderson was offered £3 to join in the arrangement. Anderson told the court he had refused the offer and had not wanted anything to do with it. Sheldon therefore told him to remain silent on the matter, a suggestion with which Anderson readily concurred. After the game, said Anderson, West had told him, 'I am not afraid. They cannot get any evidence against me.' West had won £70 on his bet.

Under closer examination Anderson admitted that initially he had denied any knowledge of the fix, but after several sessions of questioning by the commission he had finally owned up. 'I was tired of telling so many lies', he told the court. But he insisted that he had not made any bets himself and that just before the match he wanted to refuse to play. He decided against it though, because this might have alerted the directors.

Next to give evidence was Anderson's opposite number, the Liverpool centre-forward Fred Pagnam, who was now learning another form of shooting in the Royal Garrison Artillery. Pagnam said that Sheldon had told him of the arrangement while they were travelling in a taxicab on the way to Old Trafford. The score was to be 2-0 and each player would receive £3. Pagnam had refused and threatened 'to bang one in', but Sheldon warned him that if he did he would be 'bloody well finished' at Liverpool.

Nevertheless Pagnam did try, and was duly warned when he came close near the end of the game with a shot against the bar. How different this whole story would have been had the shot gone in, a thought which no doubt crossed the minds of several of the players then sitting in the court.

Another Liverpool player not part of the arrangement was the captain, Ephraim Longworth. He said in court that the game was definitely fixed and that at half-time he had warned his team-mates to play the game or there would be trouble. No doubt Longworth remembered the fuss over the game against Chelsea in 1913. Donald McKinlay, another who had played in both games, said in the witness box that he too had refused to have anything to do with the fix. Sheldon had told him 'to lie down' during the game.

Sheldon also approached Robert Purcell, the right-half, who immediately agreed to join in. Purcell then telephoned a friend in London and told him to put a £1 bet on the result. He later took half the profits of the 6-1 winnings, which of course were small fry compared with West's alleged investment.

Billy Meredith, United's famous winger and now also a licensed victualler in Longsight, said in evidence that he had no foreknowledge of the plan, but once the game was under way he realized something was wrong because no one passed to him. No doubt aware of

Meredith's past experiences with attempted bribery (see Chapter Two), his subsequent rehabilitation and his prominent role in the Players' Union, the other players had very wisely decided to keep the whole arrangement from him. Meredith remembered asking his goalkeeper during the match if he knew anything, but as Robert Beale said when he was called to the witness box, all he knew was that before the game Sheldon had told him that he would be enjoying a quiet afternoon.

And so the court hearing continued, the witnesses becoming less well known to the public as the afternoon drew to a close, and another day's proceedings began the following morning. The referee and linesmen gave their versions of the match, followed by the United secretary/manager John Robson. Each agreed that the match was fixed.

Robson told the court that in a fit of anger after the game he asked West why he had kicked the ball out of play all the time. West apparently replied 'What would you do if you had a number of matches to play in a few days?'

One witness described the match as 'a very weird exhibition' in which 'neither team seemed to care what became of them'. A part-time bookmaker, Mr E. Giles, said he had taken a number of bets on the game. Bets on results were common enough, but on the actual scoreline were rare. Had he not suspected something and refused to accept further bets he would have lost as much as £500. As it was he lost £150, and that was quite enough.

Only on the third day of the hearing was a member of the commission called into the witness box. It was the diminutive, apparently frail figure of Charles Sutcliffe, the little lawyer from Lancashire who never seemed to tire of his extensive work for the League. In his opinion, and after wide-ranging research, Sutcliffe was convinced that West was prominent among the United players in this 'squaring'. He reminded the court that Sheldon admitted that West was one of the original plotters at The Dog and Partridge, and although he was unable to give any specific examples, Sutcliffe also said that West's evidence at the enquiry had been contradictory. He was not accusing West of having made a bet himself, but there was no doubt that several of West's friends had done.

Finally, it was the turn of the judge, Justice Ridley, to sum up. The FA, he said, had a duty to report the findings of its commissions, because '... these football matches were of general interest in the North of England' (a remark not destined to go down well with Southerners in the court). He said that when the commission first tried to make a report on the matter it chose not to implicate West, yet had its report declared the match to be fixed without actually implicating someone from the Manchester United team, not only would the commission have looked ridiculous but it would also have been guilty of malice.

On the question of whether West had been libelled in any of the newspaper articles, the judge considered the reports to have been 'fair comment', since they merely represented the facts as stated in the FA's judgement.

And so he came to a verdict. Not surprisingly, after all the evidence and the judge's comments, Enoch West lost his case on both counts. No libel was proved, and the FA ban still stood. Presumably West would now drop the whole matter and shy away from any further publicity which would surely only serve to damage his reputation further. Had the public not heard and read enough to be convinced that justice had been done?

In fact there was very little reaction to the case. A solitary letter to *The Times* on July 12, from the aptly named Dean J. E. C. Welldon of Manchester, noted how West's case had not failed 'to excite very serious disquietude'. (Welldon was a former headmaster of Harrow who boasted with unconcealed glee that he had once spanked Winston Churchill. He later became the outspoken Bishop of Durham, as we are reminded in Chapter Four.)

'Gambling is a poison which vitiates the very soul of athletic games', wrote the Dean. Sport had to be liberated from gambling, especially when the 'nobler moral spirit' evoked by the present War called for 'the very elevation of sport'.

For Enoch James West the War did eventually call, soon after his unsuccessful court action. But he was lucky, being billeted as a driver to the then safe posting of Ulster, where he apparently tried to play football under the pseudonym of Reeve, before being found out and stopped.

That might well have been the very last we ever heard of Enoch 'Knocker' West. But, as those who knew him were to remark in later years, he was nothing if not a persistent man.

Apparently still convinced of his innocence, on 11 February 1918, in the Court of Appeal, West argued against the previous court's decision. This time he was successful on one count. A new trial was ordered on the question of whether the newspaper comments were defamatory. On the question of the FA ban, West's appeal was turned down.

But a new hearing would take eleven months to materialize, and so let us leave Enoch West temporarily and take notice of two important events.

The most important was of course the Armistice and the return of all the surviving footballers to civilian life. Those still young and fit enough went back to their clubs, while both the FA and the Football League started to pick up the pieces after three barren years. West went back into the Ford factory.

The other significant event as far as our history is concerned occurred before the Armistice, when in March 1918 a former Manchester United footballer was charged by the police of 'having conspired with persons unknown who had made bets on the results of various matches'. The former player was none other than West's old team-mate, George Anderson.

Anderson, who had claimed to have no personal involvement in the Good Friday scandal, also denied the charges on this occasion. They were absurd, he said. He had never betted. There must have been a conspiracy against him.

He was presumably referring to the signed evidence given by seven current professionals. Thomas Fleetwood of Everton alleged, for example, that Anderson had called on him in January and offered him £10 if Everton lost or drew their game against Blackpool. A similar offer was made by an unknown gentleman, referred to in the hearing only as 'the Jew'. Fleetwood reported the matter to his club, which instructed him to meet Anderson again and take £20 from him. Everton then won the match comfortably 7-2 and Anderson demanded his £20 back.

William Gault, also of Everton, was allegedly offered £60 for the Blackpool match by Anderson, while David Wilson, the captain of Oldham Athletic, claimed that Anderson and 'the Jew' had called on his shop and offered him £20 if Oldham lost their match against Blackburn Rovers. Wilson reported the approach to his directors before leading his team to a 2-0 victory. Similar stories were told by four Manchester United players, Meehan, Woodcock, Silcock and Ellis.

Some reports suggested that Anderson was 'working for a big (betting) firm in Scotland', which may well have been the case, because at the very same time Anderson had allegedly approached the seven players, various other players in Lancashire received this same curious missive from two apparently separate firms of Scottish accountants.

Each letter began:

'Sir,
  I understand that you are a reliable man – one whom I can thoroughly trust.'

There then followed an offer of £50 to throw a particular match!

Although the letters bore signatures and addresses, a further investigation by the Football League proved these to be bogus. Perhaps they were Anderson's handiwork, or, if Scottish betting interests were active in Lancashire at the time, it was certainly feasible that Anderson had acted as a go-between.

At his trial for 'conspiracy to defraud' in April 1918 Anderson was described as a former warehouseman who was now living on savings of

£400. He denied working for bookmakers, although he could not deny having run in a foot handicap race under a false name.

After hearing the evidence the jury took an hour to reach a verdict of 'Guilty', and taking Anderson's former good conduct into account Justice Salter passed sentence of eight months imprisonment with hard labour. It was a tragic fate for a former player of such promise, who, at the age of only twenty-six might otherwise have renewed his career at the end of the War.

A month or so after Anderson left prison, Enoch West was back in court again. On 15 January 1919 his second attempt to win libel damages began, this time with Justice Darling in charge of the proceedings. Much of the same ground was covered in this hearing, but the libel charges were aimed differently.

Hulton newspapers had reported at the time of the FA's judgement that the committee had been divided on one issue, that of which players were to be punished. Reports suggested that the FA had acted only where total proof was found, while other players had escaped punishment because of inconclusive evidence.

On 27 December 1915, therefore, *Athletic News* commented 'it is only on that basis that we can possibly understand why four times as many Liverpool players have suffered compared with Manchester United's solitary defaulter!'

West claimed that this remark was 'unfair comment'.

At the first commission meeting Charles Clegg had apparently said that there seemed to be little evidence against West, and there had been a unanimous vote not to punish him without further information.

In his defence West told the court that at the time of the match in question he had only been three months away from a promised benefit, so he was hardly likely to have jeoparized possible earnings of up to £2000. He then made a surprising accusation. He claimed that Manchester United had deliberately sanctioned the allegations against him in order to avoid paying out his benefit money. It was a wild charge, and fortunately for him not taken seriously.

Patrick O'Connell was again called into the witness box, as was Charles Sutcliffe, but little new information emerged; O'Connell repeated his denials, Sutcliffe retold the story of the investigation. The League official did concede that at one stage of the enquiry West's name had been struck off the list of guilty players, but also revealed how some of West's own evidence to the commission had been contradictory. For example, although West at first denied playing defensively in the second half, when shown press reports suggesting otherwise he then claimed that O'Connell had told him to play back. O'Connell denied giving such an instruction. West had also told the commission he had no relatives in Hucknall Torkard. This, too, was a lie.

Inevitably, the outcome of this final trial went against West, and this time he was also ordered to pay costs. Essentially he had never looked as if he would win, but then no one had expected the action in the first place, let alone an appeal or a second trial. Nor was it ever known how West could have financed such extensive legal action.

But those who knew 'Knocker' West were not surprised at his behaviour. One of his sons, Jimmy West, said of his father, 'He was always very persistent. There was never any messing about with him. He always stood up to the authorities. If he was living today he would be a Communist.'

So was Enoch West perhaps a committed ideologist with a serious grudge against the establishment? Another of his sons, Eric, who had a short professional career himself with Grimsby Town, suggests otherwise. He says his father was only interested in 'beer and billiards'.

One thing was certain. 'Knocker' West never renewed his contacts with football after his last defeat in the courts, even when the four Liverpool players banned with him were, in recognition of their army service, given the opportunity of apologizing for their behaviour. Purcell, Miller, Fairfoul and Sheldon each duly expressed their regrets, and with the exception of Fairfoul all went on to play for Liverpool after the war. Purcell made only two more appearances in the first team, while Jackie Sheldon played a further seventy-two games until a broken leg ended his career in 1921. The club even granted their reformed sinner a benefit.

Tommy Miller made a superb return to football, scoring fifteen goals in his first twenty-four games for Liverpool. Indeed, he was so impressive that he received his first cap for Scotland in 1920, and won two more after he had been transferred to a new club, ironically Manchester United (he was joined at Old Trafford by another of the Liverpool players who took part in that fateful Good Friday match, Jimmy Nicholl).

Because of his challenge to the FA West was probably never given a chance to apologize, though it is doubtful he would have taken it anyway. Not once during his lifetime did he ever admit any guilt. Nor can we ever entirely dismiss the possibility that despite all the evidence West may indeed have been innocent.

But however guilty or innocent he was, the emotional scars remained with West for life and undoubtedly had a lasting effect on his personal circumstances. In about 1927 he left his wife and six children and went South to Ford's new factory in Dagenham, Essex, where he remained until his retirement after the Second World War.

His last years were spent near to Old Trafford in Walnut Street, Salford, but despite having his FA ban finally lifted by the general amnesty of October 1945, at the age of fifty-nine, he stayed away from football. Of Manchester United he once told a newspaper reporter, 'I don't want to go near that place again.'

'Knocker' West's penultimate appearance in the newspapers came in October 1960. The footballing world had just been shaken by the revelations of former Welsh international Roy Paul, in the *Sunday People*, and a full League investigation into bribery allegations was just getting under way (see Chapter Eleven). The *Manchester Evening News* went to see West, who was then seventy-four years old, but still active and forthright.

'It is unbelievable the amount of corruption and back-biting that goes on in a dressing room', he commented. Those players who admitted to taking bribes, as Roy Paul had done, were wrong, said West. 'If a player is approached and asked to fix a game he should agree and then go straight to the FA.'

Before anyone could ask why he had not done this himself forty-five years before, West repeated the fact that he was innocent. 'My career was ruined', he said, defiant as ever.

'Knocker' West last made the news in September 1965. At the age of seventy-nine in Eccles Hospital he lost another battle, against cancer.

4
Dear Sir, I Must Protest . . .

'MORE selfish or more unsportsmanlike conduct it would be difficult to conceive. The League Committee, in abetting it, are guilty of an even more serious offence against what used to be the accepted and honourable traditions of sport and fair play.'

Association football rarely commands the attention of *Times* leader writers, but, as the extract above exemplifies, when the occasion did arise, at least in the years before the Second World War, any attack upon good old amateur sport by those tainted, ungentlemanly professionals was as good a topic as any to get 'The Thunderer's' hackles rising.

This particular tirade against uncricket-like football dates from *The Times* of 18 November 1922. It was written in a bout of moral indignation aroused initially by letters from two men, one a former Corinthians footballer, Stanley Harris, the other J. E. C. Welldon, the former Dean who was now Bishop of Durham. Each had complained only a few days earlier that in football, sport was now only secondary to financial profit, be it from the buying and selling of players or from betting on games.

'Where the love of money comes in', wrote the Bishop, 'the love of sport for its own sake dies out.'

This was hardly a stunning revelation or a worthy analysis. Nor was it apparently based on any first hand experience of attending professional games, but the leader writers accepted the two men's evidence without question or investigation. On November 7 *The Times* called for the 'suppression of the football bookmakers who . . . prey on the gullible public'. One could have said that *The Times* was a touch too gullible itself, but, as is so often the case, once the newspaper saw fit to give the matter space on its editorial and letters pages, football's woes immediately assumed grave proportions indeed.

Serious enough at least for the *Athletic News* to counter with its own opinion a few days later. Even though it was doubtful whether either Harris or Bishop Welldon had actually seen any betting at a Football League game, said the *News*, was it not ridiculous to castigate the entire professional body just because some people liked to place bets on results? Test matches, the boat race, even general elections were subject to betting among the highest in the land. With its usual poetic verve the *News* mused on the Bishop:

'O shame, where is the blush? Religion weep!
If such the shepherds, what must be the sheep?'

There the matter would have rested no doubt, until some other morally righteous individual saw fit to deride football betting while conveniently omitting to mention any of the more privileged punters at Ascot or Epsom.

A few days after the letters appeared in *The Times* however, as if by divine intervention, an incident occurred which was to bolster the Bishop's case admirably. Furthermore, it was handed to the nation's small but influential anti-professional lobby on a gilded plate by none other than the Football League.

At the centre of the row was Plymouth Argyle, amateurs themselves only nineteen years previously and members of the League for just two years. Argyle were in November 1922 top of the recently-formed Third Division South, having finished the season before in second place. Excused from playing in the preliminary rounds of the FA Cup as a result of this good placing, Argyle found themselves with a free Saturday afternoon on November 18.

Who better to play in a friendly, therefore, than the famous amateur team, Corinthians? Not only would it be an interesting test of Argyle's footballing strength, but it would also give the players a chance to visit the venerated Crystal Palace stadium, where Corinthians had only recently based themselves (Crystal Palace – not to be confused with Selhurst Park – had from 1895 until 1914 been the home of the FA Cup Final and was only just back into use for football after spending the war years as an army depot). In addition, which set of provincial players would not welcome the opportunity of a London jaunt?

Accordingly, the Plymouth secretary-manager Bob Jack, father of the famous trio of brothers, David, Robert and Rollo (all of whom he sold to Bolton Wanderers) made the necessary arrangements with the Corinthians and looked forward to a pleasant break from the rigours of a League season.

But it was not to be. On the same day that Argyle were due to play the friendly, Crystal Palace FC were entertaining Barnsley in a Second Division fixture at their new ground, the Nest, less than two miles from the old Crystal Palace grounds. Palace manager Eddie Goodman complained to the League that because Argyle's visit would reduce the gate at the Nest, the match against Corinthians should be rearranged so as not to clash.

Football League Secretary Tom Charnley agreed. Argyle's action was an indirect threat to the welfare of another League club and so the friendly should not proceed. There was a precedent for this, Charnley said later. The League Management Committee had once prevented Chelsea from hiring out Stamford Bridge for an inter-universities game on the same afternoon that Fulham had a home match.

Reluctantly Bob Jack sent a wire to the Corinthians' Honorary Secretary Geoffrey Foster informing him that Argyle had to cancel the game owing to a League ruling. Foster was outraged. What right had a professional body to interfere with the freely-arranged fixtures of an amateur club? One might put it more bluntly: what right had a bunch of Northern tradesmen to mess up the sport of a few honest Southern gentlemen? Immediately, Foster wired his reply. The Corinthians would not accept Argyle's withdrawal without further explanation.

The following day Jack cabled back, explaining Crystal Palace's objections and the League's subsequent instruction. 'We have no option', said Jack.

Foster was even angrier now. If a local professional club could prevent the staging of another football match on its doorstep, merely because it feared a lower financial return, what hope would there be for any successful amateur team in the country? Clearly he could not allow such a precedent to be established, for the sake of all amateurs.

'Must hold you to your engagement', said Foster in his swift reply. Jack wired back the day after, just twenty-four hours before the game was scheduled. 'Regret definitely impossible'.

Argyle remained in Plymouth.

So Foster turned at once to his natural ally, *The Times*, whose Saturday edition, as indicated by the leader column we quoted earlier, was equally indignant. The League's 'astounding' action, said *The Times*, reinforced exactly what the Bishop of Durham and Stanley Harris had so recently written. This was a 'Football League scandal', in which the tyranny of the League was matched only by the selfish attitude of Crystal Palace, who feared for their own gate on an afternoon when there were other important Cup ties being played in London.

The *Daily Telegraph* was similarly perturbed. 'It is difficult to believe such unsportsmanlike behaviour', wrote a correspondent. Down in Plymouth the *Western Independent* called it a 'football sensation', which had aroused 'indignation in the amateur world'.

But although Argyle's chairman, Mr Elliot Square, was most upset, his club would nevertheless abide by the League's decision. At the same time, manager Eddie Goodman tried to put Palace's point of view. 'Supposing we went down to Plymouth', he told the *Independent*, 'and fixed up a match there to clash with one of theirs. There would be the same objection made to it that we are making now.'

His argument was lent extra weight on the Saturday afternoon in question, as a larger than normal crowd of 12,000 turned up at the Nest to watch Palace beat Barnsley 2-0. Come Monday, however, and the *Athletic News*, in most respects the voice of the League, published in Manchester, tore into *The Times*, the voice of another establishment which emanated from London.

Condemning 'hysterical commentators' the *News* wrote that Argyle had broken one of the original rules of the Football League, an undertaking not to jeopardize fellow members. 'The League had no choice, and because the officers acted as bound by law and custom, they have been compared with the Bolshevik rulers of Russia! What next?' (The Bolsheviks were at that very time in the midst of a dour but ultimately successful struggle to control the old Russian Empire.)

On the same day the Corinthians gave vent to their anger by complaining most heartily to the FA. 'It is almost unnecessary to submit the disastrous consequences which must ensue, not only from the cancellation of this particular match, but from the official recognition of the principle which it involves.'

The complaint, recorded in *The Times* of course, also noted that the Corinthians had an arrangement with the owners of the Crystal Palace grounds, so that both the club and the owners had suffered loss of revenue as a result of the Argyle match being cancelled.

Surprise, surprise, noted *Athletic News* a week later. In one breath the League is condemned for putting money before sport, in the next the Corinthians complain that they and their landlords have suffered financial loss. Meanwhile, back on the letters page of *The Times* the amateur sportsmen continued to froth.

Football is a sport, not merely 'a money-making machine', wrote R. A. L. Mackenzie of London NW11. In future, he asked, would every non-League club have to apply for special permission to play a game on the same day a League match was being staged nearby? He deplored the League's action.

Another Southerner, P. Liddell of Winchester, described the cancellation of the match as a 'death blow' to professional football. His sympathy went out to Geoffrey Foster, who had done so much to help revive amateur football. Surely the man was owed an apology by the League and Crystal Palace FC.

'Can it be possible', Mr Liddell asked rhetorically, 'that next summer Lords' will object to Surrey CC having a match at The Oval on the same day, for fear of losing gate money?' Of course not, he wrote. Cricket would never descend to such a 'disgusting and degrading state' as football.

Foster himself wrote a letter, but this time to *Athletic News*.

Amateurism had been attacked and the Corinthians arrogantly treated. 'This tirade is terrifying', he wrote. The Football League has dictated to the public.

But *Athletic News* was still unmoved. This incident had 'aroused the indignation of London newspapers, ever eager for sensational news and ever ready for an attack on the League, which is merely a federation of professional clubs'. In its opinion, Plymouth Argyle had no right to arrange the game. They must have seen the Palace game on the fixture list beforehand and have known the detrimental effect their own match would have had on gate receipts at the Nest. This would have harmed not only Palace but Barnsley also. 'Argyle (are) the culprits, not the League', *Athletic News* judged.

Nor had the matter anything to do with an attack on amateurism, it was purely a question of gate receipts. 'Mr Foster knows. We all know. It is well not to deceive ourselves and to swallow bunkum.'

Like all 'honest folk' the Football League only wanted to pay its way. If that be 'ugly commercialism', it was a doctrine which had universal approval, and that was the end of the matter as far as *Athletic News* was concerned.

But Corinthians still expected the FA to take some action. It was, after all, the guardian body of all English football, both amateur and professional. In the meantime, however, a still unpacified Foster rearranged the friendly with Plymouth for Saturday, December 2, when Crystal Palace were playing away at Blackpool.

Perhaps Palace's fears had been justified however, for an estimated crowd of 5000 attended the game at the old stadium. Plymouth won 2-0, though according to *The Times*, Lieutenant K. E. Hegan for the Corinthians was the best forward on the field. How nice it had been, suggested the correspondent, that the 'old familiar wooden supports on the grass banking were patronized as in the days of the Cup Finals'. Suffice it to say that the *Athletic News* reported only the result of the game.

Ten days later the matter came to an end. The FA issued an eight page pamphlet in which it was plainly stated that 'most of the comments on this affair have been the very dregs of nonsense'. Argyle were newcomers to the League and, it transpired, had not realized that the League's ruling on arranging fixtures had also applied to amateur opponents. (In this they were hardly blameworthy. The regulations only stated vaguely that 'Clubs shall not arrange matches until after the League fixtures have been settled'. Did that mean that once the fixtures were finalised clubs could fill in any empty dates, or that no other games could be arranged until every League fixture had been completed?)

It was also suggested in the FA pamphlet that Argyle had somehow believed that the Corinthians still played at Queen's Club, West Kensington, although even if this had been the case it would hardly have eased matters since both Fulham and Chelsea's grounds were close by.

The FA did however, order Argyle to pay the Corinthians the £10 sum which had been demanded as token compensation, and on December 16 Bob Jack sent the cheque.

There were newspaper reports suggesting that John McKenna, President of the Football League and a vice-president of the FA, had said that in future the authorities should simply let any game proceed and then afterwards order the offending club to pay the balance of gate receipts in compensation.

But despite the weeks of argument and protest in the newspapers, there was no amendment to the rule until the start of the 1927–28 season, when a clause was added on to the original regulation, prohibiting clubs from 'improperly interfering' with other clubs' home fixtures. Nowadays this comes under regulation 24 of the Football League, which prohibits any member from arranging games beyond the competition without first obtaining the League's sanction.

If this curious little episode had any significance beyond mere clarification of the rules, it was, surely, that the League had showed itself to be prepared to act as a monopoly whenever necessary – that is to treat League clubs and the product they offered as a quantity to be distributed under its jurisdiction only, in deference to no one, whatever limits this placed on fellow members of the FA.

In this, the League was behaving no differently from dozens of other organizations which sought to protect their own interests, no doubt many of which were faithfully represented in The Times, but because it was football and because the perceived victim was amateurism, it was widely viewed as an outrageous affront to sport. In fact, 'The Thunderer' had for once done real sport an injustice.

In one respect, however, the whole affair had a highly desirable sequel. The Corinthians had become so frustrated with their limited fixture list and the difficulty of arranging matches against top opposition that only a few weeks after the Plymouth incident the club broke one of its own golden rules. Ever since its formation in 1882 as a club for ex-public schoolboys and university men, Corinthians had determined never to play a competitive match, with the exception only of charity shield matches.

After the treatment they received from the League in November 1922 the club discarded this rule, and in January 1923 played in the FA Cup for the first time ever. This was a genuinely intriguing departure, since previous Corinthian teams had shown in friendlies against top professional teams – Blackburn Rovers in 1884, Preston in 1889, Aston Villa in 1900 and Bury in 1904 – that they were once strong enough to beat even the FA Cup winners and the League champions.

But although Corinthian players still occasionally appeared for England during the 1920s, the football world had changed dramatically since those famous victories. So how would the present crop of Corinthians fare against modern professionals?

In fact, the amateurs were by no means disgraced in their first few years in the competition. Huge crowds flocked back to the Crystal Palace grounds for many an epic Cup tie against League opposition, almost as if the old stadium were trying to prove itself in competition with its newly completed successor across the River Thames at Wembley Park. There was victory again for Corinthians over Blackburn in their second season of competition, and in 1926–27 the amateurs reached the Fourth Round, only to suffer defeat against League Champions Newcastle United in the last fifteen minutes.

Ironically, Corinthians stayed at the old stadium longer than Palace remained at the Nest. Two years after their argument with Argyle the League club moved a short distance to their present ground at Selhurst Park, which is also very close to the Crystal Palace grounds, now home of the superb national Recreation Centre. So Palace's rival attractions nowadays are more likely to be famous athletes like Sebastian Coe or Daley Thompson than Devonian footballers.

Sadly, Corinthians' strength and appeal as competitors against professionals diminished in the 1930s. Just before the Second World War they amalgamated with the Casuals, and as Corinthian Casuals FC have been competing ever since, in both league and cup competitions while flying the amateur flag until their centenary in 1983 and beyond.

Plymouth, for their part, appeared to have been jinxed by their 1922 experience. An unparalleled run saw them finish as runners-up in the Third Division South for no less than six seasons in a row, followed by two seasons in 3rd and 4th place respectively, until finally in 1930 they won promotion to Division Two.

Perhaps the Bishop of Durham had said something . . .

5
Getting the Right Result

H OW would you react if you discovered your favourite team had been relegated because a game involving fellow strugglers had been fixed? Or your club had missed out on promotion because of an arrangement? Would you even recognize a fixed game if you saw one?

In this chapter we look at some of the attempts between 1919 and 1952, successful and unsuccessful, to arrange the results of important games in the Football League, for the benefit of certain clubs rather than gambling interests. Some of the men involved in the rigged games sought to avoid relegation, some wanted to secure promotion. Sometimes the offer to fix a game has been laughed off, sometimes it has been eagerly accepted. Not all the players or officials need have known, though many might have suspected.

Only if there was someone at least suspicious or brave enough to report the matter, and only if whoever heard this report has then passed on the information to the FA or the Football League has there been an enquiry. The other occasions, if indeed there have been any, belong entirely in the realm of conjecture.

Before we study individual cases however, it is important to look at football's own internal system of justice – many claimed injustice – by which a joint FA/Football League commission of enquiry would investigate an alleged serious infringement and then pass judgement.

For a start there has not always been a right of appeal. All FA and Football League judgements were (and are), however, subject to the law, and if a player or official felt aggrieved he could, with the right case and resources, seek redress in the courts. In practice this happened only rarely – Enoch West's unsuccessful attempt was one example – and only on a few occasions have FA rulings been overturned (see Chapter Eight). This is not to say that the football authorities were always right, or indeed that all the guilty men were punished. Several may have escaped because of a lack of evidence.

High-ranking lawyers were invariably well represented on FA and Football League commissions; men like Clegg, Sutcliffe, Cuff, and Brook Hirst were respected solicitors (as are many of today's officials), and they were well aware of their limitations and responsibilities. Remember Sir Charles Clegg's words: 'Never let us do anything that we cannot justify, if need be, in a court of law.' Sir Frederick Wall added,

'The football community has to trust the FA.' And so it did, usually. For example, few people had believed that Billy Meredith was guilty of offering a bribe in 1906, but a year later they discovered the FA had been quite right to ban him.

But at the time of the Meredith decision, and on several similar occasions in later years, the FA's judgements often seemed harsh and even ill-considered. This was mainly because for many years neither the FA nor the Football League seemed to develop any acumen for public relations. In the majority of cases concerning bribery and corruption the public was given only the briefest of statements with no further explanation (the Good Friday 1915 match report was an exception). It was then up to the press to sort out the resultant confusion of rumours, accusations and denials.

Such was the aftermath of the Travers case at the end of the 1921–22 season. Bernard 'Barney' Travers was a tall, strong and immensely popular centre-forward whom Fulham had bought from Sunderland in 1921 for £3000, equal to the record fee set a few months before. He proved a worthwhile investment, however, with twenty-eight goals in forty-five appearances.

On 18 March 1922 Fulham had a vital away game with South Shields (later to become Gateshead) at Horsley Hill. Both clubs were chasing the Second Division leaders, but the London side, in fifth place, had possibly their best chance of promotion for several seasons. With ten matches to play Fulham were four points behind second placed Stoke.

Fulham's left back in those days was a Scot called Alec Chaplin, who began his career with Dundee Hibs and had come to London to work in an aircraft factory during the First World War. He and his family actually lived in the Craven Cottage at Fulham's ground. Alec, who was ninety-three in 1984, remembers the game against South Shields.

'It was an important game', he recalled sixty-two years later, 'because we'd been going well and had a chance of winning the League.' Chaplin and the team travelled up to Horsley Hill just before the game, but he remembers that Barney Travers met them at the ground. There was general impression that Travers, who hailed from the North East, had been sent up a few days beforehand, although no one at the time knew why.

'I knew one of the South Shields players, a chap called Hutchinson who I remembered from junior football days, and as the players went onto the pitch before the match I went over to him, and I'd hardly got talking to him when someone pulled him away. I thought nothing about it. I thought he was getting instructions maybe', said Chaplin.

According to *Athletic News* 'Travers was a clever bustling leader' of the Fulham attack that day, whereas the South Shields Gazette commented that up to half-time Travers 'had scarcely been in the picture', thanks to some tight marking. Chaplin's defence, said the Gazette, had been 'heroic', but not enough to prevent the 12,000 spectators seeing South Shields deservedly win the game 1-0 (and they finished the season in sixth place, just ahead of Fulham).

After the match, Chaplin recalls, there was talk of there having been an attempt to 'square' the result, and he then realized that Hutchinson had not been allowed to talk to him because the South Shields players were afraid of a Fulham player making another illegal approach.

South Shields hardly waited a moment. They reported the matter so quickly that by Sunday the FA had set up a joint commission of enquiry with the Football League, and this met in London on Monday. The hastily-gathered commission heard evidence from Alf Maitland, the South Shields left back, that Barney Travers had offered him £20 to lose the match. He swore this to be true in front of a Commissioner of Oaths, although Travers' own evidence directly contradicted Maitland's.

Had the ninety minute enquiry been conducted in a court of law we would have known more of the facts, but such commissions always investigated in camera. Thus, when the FA's decision was announced nearly three weeks later on April 8, on the morning of the England v Scotland match at Villa Park, there was only the briefest of statements – Bernard Travers of Fulham was permanently suspended from football and football management.

Understandably there was consternation. One of the most expensive footballers in the British game, and one of the most successful in goalscoring terms, was reported to have offered £20 to fix a game. 'A man in his station does not put down £20 to gain a bonus of £2 for a win', commented *Athletic News* warily. Alec Chaplin agrees. 'He couldn't go up there and bribe anyone with what he earned.' Nor, according to Chaplin, did Travers seem the type of person to have initiated such a move himself. There had to be others behind him, *Athletic News* believed, and therefore the commission was duty bound to release more information so that Travers alone would not have to pay the price for other people's wrongdoings.

Of course, this information never came. The FA remained silent on the matter, even on the question of whether Fulham themselves had been implicated. This was an unusual omission, since in previous cases of attempted bribery the clubs of players involved had been publicly exonerated from blame. Instead Fulham's name was not cleared, although the club did state that no charges had been levelled. They also denied that the club was helping Travers financially through his misfortune.

There was, however, a very strong suspicion among people close to the club that Travers, as a local lad, had been sent to South Shields by a Fulham official to offer the bribe, and that the manager Phil Kelso, if not the instigator, was certainly aware of the plan. If this were true, Travers had indeed been made a scapegoat.

While Fulham counted their losses, Charles Clegg of the FA mistakenly put the whole affair down to gambling and made a predictable pronouncement. Players were warned once again that betting on matches was contrary to FA rules and that if approached by gamblers they should contact the authorities immediately. But Clegg made no mention of what a player should do if his own manager or chairman made the approach.

For Travers, possibly a naive young man, the lesson was the harshest any footballer could possibly receive. An attempt to relaunch his footballing career in Spain failed when it was quickly discovered why he had left England and so, forbidden to carry on, Barney Travers returned to his family in their Sunderland cottage. There he immersed himself in the family fruit business (which still thrives) and as his son recalls, he was always known as a happy man with many friends. He certainly appeared to carry no long term grudges, and although he rarely went to see football he was said to have been very pleased when in October 1945 his lifetime ban was lifted as part of a general amnesty after the Second World War. He died about ten years later.

While Barney Travers' punishment should have been sufficient to deter any other footballers from such an act in the future, there were several players who must have followed the proceedings with a distinctly uncomfortable feeling that it could so easily have been them.

Almost a year after the Travers case, in March 1923, just a few weeks before that historic first Cup Final at Wembley Stadium, another 'Football Sensation' was uncovered. This time, however, it involved a game which had taken place some years before, and if the Travers case was unfortunate, this new scandal was potentially catastrophic.

The first hint of trouble came in an article in the *Sunday Chronicle* on 4 March 1923. Apparently the Football League Management Committee had received a lengthy letter from an unnamed source, making serious allegations about a match played at the close of the 1920–21 season. The teams involved were said to be from the North and the Midlands and apart from the fact that the letter challenged 'the bonafide character of the result' nothing more was known.

But news travels fast in footballing circles, and the following evening the *Midland Daily Telegraph* revealed that the *Sunday Chronicle* article was referring to a match played on 26 March 1921 between Coventry City and Bury at Highfield Road, but the allegations were unclear and the reports shrouded in mystery. The most that could be confirmed was that such allegations had been heard before, a long time ago, and that they arose from a casual conversation in a certain board-room.

Coventry City's acting president, David Cooke, claimed to know nothing of the allegations. 'I was never more surprised in my life to read such a ridiculous thing', he told the local press.

Twenty-four hours later the rumours were beginning to assume awesome proportions, as the FA announced from Cardiff that a joint commission of enquiry had been set up with the Football League to look into the allegations. 'The Football Association moves in a mysterious way its wonders to perform', wrote an obviously bewildered 'Nemo', the Midland Daily Telegraph's football correspondent.

Many familiar faces were chosen to sit on the commission: Charles Clegg would be the chairman, assisted by Charles Crump, John McKenna, John Lewis, Charles Sutcliffe and from the Midland League, Arthur Kingscott (who we shall read a lot more about in Chapter Six). The only person known to have been called to attend the enquiry as a witness was Harry Pollitt, Coventry's secretary-manager at the time of the game in question.

But was it the game everyone thought? From Preston, home of the League headquarters, came a report that the 26 March 1921 match was not the one at the centre of the enquiry. The scandal was really about Coventry's fixture with Bury on 1 May 1920.

On 9 March 1923 the commission held its first meeting, at the Grand Hotel, Manchester, with so many present and former players and officials in attendance that the anteroom was quite congested. Bury alone brought a party of twenty men to the hotel, including several players. City brought only one player; George Chaplin, a Scottish international full back who was, coincidentally, the older brother of Alec Chaplin, the Fulham defender we encountered in the Travers case. One by one the witnesses were called into the commission's presence, first the Bury representatives, then Coventry's, until after four apparently gruelling hours the meeting was adjourned.

Still it was not entirely clear to outsiders what the exact allegations were, although the FA secretary Frederick Wall did intimate that a substantial sum of money had changed hands in order to 'square' an unspecified match. Another report told how certain individuals confirmed that there had been talk of rigging a result, but that it had been 'mere bravado'.

The next days' crop of rumours suggested that the 'fixed' match had in fact been played in 1919. It was also whispered that the allegations had emerged because of differences among the Bury directors. Apparently allegations of match rigging had been made from time to time at various board meetings, until eventually certain Bury directors had become so tired of the gossip that they decided to inform the League in the hope of instigating an enquiry to clear up the whole matter.

Certainly the affair had aroused widespread interest and speculation. 'For a week or more', reported the *Bury Guardian*, 'it had been the chief subject of conversation in the streets, clubs and private company.'

The enquiry was by now assuming unexpectedly serious proportions. Despite his ill-health, a former Coventry director called Carpenter made the trip to Manchester, while others attended at great personal inconvenience, including present officials who had joined Coventry since 1921 and had no knowledge of the events. But after sifting through the evidence, as often occurred with joint FA and Football League commissions, there was then a long wait. Perhaps the members felt it best to wait until after the Wembley final. Perhaps, as a secret visit to Highfield Road by FA officials suggested, there was still more to find out.

In the meantime there were two significant events. On March 21 the entire Bury board of directors was voted out by the shareholders. The stated cause was not the current enquiry hanging over their heads, but general mismanagement, a controversial admissions policy for Cup ties and some ill-considered team selections. Nevertheless the outgoing chairman entreated his opponents to wait until the commission had proved the directors innocent; he knew very well how it would seem if the shareholders were seen to ditch the board in this hour of crisis.

Three weeks later, a day after he had seen the Scotland v England match, Charles Crump died. He was eighty-three, a senior vice-president of the FA and a genial man, well-loved by all in football. His death would delay the commission's decision still further.

So, while we wait for the wise men of football to make up their minds, let us look back at the match or matches which, we are now fairly certain, were the ones being investigated. They took place on 28 April 1920 and 1 May 1920, and were indeed between Coventry City and Bury.

The 1919–20 season had been a disastrous one for Coventry City, their first ever in the Football League. Up until the end of April they had not been out of the bottom two places in the Second Division, and if they were to avoid seeking re-election – which they would have had to do regardless of the forthcoming formation of the Third Division that summer – Coventry needed at least a point from their penultimate match at Gigg Lane on Wednesday, April 28. Bury themselves were just behind the Second Division leaders and had a slim chance of finishing fourth, but no higher.

Meanwhile Lincoln City, a place above Coventry but with an appalling goal average, could only watch and wait with bated breath. As the Coventry players trained at Blackpool before the Bury game, the *Midland Daily Telegraph* reported, 'Coventry City are leaving no stone unturned, neither are they trusting to elements of luck, to get away from the danger zone.' Little did the reporter realize how close to the nub his comments were.

Whatever the nature of Coventry's preparations, they had the desired effect, for the team managed a splendid 2-2 draw at Gigg Lane that evening, in an exciting and closely-fought game. George Chaplin was described as the best back on the field.

But Coventry still had to win their last game, at home to Bury three days later on Saturday May 1, to be absolutely safe (the 1919–20 season was the first of five played after World War One in which the League experimented by having clubs play each other at home and away on consecutive match days. It was also the first in which the season was officially extended into May). So the Coventry team stayed in Blackpool for extra training while the chairman, Fred Lee, urged the supporters to come on Saturday to cheer their favourites. He also expressed great confidence, perhaps too great, that Coventry would beat Bury at Highfield Road.

Sure enough, in front of wildly enthusiastic, packed crowd, Coventry won the day 2-1 after being a goal down at half-time, and thus finished two points ahead of Lincoln, who were now forced to seek re-election. It had been a close, thrilling end to Coventry's first season in the League, and the first season of organized football since the First World War.

There was great sympathy all the same for Lincoln, who despite finishing above bottom-placed Grimsby Town, failed to gain re-election for the third time in their history, and to rub salt into their wound, whereas they were not even admitted to the newly formed Third Division, their Lincolnshire neighbours, Grimsby, were. The following year, as Lincoln played in non-League football, Coventry fared even worse and finished in 21st place, but were not relegated because that year only one club, Crystal Palace, was promoted from the Third Division.

By the time the match-fixing scandal broke in March 1923 Lincoln City were happily restored to the League, in the Third Division's Northern section, while Coventry were hanging grimly on to their Second Division status. Nevertheless one can easily imagine how Lincoln and their supporters reacted when the validity of those final games of the 1919–20 season was challenged, and how doubly enraged they became when, after much deliberation, the results of the enquiry were eventually announced on Monday, 28 May 1923, at the Connaught Rooms in London.

The commission's findings were indeed shattering. Frederick Wall's typically brief statement suggested that the commission had not been able to ascertain all the facts – hardly surprising if both clubs were implicated – nor did he reveal who had informed the League, or why it had taken three years for the scandal to be uncovered.

Nevertheless the commission had found out enough for the FA to conclude that a total of ten men were guilty of arranging a game between Bury and Coventry City in 1920. In view of the previous judgement of 1915 there was only one possible sentence. They were all banned for life from football and football management.

The men found guilty were, for Bury: J. W. Horrocks, the former chairman, and F. Read, a former director, both of whom had just been voted off the board; W. S. Cameron, the secretary-manager, plus J. Allan, R. Perry, W. N. Ritchie and J. Goldie, all players who were no longer on Bury's books. For Coventry City lifetime bans were imposed on J. Marshall, the chairman, David Cooke, the former director and George Chaplin, the captain. In addition, each club was fined £100 and another Bury player, T. Cornthwaite, the former goalkeeper, was suspended for twelve months.

Not since 1906 had the wrath of the FA fallen so mightily upon individual clubs, but on that occasion the 'crimes' were irregular payments, which most people in the game recognized as being fairly commonplace. This scandal was in many ways far more damaging to the game's reputation, because it involved not only players but managers and club directors in the deliberate rigging of a match result. One could perhaps forgive Leeds City, expelled from the League in 1919 for financial irregularities. Barney Travers' one foolish act was most regrettable, and one could understand how one or two impressionable players might be caught in a bookmaker's web. But two sets of directors? Such involvement had never been proved before.

Furthermore, in fining each club only token amounts the judgement had the effect of accentuating the guilt of those individuals named by the FA. This was deliberate. The commission felt that since both Coventry and Bury were now run by different boards and had largely different playing staffs it would have been unfair to penalize them further. This was certainly true in Bury's case, but not for Coventry.

City were to lose their long-serving and popular captain, George Chaplin, who was quick to proclaim his innocence. 'It has hit me harder than anyone', he told the press. 'In twenty years of football I have never had a complaint of any kind made against me before.' In such bitterness and controversy ended a long career, with Chaplin suffering further by missing out on a promised benefit, due the year after.

A greater loss in the long term was David Cooke, who, though no longer a director, was at the time acting president of the club. For years a generous and active worker behind the scenes, Cooke had only recently saved Coventry by personally paying off a substantial bank overdraft. The censure on him was probably the most crushing. Cooke refused to comment on his ban, while Jack Marshall stoutly denied the charges. 'If any money was paid out, I am ignorant of the fact. I know nothing about it.' However, details in the original letter to the Football League suggested otherwise.

It was later revealed that witnesses had allegedly heard Marshall say at Rochdale that fixing the Bury match had cost Coventry several hundred pounds. It was also said that during the second half of one of the matches in 1921 Marshall had been seen in discussion with a Bury director, Mr Helm. Marshall admitted he had been speaking to Mr Helm, but that the topic of conversation had been the sale of a motor car.

The former Bury director F. Read also denied his involvement in the fix, as did W. S. Cameron, the Bury secretary-manager, who was reported to have been thunderstruck at his lifetime ban. Nothing had been proved against him, he said. J. W. Horrocks was equally shocked. 'The findings of the commission came to me as a great staggerer. I have never known in my twenty years' experience of football a greater miscarriage of justice.' Horrocks faced the additional humiliation of having his name struck off the list of men up for re-election to the Football League's Management Committee, many of whose members were said to have been in favour of expelling both Coventry and Bury from the League.

In reality it was extremely hard for any onlooker to know the whole truth, especially after the misleading series of rumours which had preceded the FA's judgement. Even the FA's final statement added to the confusion. It said that the match which had been fixed was at Bury – meaning the 28 April fixture – and that an arrangement had been made for Coventry to win. If that were the case the fix did not work, because that match resulted in a draw. Did the FA not mean the second game, at Highfield Road? It was all rather confusing, and the FA hardly helped to clear the air by refusing to release more evidence.

One thing was certain. There had been an attempt to arrange one result, and money had changed hands. One of the suspended former Bury players admitted that although he had known nothing of a fix before the game (he did not say which game) a man had approached him afterwards saying 'I have something for you.' The man then gave him £15. When asked what it was for the man replied hastily, 'Oh it's all right', and walked away. The player conceded therefore that there must have been an arrangement, and that since he had kept the money and told no-one, he could hardly complain about the penalty.

Predictably, a few days after the judgement, in June 1923, Lincoln City lodged a formal complaint with the Football League, demanding their right to return to the Second Division. Equally predictably the League refused, on the grounds that the 'fixed' game, which it referred to as the draw at Gigg Lane, had no bearing on Coventry's final position. Technically this was true because Coventry won the next match. Even without the draw at Bury, Coventry would have still stayed up, because Lincoln had a worse goal average.

Nevertheless, Lincoln could argue that Coventry might not have won the second game at Highfield Road had they not received the confidence booster of that draw at Gigg Lane, and that morally therefore Coventry had no right to their current status (this was assuming that the victory at Highfield Road was not rigged also).

Lincoln's unsuccessful appeal was not quite the end of this unseemly business. In January 1925, again without warning, the Coventry v Bury case was reopened, with the result that Mr H. Pollitt, the former secretary-manager of Coventry, was also suspended permanently from football. If there was any consolation for Lincoln it came in the 1925–26 season, when Coventry, who had eventually dropped down to join Lincoln in the Third Division North, finished one place below them, in sixteenth place.

Meanwhile Barney Travers' old outfit, Fulham, were struggling in the Second Division, and at the end of the 1927–28 season were fighting to avoid relegation, ironically, with South Shields. Sensing Fulham's desperation, a director of Oldham Athletic was heard making an offer to one of his opposite number in the Craven Cottage boardroom, just before the two teams were due to play.

Having suffered once before, and no doubt aware of how the Coventry v Bury scandal had leaked long after the event through boardroom chatter, Fulham had no hesitation in reporting the matter, and a commission was appointed. Meeting in Sheffield on May 23 it decided that Mr A. M. Barlow, director of Oldham Athletic, 'made a proposal of a serious character . . . calculated to affect the result of the match'.

Barlow thus became the last Football League director to be banned for life after being found guilty of trying to rig a match. Honest Fulham were relegated, but at least with a clear conscience, and a commendation from the FA for fulfilling their duty.

Incredibly, however, Fulham might also have had a grievance similar to Lincoln's, because only two months later in July 1928 yet another joint FA and Football League commission had to investigate a matter of match fixing. This time the allegations were against Mr P. Proudfoot, the manager of Second Division Clapton Orient, who had just escaped relegation by finishing one point above unlucky Fulham.

These were worrisome days indeed for the League as a succession of managers and officials was asked to testify before the commission in Sheffield on July 27. Had Proudfoot made 'certain proposals with the object of procuring the results of certain matches'? Mr A. Chadwick, the Southampton manager, was called in, as were the Northampton and Brentford managers, Jack Tresadern and Harry Curtiss. This time however, the FA could prove very little, and because the charge was so serious they felt unable to impose the full penalty.

Instead, Proudfoot was suspended for six months for his involvement in illegal payments at Clapton, while the FA openly expressed their dissatisfaction with the evidence of the other three managers. Clearly there was much more to be said, and much to lose in saying it. (Clapton cannot have been too put off, however, because Mr Proudfoot returned for two more spells as Orient's manager between 1930–39).

In retrospect, who can fairly judge the young, naive and often impressionable footballers who became unwittingly entangled in such affairs? Or the managers and directors who appeared to have been driven to their misdeeds by a fear of failure? So rarely was the public ever presented with hard facts, so blurred was much of the known evidence.

An important observation we can make is that none of the convicted individuals mentioned in this chapter ever sought to challenge the FA's judgement in a court of law, as was their right. But then, to working class men like Travers and Chaplin, might it not have seemed as if the ageing gentlemen of the FA and the bewigged gentlemen of the courts were indeed one and the same, part of a hostile establishment? Court appeals also cost money, at least beyond the slender means of a footballer suddenly deprived of his main source of income. Or were the accused and convicted footballers so deeply discouraged from defending themselves further by their own sense of having been dealt an injustice?

Or were they simply all guilty? If they were, we should also ask whether the FA was always justified in depriving these men of their livings in football. Those individuals we saw in Chapter One, convicted in the courts of having attempted to bribe footballers, received relatively light sentences. A few months in prison was hardly the same as being kept from your chosen profession for a lifetime.

Any lesser punishment, however, might have been interpreted as weakness on the part of the authorities. When the football scandals of the mid-1960s were revealed (see Chapter Eleven), there was no doubt that the FA's lifetime bans on convicted players had a most salutary effect on the rest of the profession. It is inconceivable that the punishments handed out to Travers, Chaplin and the rest during the 1920s did not have the same effect on their contemporaries.

Finally, we should consider whether the FA was actually doing the game an indirect disservice by withholding from the public eye all the unsavoury and shocking truths about the game it purported to govern. Of course it was unpleasant for the national sport to have its dirty linen washed in full public view. Of course it was important that the public should not form an impression that all football was crooked. Nevertheless, it is arguable that a better-informed public would have been that much more vigilant, while players and officials might have been warier too. They might also have been encouraged to speak out more boldly when they met with an attempt to fix a game.

As it was, the perceived method by which the authorities judged such matters as match fixing probably alienated more players and officials than it impressed. No one liked to see a fellow professional dealt with in an apparently draconian manner, innocent or guilty. Furthermore, by revealing so little, the FA made it a great deal easier for guilty men to plead their innocence in front of a sympathetic public.

Since those occasional, but nonetheless tormented moments in British first-class football in the 1920s, until the late 1950s there were very few allegations of match rigging, and no recorded convictions or suspensions. Why was this? If we were to presume, regretfully, that match rigging was indeed an inevitable part of the game – albeit only a very small part – there are three possible answers. Either the 'fixers' were becoming more subtle, the FA had lost its teeth, or the tough stance taken by the authorities in the 1920s really did have the desired effect on future generations.

Essentially, there were few substantial changes in either the financial or social status of most players in the years from 1928 until 1961. At the same time the popularity of gambling rose enormously, as a boom in pools revenue indicated (see Chapter Seven). So if match rigging did take place during the period 1928–60 it would have been for the same reasons as it occurred before 1928 – for gambling profits, to ensure promotion or to avoid relegation. (One former professional claimed that it was also possible for a match to be rigged in order to help a neighbouring club avoid relegation, on the grounds that 'it was helping your mates' and it guaranteed potentially lucrative derby matches the following season).

One only has to read the popular Sunday newspapers of the 1950s, for example, for a whole stream of 'frank and honest' revelations about fixed matches, usually by former professionals anxious to sell their story. It is extremely difficult to confirm if any of these stories were true, or whether they had been sensationalized out of proportion by the newspapers, mainly because the revelations never actually mentioned specific games.

However, there is at least one former professional – and possibly dozens more – quite willing to admit to having taken part in or witnessed particular 'rigged' games.

Ken Chisholm was an exuberant inside forward who played 328 League games and scored 132 League goals for six clubs between 1947–57. Born in Glasgow, he began playing with Partick Thistle, coming south to play for Leeds, Leicester, Coventry, Cardiff, Sunderland and Workington, before finishing his career in the United States. Known, not surprisingly, as soccer's 'Happy Wanderer', Chisholm was always a strongly independent man who was never afraid to take on managers or the authorities. He recalls two matches which he knew were definitely rigged.

The first occurred on Saturday 7 May 1949, a week after Chisholm had played in the FA Cup Final for Second Division Leicester City. Leicester, the underdogs, were beaten 3-1 by Wolverhampton Wanderers and were then faced with a testing programme of three League matches in a week. After two of those games ended in defeats they travelled to Cardiff needing just one point to avoid the ignominy of becoming the first-ever Finalists to have been relegated to the Third Division.

But there was one crucial coincidence. Their opponents, Cardiff City, also needed one point, not to avoid relegation but to put them into fourth place in the Second Division. This would entitle the Welsh team to 'talent money' (they had no chance of finishing in third place).

In their last home match of the season on the Thursday evening after the Final, Leicester lost 3-0 to promoted West Bromwich Albion. The Cardiff fixture was their fourth game in eight days and morale was low, with a first team squad already badly depleted through injuries and their scheming centre forward, Don Revie, still unavailable. Both physically and psychologically therefore, the game at Ninian Park represented a considerable hurdle. After Wembley, noted the *Western Mail*, it was like going 'from the sublime to the ridiculous'.

In contrast, their relegation rivals Nottingham Forest were in tremendous form, with a late-season burst which had earned then eleven out of a possible fourteen points. Forest would survive if they could beat Bury at home while Leicester lost away at Cardiff. Added to the fact that Cardiff had a good home record, Leicester's task seemed beyond them.

Manager Johnny Duncan made seven changes from the side beaten by West Bromwich, so that only five of the previous week's Cup Final team were still fit or in favour by the time Leicester arrived at Ninian Park. Chisholm himself was a doubtful starter, having sustained an ankle injury, and seemed likely to miss his first game since joining the club three months earlier from Leeds United. Nevertheless, desperate for scoring power, Johnny Duncan asked him to try a fitness test even though he was patently far from fit. Chisholm agreed because the game was so crucial, but on returning to the dressing room after a few trial sprints along the touchline, he was stopped from getting changed for the game. Somewhat taken aback by this sudden change of heart, Chisholm recalls how he was taken to one side and told that an arrangement had been made for the game to be drawn and so there was no need to injure himself further.

Writing of these events several years later in his unpublished auto-biography *There's Another Way to Live*, Chisholm will not reveal who made the arrangement, or how many or which of the players were involved, but he confirms that it was neither the managers nor the directors of either club. Nor, in this instance, did any money change hands. It was simply an agreement that the match should be a 0-0 draw.

Being a keen gambler, Chisholm immediately dressed, left the ground and telephoned a bookmaker in Glasgow with whom he kept an account. In those days it was still possible to bet on an individual match, with the odds for a draw being 5-2, so Chisholm decided to bet £250 on the game (it was contrary to FA rules for a professional to bet on a match, though this rule was regularly flouted). Chisholm also advised the bookmaker to hedge the bet to a bigger bookmaker – that is, to transfer the liability – since he was certain of the result.

Back at Ninian Park the arranged 0-0 draw got under way and soon began to irritate the 35,000 crowd. Chisholm remembers sitting on the bench feeling extremely embarrassed, as the crowd started shouting remarks like, 'Give them a point, keep them in the Second Division, they got to the Cup Final!'

Indeed there was a great deal of sympathy all round for Leicester, the gallant losing finalists and Second Division strugglers beset with injury problems. Billy King of the *Leicester Evening Mail* wrote in his match report of 'the almost desperate anxiety of the Welsh crowd to see Leicester grab a point'.

The match was, he wrote, 'A polite, drab encounter . . . on both sides a great deal of loose play kept the standard of football at a low level. It was a tame spectacle with both sides behaving so far as though in an exhibition, and the crowd were getting restive.'

King was not alone in his condemnation of this curious match.

'Citizen' of the *Western Mail* described Leicester's performance as 'amazingly inept'. The match, he wrote, 'was just a story of missed chances, half-hearted tackling and ultra-polite tactics from start to finish'.

For part of the ninety minutes the crowd were slow-handclapping the players, while the biggest cheers seemed to come from Cardiff supporters urging on Leicester.

In Chisholm's own words, this is how the game proceeded: 'The play was all in midfield and no-one was tackling hard. A high swirling ball came over into our eighteen-yard box, late in the game, and one of the Cardiff players obviously attempted to head it over the bar, but the wind caught the ball and it dipped into the top right hand corner of our net.'

From then on, with sixty-five minutes gone and the agreed 0-0 draw no longer possible, Leicester had to make a game of it. At least they had the crowd's support. As James Stephens wrote in the *Leicester Mercury*, 'Many people behind the Cardiff goal urged them on by shouts and gesticulations.'

There was even greater urgency when it became known that Forest had beaten Bury – their match had kicked off fifteen minutes earlier – so that Leicester had to equalize to stay up. 'You have never seen panic like it', remembered Ken Chisholm.

But the arrangement was not forgotten. With just thirteen minutes left to play the Leicester centre-forward Jack Lee equalized. Leicester won a corner, and as the Cardiff defence watched it drop into the area Lee struck the ball with such little force that as it bobbled over the diving goalkeeper it hardly reached the back of the net.

'Lee's goal aroused the biggest cheer of the afternoon', wrote Stephens. According to the *Western Mail* it was scored 'with the home defence showing unnatural reluctance to go into the tackle'. Thirteen minutes later the final whistle blew and Leicester were safe.

'Not for a long time have I seen such a "friendly" atmosphere prevailing in a game', wrote 'Citizen' afterwards. '. . . and when the final whistle blew, players of both sides shook hands as they walked off the field together'.

A common enough end to a game one might think, so why did he stress the point? Did the press have their suspicions? Leicester's manager Johnny Duncan told the reporters, 'The last thirteen minutes of the season were the worst I have ever known. I just did not know where to look.' Chisholm later put it differently. 'Everyone felt guilty because it was so obvious.'

Nevertheless Ken Chisholm won his wager, Cardiff's players received their £20 'talent money' and to popular acclaim Leicester stayed in the Second Division. As the *Sunday Dispatch* reported the next morning, there was indeed widespread joy that Leicester, the plucky, gallant losing Finalists, had survived, and on Monday morning Filbert Street was flooded with messages of congratulation, apparently from almost every Football League club. This was hardly a consolation for Nottingham Forest, however, who went down into the Third Division for the first time in their history. Had Leicester been defeated in a true contest Forest would have stayed up.

With hindsight it seems incredible that despite the press reports, despite the result and both teams' performances, no challenge was ever publicly voiced. Neither the Football League nor the FA showed any interest in investigating, nor did Nottingham Forest make any complaint. This fact alone is perhaps the most startling of the whole affair, especially as the game apparently aroused some suspicion among other footballers of the period.

The second time Chisholm was involved in what he describes as an arranged game took place three years later, but on this occasion, on the last day of the 1951–52 season, he actually played. Coincidentally Chisholm was by then a player with Cardiff City, who needed to win their last home game of the season against Leeds United in order to gain promotion to the First Division.

Cardiff were two points behind second placed Birmingham City, who had finished their programme, but the Welsh outfit had a slightly better goal average. For their part, Leeds had no chance of promotion or a 'talent money' placing, so, according to Chisholm, another arrangement was made among certain players, just to make absolutely sure of Cardiff's promotion. The Welsh team were strong favourites to win the game anyway, especially in front of 50,000 enthusiastic supporters at Ninian Park.

The match took place on Saturday 4 May 1952, on the same afternoon as the Cup Final between Newcastle and Arsenal, and there were six players in the Cardiff side that afternoon, excluding Chisholm, who had played in the match against Leicester almost exactly three years before. None of the Leeds officials knew of the arrangement, which resulted in Cardiff being allowed to win easily by 3-1, with Chisholm scoring the third goal in the fifty-fifth minute.

Thus Cardiff were promoted above Birmingham City, by just 0.137 goal average. Had Leeds managed at least a draw at Ninian Park, Birmingham would have gone up instead.

Ken Chisholm does not retell these events with any great pride, nor in an attempt to scandalmonger. 'Before people get hot under the collar', he writes in his memoirs, 'this kind of "arrangement" was commonplace towards the end of every season in those days, and I know of many similar cases where points were given away to save clubs who commanded good support from being relegated, and also to get promotion.'

Chisholm's account was chronicled more than thirty years after the events, but it had been carefully noted down by him long before. He was offered no inducements or incentives to reveal or embellish any of the details. We must ask therefore, how many other crucial matches have been subject to arrangements between two sets of players? How many promotion and relegation issues have been settled entirely by illegal payments or mutual agreements?

There were occasions, sensationally exposed in the Sunday newspapers, when such offers were alleged to have been made, but laughed off. There must surely have been others taken seriously. It is my view, however, that the problem was not as widespread as several former players have suggested. Undoubtedly there were more arranged games than we will probably ever know about, but not many. The professional players' grapevine was a strong one. Rumours spread fast, and it would have been difficult to keep the FA and Football League in the dark for long.

Even so, the events recalled in this chapter make for chilling and dispiriting reading for the followers of teams such as Lincoln City, Nottingham Forest and Birmingham City, who each suffered as a result of arrangements.

6
Arthur Kingscott and the Rebounding Ball

COMPARED with previous years, the 1933 FA Cup Final was an uneventful affair. Everton, the favourites, enjoyed a comfortable 3-0 win over Manchester City, one of the goals coming from team captain Dixie Dean. City's goalkeeper Langford was blamed for two of the goals but otherwise the only other noteworthy feature was the fact that for the first time officially the players wore numbers on their shirts.

That was on April 29, and with a few days of the season remaining attention immediately turned to the title race, with Arsenal, en route for the first of their three successive Championships, successfully holding off a challenge by Aston Villa.

But one man was not content to let the Cup Final be forgotten. He was the referee, Mr E. Wood of Sheffield, and he was angry, not with the result but with the conduct of another former Final referee, Arthur Kingscott, then aged sixty-nine and one of the most powerful men in world football.

Wood's complaint and the inquiry which followed aroused such a commotion that for a brief moment the entire leadership of the FA was put in question, while the long and devoted career of Arthur Kingscott was completely and cruelly destroyed. And it was all because of a single, laced-up leather football.

By tradition one of the referee's tasks at Wembley is to select the match ball. But in 1933 and all previous years different conditions prevailed. The balls brought to Wembley used to be clearly marked with brand names, so that the referee knew exactly who had manufactured the ball of his choice. Naturally, this put him in a difficult position, because everyone knew just how great were the advertising benefits to be gained from supplying a ball for the Cup Final.

Even so, until 1933 the referee's complete impartiality in this matter was never challenged, but in the weeks leading up to that year's Final there were rumours that some manufacturers were indeed trying to exert a bit of gentle persuasion on Mr Wood. Apparently in certain circles it was not unknown for referees and linesmen to compare the fruits of such persuasion with each other. One linesman went on record to say that a former Cup Final referee had boasted of a leather dressing case his wife received from the firm whose ball he chose for a semi-final.

Another linesman, from the 1930 Cup Final, recalls the referee, Tom Crew of Leicester, sending a telegram during half-time. 'I've chosen your ball', he was alleged to have said, perhaps expecting some reward to follow.

Arthur Kingscott held many posts in his forty-year period at the FA, and 1933 found him most notably as Honorary Treasurer, a post he had held since 1918, and chairman of the prestigious Final Tie committee. A former League referee himself (he officiated at the 1900 and 1901 Finals) Kingscott was well aware of rumours circulating about referees, and so, being a scrupulously honest man who also rather liked to impose his authority, he decided to take action.

On the afternoon of the Final he entered the referee's dressing room at Wembley and handed Mr Wood a pre-selected match ball. The referee's traditional privilege had been denied! Words were exchanged and that, thought Kingscott, was that. The match went ahead, but although Kingscott soon forgot the incident, Mr Wood did not. His integrity had been impugned by a high official, for Kingscott was a member of English football's highest body, the FA Council. It just would not do.

Events moved silently at first, until the story finally broke two months after the Final, on July 23. Writing in the *Sunday Chronicle* the former referee and contemporary of Kingscott, J. T. Howcroft of Bolton (whom we first met in Chapter Two) revealed that contrary to existing regulations an official of the FA had taken it upon himself to select the Final ball, and in so doing had used words which struck at the character of all referees, past and present. No names were mentioned and for the next two-and-a-half months no more was heard of the case.

Even if the report were true, past events suggested most strongly that if a member of the FA Council had been at fault, his fellow members would do their utmost to keep the dispute from the public eye. At the court of the FA, as we have seen, there was no public gallery. Besides which, they all knew Arthur. Surely a few quiet words behind the scenes would settle matters. At worst, if indeed he was guilty all they had to do was fail to re-elect him at the next meeting.

So it was, when, to Kingscott's complete amazement, the FA took the major and totally unexpected step of calling for a special commission. A special commission, just because of a leather football! It seemed ridiculous. (Incidentally, one of the Association's officers who demanded redress was Tom Crew.)

Nevertheless Kingscott could hardly have been too concerned. On the commission, which was to sit at the Victoria Hotel, Sheffield, on

October 20, were the very men with whom he had been governing football for decades.

His own record had been exemplary. Since becoming Honorary Treasurer he had seen the FA progress from near bankruptcy after the First World War to a large and prosperous organization with assets of over £120,000. He had personally organized and led several England tours abroad, and he was the first man to have invited foreign teams to England for return matches. He could also claim with every justification to be the man who had introduced the great Derby County and England forward Steve Bloomer to first class football. So high was his standing that on Cup Final days Kingscott was often to be seen as an official escort to the King, a much-coveted role. Coincidentally, in view of the 1933 Cup Final incident, he was also credited by some with being the first man to suggest the numbering of players.

Stories from Kingscott's twenty-one years of refereeing portrayed him as a stickler for discipline – he had never tolerated any dissent from players – and he was in the records as being the only man to referee two First Division games in one day, at Wolverhampton and West Bromwich in 1893. Following in his footsteps came two sons – Harry, who had refereed the 1931 Cup Final (in controversial fashion also) and Cecil, who had just graduated to the League's list of linesmen.

Beyond the FA, Arthur Kingscott was the co-founder and president of the Midland League, an active, community spirited resident of Sawley, near Nottingham, where he was a churchwarden and a freemason, and until his retirement he had been an accountant with the Midland Railway in Derby.

In short, Arthur Kingscott was a model citizen, a dedicated administrator and a pillar of the FA. Indeed, of the elected Council in 1933 only Sir Charles Clegg, the President, Mr A. G. Hines and William Pickford had been involved longer than Kingscott, who first joined the FA in 1894.

Clegg was now eighty-three and completely deaf. Known in his heyday as 'Emperor Clegg' and 'The Cleggislator', he had played in England's first ever international in 1872, an experience he hated because the southern snobs who made up the rest of the team would not pass or even talk to him, a mere northern solicitor. A total abstainer, as was his great friend Kingscott, and a man of few words, unlike Kingscott, Clegg had commanded the respect of all who met him, but now he was losing his grip on power, and was so frail that whenever he travelled he depended entirely on the supporting arm of Arthur Kingscott.

The Secretary of the FA at this time was Sir Frederick Wall, then aged seventy-five and perhaps the most influential man on the Council.

With his drooping white moustache and his strict, formal, some said pompous manner, he embodied the spirit of the FA, where he had worked since 1895. A stickler for tidiness, when everyone else used fountain pens, Wall used a quill, and seldom was he seen without a silk topper or a bowler hat. Perhaps one of his most memorable legacies was the introduction of his favourite hymn *Abide with Me* as part of the Cup Final pre-match community singing.

As the only paid member of the Council, earning £1200 a year, Wall would have had the closest working relationship with Kingscott, who, as Treasurer, was in charge of the cheque-book.

Both Clegg and Wall attended the enquiry at the Royal Victoria Hotel although only Wall, as Secretary, sat on the commission. In the chair was William Heard of the Middlesex FA, a staunch supporter of the Society of Referees, and there were six other members. Clegg looked on, joined by another of Kingscott's friends, the seventy-year-old Football League President, John McKenna, and another veteran of the FA, William Pickford. The youngest member present was fifty-five-year-old Amos Brook Hirst, a Huddersfield solicitor strongly tipped to succeed Sir Charles. Finally there was Arthur Kingscott himself and Mr Wood, the first time either had met since that fateful encounter at Wembley.

Mr Wood's account was the first to be heard. 'A little time after my arrival at Wembley, Mr Kingscott entered my dressing room and asked where the balls were that had been sent for selection. I told him I had not seen any, and none were brought in. He then told me "that as the Council had heard you referees are making money in choosing balls for Final Ties, they had decided to appoint him to choose the ball for the Final". I resented this remark very much, and told Mr Kingscott "if that was the opinion the Council had of their referees, honoured to take FA Cup Finals, I was pleased they had relieved me of all responsibility in the matter". The ball was later brought into the dressing room.'

Kingscott, with all the assurance of a man on home ground, denied ever having used the words attributed to him. 'The committee is engaged on the most grotesque enquiry ever undertaken by the Football Association, and my explanation will show that on innocent incidents they are using heavy machinery to burst a bubble . . .'

Recalling the events leading up to the match, Kingscott told the commission how he had selected the ball at the request of John McKenna, who, he said, had taken it upon himself to act on behalf of the Emergency Committee, in order to scotch 'the ugly rumours afloat' concerning referees. Kingscott professed himself to be astounded at the course events had then taken, because on the afternoon of the Final he was sure that Mr Wood had cordially agreed with his own judgement.

But friend though he was, McKenna was not going to let Kingscott's account go unchallenged. 'Mr Kingscott makes a mistake', he began. Clearly the enquiry was not going to be plain sailing for the Honorary Treasurer after all. McKenna informed the commission that on the Friday before the Final he had told Kingscott that *only if the rumours were true* should someone else select the match ball. He repeated this on Saturday.

Then Sir Frederick Wall spoke. 'After the luncheon at Wembley, I met Mr Kingscott in the corridor. He said the Emergency Committee had instructed him to select the ball because of rumours that referees made money out of it.' Kingscott had then asked if Wall wanted to accompany him to the referee's room, but the Secretary declined.

What followed in the referee's room was now in dispute. Kingscott denied using the words reported, but Wood stuck to his account. It was one man's word against another, and Kingscott was, after all, an FA man. Surely they would believe him.

But before anyone had a chance to comment further on the details, Kingscott spoke up once more. He admitted that the Emergency Committee had not discussed or acted upon the rumours and that therefore he had no authority to act as he did. He acknowledged that although he had been intending to talk to the President about the ball selection he had omitted to do so, despite the fact that he and Sir Charles had eaten dinner and breakfast together immediately before the Final. Even so, he was a trusted member of the Council. What could they possibly do to him?

The answer soon came. The Chairman informed Kingscott that the commission found unanimously that he had used the words attributed to him by Mr Wood and that they should be withdrawn. Kingscott was suddenly numb. His fellow councillors . . . they did not believe him! Defiantly he replied, 'You are asking me to withdraw something I never said.'

But the commission still thought otherwise. Left alone to decide the matter they confirmed their belief that Kingscott had used the words reported, had 'improperly reflected on the honour of past Cup Final referees' and had, without authority, changed the practice of selecting the Cup Final ball. Sentence was deferred. The full FA Council would have to decide.

Kingscott was, in his own words, astounded by the commission's findings when they were sent to him over a month later. His entire career was to be put in question just because of this one, admittedly thoughtless action. And his former colleagues had all deserted him.

Extremely shaken that day, November 17, he sat down and wrote a long, rambling account of what he claimed had occurred on the

weekend of the Final. But far from clarifying the situation this document would only have complicated matters. It was laced with half-
remembered quotes and almost begging in its tone. His sons, Harry and
Cecil, feared for his health and immediately decided to intervene. Next
day they travelled to see Sir Charles Clegg at his home in Sheffield and
here they were given the first intimation of how serious was the matter.
'Your father has made a mistake', Sir Charles told them, 'and there are
those who want him out of office.' There was only one way to save him.
'If your father would only withdraw his words and not adopt such a
defiant attitude and only admit that he said the words, even if he said
his memory played him false after six months, it might help matters.
But if he persists in adopting the attitude he has done, nothing can save
him.'

Therein lay the truth of the matter. Kingscott, for all his efficiency,
power and experience, had made too many enemies. It was not so much
what he had done but the way he had done it. For example, only a
fortnight after the 1933 Cup Final Kingscott led the England tour of
Italy and Switzerland. Having already conducted successful tours to
France and Canada there were undoubtedly some within the FA who
felt that Kingscott might have stood aside to allow someone else the
opportunity of foreign adventure. (On the French tour Kingscott was
remembered for having caused amusement among the host officials
with his comment after the game, 'Un bon allumette!')

But there were other grounds for resentment, because while the party
was in Rome it was reported in the English press that Kingscott had
appointed the Arsenal manager Herbert Chapman, who was travelling
as a tourist with the group, as England team manager. Had this been
true it would not only have been a high-handed action but also an
innovatory one, since the post did not officially exist at that time.

One prominent football official back in London approved, however.
When he read the reports of Chapman's alleged appointment he sent
Kingscott a telegram saying, 'Congratulations on step long overdue'
and signed himself 'Rip Van Winkle'.

In subsequent arguments about the incident one member of the FA
claimed that he had even seen written evidence of the appointment.
Kingscott claimed he had done no such thing. His version of events was
that during a function prior to the Rome match he was handed a menu
with a request scribbled on it by Chapman, asking to have a few words
with the team before the game. Kingscott wrote back, also on the menu,
that he had no objections provided the trainer did not mind. It was
probably no more than the exchange of two men bored by the occasion.

However, official anger aroused by press reports showed how ready
certain men were to pounce on Kingscott's every move. They disliked

his manner, the way he had gone on the last tour half-jokingly pro-
claiming his intention to rule the party like the new Italian dictator. As
one said later, 'The time had come when we simply could not and
would not work with him any longer.'

In addition, and most hurtfully to Kingscott, when the Final ball
controversy erupted there was an unspoken inference that perhaps as
Honorary Treasurer he had not been entirely honest. This was simply
because no-one in the FA ever actually stated in public, until after the
final judgement, that Kingscott's handling of the funds had never been
in question.

On the contrary, not only had he never misused the FA's money, but
it also seems certain that he was too strict and vigilant for some of the
members. Apart from Wall, none of them were paid apart from travelling and day-to-day expenses, so the refusal of a request here and there
could have soon led to animosity.

Curiously, perhaps his worst enemy was not on the Council. A report
in the Sunday Dispatch on 17 December 1933 made a tantalizing
reference to 'the mysterious figure of a woman . . . who is said to have
dominated football's legislators . . . it is rumoured that a woman played
a big part in bringing the trouble to a crisis'.

Until now the identity of this mysterious woman has never been
revealed. In fact she was no femme fatale who had enchanted the aging
gentlemen of the FA. She was the second wife of Sir Frederick Wall, a
former barmaid several years his junior. According to some contemporaries she was a woman of extravagant tastes, rather too fond of a
flutter and not averse to barging into a Council meeting to demand her
embarrassed husband's attention (the Walls lived in an apartment
above the FA headquarters). She also made wonderful jam tarts and
ham rolls for attending Council members, some of whom it was said
she would corner for a loan or two once in a while and others with
whom she would share racing tips. Certainly, if the puritanical Kingscott, as Honorary Treasurer, had refused to accede to any of Mrs Wall's
demands it would not have helped him.

As Kingscott said in the Sunday Chronicle, 'For some time I have
known that I was treading on unpopular ground in certain matters
connected with the FA, but that did not deter me from my duty. I had to
make many decisions which may have been unpalatable to some of my
colleagues . . .'

McKenna agreed that Kingscott might have been in some way the
victim of a vendetta and that certain members would take the first
chance of getting rid of him. But despite knowing all this, Kingscott
still found it hard to modify his blustering manner.

When Harry and Cecil returned from Sir Charles' home in Sheffield they begged their father to change his attitude and write to the FA admitting his error. Unfortunately, however, Kingscott had already sent off to Sir Frederick his first letter, written in the heat of the moment. After much persuasion, Harry and Cecil prevailed upon their father to write another letter, this time confessing his 'guilt' in the affair of the Final ball, even though this ran counter to his strong sense of justice.

Kingscott's second, painful letter said, 'I must have made use of the words attributed to me, and herewith unreservedly withdraw them. After a lapse of six months my memory must undoubtedly have failed me, but my purpose was honest and was done as I thought in the best interests of the game.'

In sending his sincere regrets Kingscott probably thought that the matter would be settled, but in reality he had almost certainly signed his own expulsion order, for Sir Frederick now had both letters before him, and one contradicted the other. It was just the evidence Kingscott's enemies wanted.

Knowing this, Cecil wrote to the Secretary asking for the return of the first letter. 'As he is suffering from a severe nervous breakdown, he was not in a fit condition to draft such a reply.' But Wall was unmoved. He wrote back, refusing Cecil's request.

The final blow fell on Monday, 11 December 1933.

As announced by the commission in Sheffield, the FA Council was to decide what action to take on its findings. When the Council did eventually meet, at Lancaster Gate, Kingscott took his seat as usual, and sat through several items on the agenda as the meeting progressed in normal fashion. There was an application by Folkestone FC to become full members, a request from Tottenham Hotspur to play a charity game in Paris (refused) and perhaps the most exciting event of any FA meeting, there was the suspense-filled draw for the Third Round of the FA Cup. Eventually, the meeting arrived at item number ten on the agenda. All seventy-three men sitting in the chamber must have stirred uneasily in their seats as the chairman read out the report.

In view of the findings of the Sheffield commission ordered to enquire into incidents arising at the recent Cup Final, Arthur Kingscott was asked to resign.

There must have been some anxious moments as all eyes turned to await the Honorary Treasurer's response. Would he do the honourable thing and go quietly? Not Arthur Kingscott. He refused to resign and demanded to face the Council with his own side of the story. How his opponents must have squirmed with displeasure. But they had no choice and sat back as Kingscott read out a long statement.

Unfortunately he told them nothing new. It was exactly what he had written under great stress only three weeks earlier. The Council, he said, should consider the strain placed upon him as Chairman of the Final Tie committee. 'I am earnestly requested by a member of the Emergency Committee . . . to take a certain course, which unfortunately I did, without giving the matter sufficient care or forethought.'

Retelling the events of that afternoon Kingscott concluded, 'I therefore earnestly appeal to our revered President, I appeal to my brother officers, I appeal to every member of the Council . . . not for mercy but for common justice.'

His was a passionate plea, and there must have been some awkward feelings among those older members who had worked for so long with the man now in front of them, desperate for acquittal.

They asked him to leave the room while the Council considered the matter further, Kingscott little realizing that it was not only the question of the Final ball which so animated his fellow councillors. In his absence, three influential members made hostile speeches against Kingscott, making charges he was never called back to answer. Some of the speeches, journalist F. Stacey Lintott was told afterwards, were 'of such violence and bitterness that they astonished many of those present'. But they were certainly persuasive, because when a vote was taken after two hours of debate only a handful of men took Kingscott's side.

Finally, cruelly and tactlessly, William Pickford emerged from the chamber and approached his old colleague who had been waiting, in what emotional state we can only guess, in an adjacent room. Pickford was blunt.

'Kingscott, you are no longer Treasurer of the Football Association', he said, and with that, he took away the cheque books and papers Kingscott had been clutching.

So ended 40 years of service to the FA.

'As I saw him pick up his papers from the top table and leave the council chambers', said a member afterwards, 'I realized that it was the last we should see of him in an executive position, and I suddenly became cold, as if iced water had been thrown down my back.'

The *Daily Sketch* correspondent saw him leave. 'He slowly made his way down the grand staircase of the FA offices in Lancaster Gate. He was alone. He presented a pathetic figure, visibly moved by the terrible shock he received.'

His voice shaking, Kingscott called out to the waiting pressmen, 'Where's Ivan Sharpe?' But Sharpe, the *Sunday Chronicle* football correspondent who had been his lifelong friend and confidante was not there.

Another journalist friend was, however. W. Capel Kirby wrote, in the *Daily Dispatch*, 'At the bottom of the staircase he turned into an anteroom, apparently to avoid the sympathetic gaze of his colleagues who were gathering in the vestibule, preparing to leave the building. It was obviously a very tense situation for everybody present . . . he presented a pathetic figure to those who, like myself, have known him for so many years as a care-free, cheerily disposed man, enjoying the prime of life.'

In a neighbouring room a few members of the Council were taking refreshment, but instead of the usual jovial conversation there was an eerie silence. The official FA statement had been suitably terse also: 'That in the best interests of the Football Association Mr A. Kingscott should resign his office as hon. treasurer of the Association; failing which, his name be and is hereby removed from all committees and sub-committees of which he is now a member, and that he be suspended from his office as hon. treasurer of the Association.'

Meanwhile the journalists, many of whom had arrived merely for details of the Third Round Cup draw, clamoured for comment, but Kingscott was almost speechless. 'I cannot understand the action of the Council', he told the *Daily Mail* in a barely audible voice. 'The cruelty in football is unbelievable. I have devoted my life to the game.' He called the decision 'the most dastardly trick in the annals of sport'. It had been a mistake, he said, to believe that so many of the members had been his friends.

Then Sir Charles Clegg came into the lobby. Kingscott, as ever, offered his arm to the old President, and together the two old friends left the Lancaster Gate FA headquarters which Kingscott had helped to choose and purchase, but would never set foot in again. Outside, a waiting taxi-cab took them to their train at St Pancras. Later, when he alighted at Nottingham, Kingscott said, 'Well goodbye Sir Charles, I am going home amongst people who have every confidence in me', and Clegg, who disliked any open display of emotion, grasped his friend's hands warmly. Back in Sheffield he immediately wrote to Kingscott, bitterly regretting the Council's decision and thanking him for all his attention over the years. The deaf, white haired old man had lost his helper.

Over in Sawley, Kingscott faced another hail of questions from reporters, this time in the warmth of his comfortable sitting room. Standing with his back to the fire, wrote one journalist, Kingscott's stocky figure radiated with indignation. Another reporter noted that as he spoke, above the mantelpiece hung an illuminated address presented to him by the FA after his successful Canadian tour of 1926.

A little recovered by then Kingscott said, 'Take it from me, there is more below the surface than the general public will probably ever know about. More than that I cannot say, but the day may come when, in the interests of the game I may be compelled to speak out.' But there was little else he could do now, except face the reality of the situation and resign. Both his sons and his wife begged him to, and he agreed.

The following morning saw Kingscott's name and face splashed across the headlines in what was billed as the biggest-ever footballing sensation. But even as the scant detail emerged – the FA added nothing to their short statement – it became obvious that there had to be more to the FA's action than merely the selection of a Cup Final ball.

Public reaction was immediate. Letters flooded in offering Kingscott support. Manchester United fans considered raising a petition. England players who had considered him a lucky mascot on their tours wrote in sympathy, while most important of all to Kingscott, the Midland League officials gave him their unanimous vote of confidence.

'I wish I could unburden my soul and state what I think is the reason for it all', said Kingscott the day after, and no doubt the newspapers eagerly looked forward to a whole string of revelations. The *Sunday Dispatch* carried across its front page the headline 'Big Clean Up Of Football Demanded' with a scanty report of how vested interests were trying to prevent an enquiry, of how Kingscott alleged a vendetta, and how that 'mysterious woman' was dominating the FA officials.

But although Clegg and McKenna both expressed sincere regret, the FA predictably closed ranks. Wall refused to comment, Clegg denied any intention to resign and although various commentators claimed exclusive knowledge of a special FA meeting to deal with the affair's aftermath, ultimately nothing further was said. When the FA next met, a week after the death of Herbert Chapman, on 15 January 1934, the Kingscott file was effectively closed with the appointment of Henry Huband of the London FA as Kingscott's successor. Huband had been one of Kingscott's more outspoken critics. Meanwhile, said John McKenna, with astonishing insensitivity, Kingscott should not allow the incident to worry him overmuch.

Harry and Cecil were distraught, and acted as only their consciences would allow. Harry was due to referee the Second Division game between Hull City and Oldham Athletic on the Saturday following Kingscott's enforced resignation. Instead he tendered his own resignation to the Football League, 'in view of what I consider the gross injustice meted out to my father'. Cecil, whose League career was only just beginning, also resigned.

The loyal sons did, however, gain some hope that the FA might reconsider from the stream of letters their father received from former match officials, citing examples of how referees and linesmen had accepted gifts from ball manufacturers. These letters were collated and sent to various members of the FA, together with what Kingscott described as a 'far-reaching declaration . . . sensational in character' written by Harry concerning the 1931 Cup Final, which he had refereed. The allegations were never followed up by the FA. (In later years Cecil never once forgot or forgave those men who had sat on the Sheffield commission. He would recite their names with outrage whenever the subject was raised, which in the family and local community was often. Thirty-three years later, when his brother Harry died, Cecil was still determined to vindicate his father, but attempts to interest newspapers in his story always failed.)

For his part, Arthur Kingscott gamely attempted to tell his story in a series of articles in the *Sunday Chronicle*, but the results were disappointing and fizzled out after three weeks. He did not after all rat on his old associates, despite the heading 'Now I can tell all', perhaps because of the libel laws, more probably because of his own loyalty to the game.

Yet Arthur Kingscott never really overcame the hurt and humiliation he suffered at the hands of his former colleagues. 'I am a moral leper', he once told Ivan Sharpe in a quieter moment, although he stayed at the helm of the Midland League and continued to watch Derby County at the Baseball Ground. He also remained active in community affairs, especially in his role as churchwarden.

Kingscott died on 19 June 1937, at the age of seventy-three, three and a half years after his resignation (and coincidentally, only hours after the deaths of Lt. Col. Gibson Poole in Middlesbrough and Bishop Welldon in Durham). Ever the accountant, on his death bed Kingscott instructed his sons to pay some forthcoming bills.

Three days later he was buried in his beloved All Saints Parish Church, Sawley, where a memorial still stands, erected by the Midland League. At his funeral were managers, players and a host of officials from the Midlands area, but not one representative from the FA. One final irony took place at the graveside, where in true Cup Final spirit the mourners sang *Abide with Me*, the favourite hymn of Sir Frederick Wall.

Of Wall and all the other protagonists in this curious and somewhat tragic episode, what was their fate?

Tom Crew, the 1930 Cup Final referee and one of the committee which had complained to the FA about Kingscott's behaviour, resigned soon after the affair. Kingscott's main opponent on the Council, Charles Wreford Brown, took over the coveted foreign tours.

John McKenna died three months before Kingscott, and by a strange coincidence Sir Charles Clegg died only seven days after Kingscott – perhaps he needed his old friend more than he knew – and was succeeded as President by William Pickford, who died himself some eighteen months later.

Sir Frederick Wall survived as Secretary for just a few months after the Kingscott affair, to be succeeded by a comparatively young man called Stanley Rous, who was born in the same year, 1895, that Wall had taken office. One contemporary thought Mrs Wall's behaviour might have helped precipitate her husband's departure, though even so the Council was extremely generous, granting Wall the prodigious sum of £10,000 as a retirement gift. A year later in 1935 he published his autobiography, *Fifty Years in Football*, but far from shedding any light at all on Kingscott's treatment the former Secretary pointedly omitted any reference whatsoever to the man, writing him out of his personal history as comprehensively as the Soviets had done to Trotsky only a few years earlier.

Similarly, when Geoffrey Green wrote the official history of the FA in 1953, no mention was made of the Kingscott affair either.

No doubt many of the changes on the FA Council would have come about anyway, as younger men gradually assumed positions of power in place of the old guardians of football. But the Kingscott case was perhaps symptomatic of the young guard's impatience. The sporting world was developing rapidly into an international, commercial and cut-throat business in which men like Clegg, Wall and McKenna were often out of their depth.

The Mussolini whom Kingscott had mockingly emulated in Italy turned out to be less than a worthy model, while in Germany a new world was forming, so far from the halcyon, amateur camaraderie enjoyed by the old boys of the FA. It was becoming a world run by toughened professionals.

But had Arthur Kingscott's brief spell in the headlines been all in vain? Not quite, because on 24 December 1933 a small announcement in the newspapers declared that for 1934 there was to be a change in the method of selecting the Cup Final ball. The footballs were now going to be brought to the referee completely unmarked, so that the manufacturers' identities would be unknown.

And so the system remained until 1979 when the FA finally decided to cash in on some of the commercial benefits by signing a sponsorship deal with Mitre, for the supply of all balls and flags for major FA games. It was just the sort of business deal of which Arthur Kingscott, as Honorary Treasurer, would have approved.

7
'A Little Bit of Folly in the World'

TUESDAY, 18 February 1936; the House of Commons. Mr Liddall, Conservative member for Lincoln, stands up to ask the Chancellor of the Exchequer whether he would consider imposing a special tax on the commission charged by football pools promoters, such a tax to enable the price of beer to be lowered by one penny a pint. The object is to assist Britain's hard-pressed barley growers.

Neville Chamberlain, soon to become Prime Minister, replies, 'No sir!'

These are dark days, uncertain and menacing. Mussolini's fascist troops incur the wrath of the League of Nations by invading Ethiopia. Hitler is busy planning, as his country launches the most luxurious airship known to man, the Hindenberg, and his army prepares to take on Europe. In Spain, on February 16, the left-wing People's Front has just won the elections, and Civil War is not far off.

But there is hope too, for although George V, symbol of old Britain, has just died, his handsome and popular bachelor son, Edward VIII, succeeds him.

The footballing world meanwhile marvels at the rampant form of League leaders Sunderland, who mourn the death of their diabetic goalkeeper Jimmy Thorpe, a few days after an ill-tempered match against Chelsea on February 1. The FA sit down to evaluate a recent experiment to have two referees per game. (E. Wood of Sheffield was one of them.) Aston Villa are at their lowest ebb since the League was formed, bottom of the First Division, but Sheffield United, Tranmere Rovers and Coventry City are happy at the top of their respective divisions. Terrible weather grips the North and Midlands.

In the same week as Mr Liddall tables his question in the Commons, the Football League Management Committee calls an emergency meeting to consider the national craze that they believe could ruin football – the pools. It is the beginning of a bizarre conflict.

Every week, the League claims, British people spend £800,000 on pools, but only £48,125 on going to watch football. Over sixteen times more people gamble on the game than watch it. The pools craze has taken over factories and mills, offices and schools, affecting all ages, both rich and poor. There are stories of families broken up by husbands frittering away housekeeping money, of school children found filling in coupons, of junior club secretaries being bribed by pools promoters to distribute coupons to players in return for equipment.

Pools companies have an annual income of over £20 million and rising – compared with only £5 million from the Tote – but not a penny of their twenty per cent profit goes back into the game.

> The time has come, the Walrus said,
> To talk of football pools,
> Of fixture lists and copyright,
> Of clever men and fools.

Percy Rudd, *News Chronicle* sports editor, does not say who are the clever ones and who are the fools, but on Thursday, 20 February 1936 the Pools War is declared.

For a long time the FA and the Football League have considered betting a menace to the game. In 1892 the League forbade players or officials betting on a game. A decade later the FA banned players, officials and spectators from the same. Did this mean, FA Council member Dr Edward Morley of Blackburn sheepishly inquired, that he and his friend could no longer have their customary bet of a top hat on the Rovers winning the FA Cup? It did indeed, replied the chairman Charles Clegg, amidst great indignation.

In 1910 the Council added a rule that any player or official proved to have taken part in coupon betting would be permanently suspended from football and football management.

But football betting was everywhere. That same year it was found to be rife in the army. Pub landlords ran football lotteries, coupons were circularized all over Britain, often by the most popular workers who were picked out by coupon printers and paid a ten per cent commission. Nothing could prevent people betting on football, not even the 1920 Ready Money Football Betting Bill, which forced punters to pay for their pleasure a week in arrears but otherwise had no effect apart from giving the pools great publicity.

Then the newspapers took over, until their competitions became so popular that agencies bought up massive stocks of daily papers simply to cut out the coupons and distribute them. It was marvellous for circulation, until a court ruling on a Sheffield competition put an end to the practise in 1928, and threatened to deprive the Postmaster General of £36,000 a week in postal revenues.

Whenever it could, the FA guarded against abuse, especially in light of various bribery scandals (see Chapter Five), by prohibiting players or officials from acting as bookmakers or assistants, and by banning any pools or bookmakers' advertisements from appearing in club programmes or on hoardings at grounds. Crystal Palace were the first to be ordered to remove such a sign, in 1922.

The pools escaped further restrictions when the 1933 Royal Commission on Lotteries and Betting decided to leave football alone, despite the pleas of the Scottish FA that 'the national value of the game was of sufficient importance to warrant the complete prohibition' of football betting. They had cases of players being offered bribes because of betting (see Chapter One) and crowds barracking teams whenever there was an unexpected or suspicious result.

Sir Frederick Wall, Secretary of the FA, disagreed. He knew of only three cases of bribery in thirty years, and believed there was no open or organized betting actually at football grounds.

Whatever the evidence, tampering with one of the working man's few pleasures was not the way to win votes, especially for a government in the midst of a depression. So the Football League had to act alone.

Thursday, 20 February 1936. Having received telegrams from the League, eighty of the eighty-eight League clubs send representatives to a secret meeting at the Midland Hotel in Manchester. There are plans afoot to deal once and for all with the pools promoters.

Beforehand, the camp appears to be divided, perhaps for the first time ever on the question of pools money. For years the FA has claimed to want nothing to do with the pools, and the League has steadfastly held back from demanding any money from betting interests. Money from gambling is tainted, or such has the implication been, until now.

But a Liverpool accountant, Mr Watson Hartley, has drawn up an attractive, alternative approach, by which the League might derive an income from the pools promoters; not from actual betting, but from their use of the League fixtures, which he reckons are copyright. If the pools promoters have to pay to reproduce the fixtures some £60,000 a year could be raised, reckons Watson Hartley. This money could go towards aiding injured and retired players, improving grounds and so on. The alternative is to allow the pools to carry on earning huge profits without benefiting football at all.

Recent opinion has tended towards Mr Hartley's plan, yet to many people's complete surprise the secret gathering in Manchester decides otherwise. By a large majority the clubs give the Management Committee full power to take such action as it sees fit to put an end to football pools betting, once and for all.

If it is war, although no one yet knows what the weapons will be, the spoils are patently enormous. The League is to try on its own to suppress a multi-million pound industry. Governments might quail at the enormity of the task, yet the League appears to be confident.

Will Cuff, Chairman of Everton and one of the most formidable men in League circles, declares that pools are a menace to the game and that the Management Committee has several plans up its sleeve. Meanwhile, however, all the club representatives are sworn to secrecy.

But there are leaks. Immediately after the Manchester meeting one report has it that all the season's League fixtures are to be scrapped from now on, and that clubs will only be informed of their Saturday opponents on the Thursday beforehand. There will be no change of the home and away sequence, nor need holiday and Cup games be affected. Obviously the aim of such a plan is that the pools companies would not have time to print and distribute their usual coupons.

Are the reports true? Surely, if clubs do not find out until Thursday whom they are playing on Saturday, all their advertising, ticketing and travelling arrangements will be completely disrupted. And how will the public react to blank fixture lists?

'The whole idea is too revolutionary to contemplate', says the director of one Yorkshire club. 'It is cutting off your nose to spite your face.' Think of all the advance plans supporters make for away games, he urges . . . charabanc parties, train bookings, seats ordered at local pantomimes . . .

The Leeds United Chairman, Alderman Alf Masser is equally unhappy. He jokes that he is not yet recovered from 'the dose of chloroform' administered to representatives at the meeting, and though he abides by the pledge of secrecy, privately he has a plan.

Masser is a well-known solicitor and Leeds councillor who is regarded highly among local sporting people. He has been secretary of Headingley Rugby Union FC and is internationally regarded in the sport of curling. As a former Liberal, and now Conservative councillor he is also thought of as the father of Leeds municipal golf and Sunday municipal games. Two years ago he won wider fame for acting as solicitor to David Maskill Blake in a trial following the murder of Emily Yeomans. Also in 1934, he became Chairman of Leeds United, whose entry to the League he originally sponsored in 1920. Masser will represent a formidable opponent.

Will Cuff issues a statement. 'All the clubs are agreed that pool betting must be stopped – and it will.'

The newspapers are shocked, sceptical. If home and away sequences are to be maintained then surely the pools promoters need only issue lists of home teams, leaving the punter to fill in the away column. And even if the promoters are disrupted, the League has yet to prove that the fixtures are legally subject to copyright.

Furthermore, Scottish fixtures are unaffected. A Scottish League official says that they considered taking similar action but felt in the end it would not be worthwhile.

The Pools Promoters Association is scandalized by the League's decision, and after a secret four hour meeting, at the Midland Adelphi Hotel in Liverpool on Saturday, February 22, the legal officer Mr E. Holland-Hughes issues a statement in response. With this one statement the League's action suddenly takes on an entirely different complexion.

On 3 January 1936, announced Holland-Hughes, members of the PPA met with members of the League Management Committee. At this meeting the League claimed that it held copyright of the fixtures and mentioned that it would want a substantial sum to grant a license for their use. The PPA thought the sum was 'exorbitant and unreasonable' and having sought advice found that the League had no legal claim to copyright at all. However, the PPA was prepared to offer 'a reasonable contribution', provided it was directed to the best interests of the sport and subject to FA approval. It was while waiting for a reply from the FA concerning this proposal that the PPA heard how the League had 'decided to suppress those with whom they had been conducting amicable negotiations'.

'The League's action is a stunning blow', says a spokesman, 'coming as it did without warning. But we are not dismayed.'

Immediately the Management Committee deny the truth of the PPA's statement. Fred Rinder of Aston Villa insists that the League has never asked for any payment of 'any sort, size or description'. He claims that the PPA did in fact agree that the League held copyright of the fixtures, but had considered that the use of them on pools coupons did not infringe it.

Mr T. A. Barcroft of Blackpool FC also denies the truth of the statement, though he admits that a sum of money was mentioned at the meeting. 'Honest John' McKenna of Liverpool FC, President of the Football League for the past twenty-six years, now eighty-two years old, will make no comment on the PPA statement but says there is nothing he can do about the difficulties clubs will incur when the fixtures are scrapped.

Already the war is beginning to look suspiciously ill-motivated. If the PPA's statement is true – that the League really did ask for money but was rebuffed – then the *causus belli* is not, as Cuff said, that the pools are a menace, but the fact that the PPA would not accede to the League's demands. Or, in other words, if you won't let me play with your toys I shall ban all toys.

Alderman Alf Masser meanwhile is casting off the effects of the chloroform. He issues a protest at the Management Committee's decision. The secret meeting in Manchester last Thursday was summoned at too short notice, he complains. Clubs should have had time to confer.

Cancelling the fixtures was 'futile'; the PPA's discomfort would be trivial compared with that of the clubs and the supporters. This, says the Leeds chairman, is a matter for Parliament.

Indeed it is, because the Liberal National MP for Eddisbury, Cheshire, Mr Richard Russell, has just introduced a private member's Bill to make illegal all pari-mutuel or pools betting. It is due for debate in the House of Commons on April 3. So the League is not quite alone.

But it is unpopular. Letters pour into national and provincial newspapers, some in favour of the League, most in total opposition. 'It is only another move to spoil the small man's recreations, while people who can afford big bets on horse racing will still be allowed their amusement', comments one man in the pools stronghold of Yorkshire.

In the News Chronicle a reader calls for a boycott of League matches in protest. A club director praises the pools because they have virtually eliminated the wider menace of betting through bookmakers.

MPs are divided across party lines. The Conservative member for Macclesfield, Mr J. R. Remer, says patronizingly, '. . . to suppress football pools is such a silly thing. The football pool is a poor man's little flutter.' He admits to indulging a little himself and at that very moment is in fact awaiting winnings of 12s 6d. But his fellow Tory Mr C. G. Gibson, MP for Pudsey and Otley, says otherwise. 'It is not just a little sporting matter now, it is a gambling craze.' He personally knew of five divorce cases precipitated by arguments over the pools.

'If football pools are to be abolished,' writes A. Broughton in the Yorkshire Evening Post, 'then abolish fox-hunting and stag-hunting as well. They are just as degrading.'

Several football commentators and editorials agree on one point. Did the Football League really ask for 'an exorbitant fee?' If so, the public has a right to know. If the League wants to punish the PPA, why hurt the supporters more?

Charles E. Sutcliffe of the Football League, the long-serving official who draws up the fixture lists every season, makes the first of several pithy but ill-received remarks. He comments that the pools punter wasn't much good as a football supporter anyway. 'A spade is always a spade to him', says Cuff.

Sutcliffe is very much one of the old school. The 'little lawyer from the Rossendale Valley', as McKenna is fond of calling him (Cuff is a Lancashire solicitor too) wears old-fashioned stiff collars, has white hair, a dark moustache and gaunt features. He is the legislative giant of the League but is frail in physique. He is also a demon worker, completely unable to relax, and like so many of the present day officials was formerly a referee.

There is a complaint from afar. In Sweden apparently some 200,000 people enter British pools competitions. What would they do now? If they turned to another country's fixtures, perhaps Scotland, then English football would lose much goodwill.

Meanwhile preparations are made for what the newspapers bill 'The Big Hush' and 'the Football Fixture Farce'. Posters go up saying 'United v ?' and one pools company issues its next week's coupons with Scottish fixtures only. Another goes ahead as normal in the belief that the League would not hold to its plan. The League is however, sticking to its guns.

Monday, February 24. As the extent of the opposition becomes apparent, McKenna, Rinder and Cuff meet the FA in a lengthy conference at Lancaster Gate. Each side denies that the topic of discussion is the pools war, but after the talks Rinder reiterates the League's position. The fixtures have definitely been scrapped and no team will know who they are playing until the day before.

Up in Derby the president of Derby County, Mr W. Bendle Moor, joins Alderman Masser in protest. He says he voted against giving the Management Committee full powers to act as they saw fit. 'I held that if anything was to be done, it was a matter for the Government, and I felt it was undignified for the League to take part in it.'

That evening, over in Birkenhead, MP Richard Russell speaks at a public meeting called in opposition to the pools. Also present, Will Cuff, amid much interruption, denies flatly that the League ever approached the PPA for an 'exorbitant' sum.

But the following day there is a possible chink in the League's armour, as Management Committee member Amos Brook-Hirst suggests that the principle of accepting money from the PPA is not at stake, it is merely the amount. A large enough offer would be seriously entertained, he implies. It is now understood that an offer of approximately £50,000 per year, from a group outside the PPA, has been made, but this is not acceptable. So much for the purity of ideals.

On Tuesday evening there is a gathering of malcontents, all of them northern club chairmen, called together by Alderman Masser. Sunderland and Manchester City are two of those definitely known to have joined Leeds United in this direct challenge to the League.

It is their contention that the meeting in Manchester on February 20 went against Football League rules. Firstly, Rule 23 was broken because the fixtures were tampered with. Secondly, Rule 80 was broken because no rules can be altered at meetings other than the AGM, unless at least seven days notice is given and a full agenda supplied in advance. The Thursday meeting was convened at very short notice by telegram, without an agenda. Thirdly, stated the protesters, Rule 3, which holds that no associate members can vote individually – that is,

Third Division clubs have a collective vote – was also broken, since each of the Third Division club representatives voted at the meeting.

Because of these irregularities, Alderman Masser calls for a meeting of all clubs, but to exclude specifically members of the Management Committee. Is this Civil War?

No, replies Masser. It is just an attempt to reverse the Management Committee's ruling on the fixtures.

Fred Howarth, Secretary of the League, says there is no need for an outside meeting of rebels. Rule 14 provides for special meetings of this nature to be held within the framework of the League. Masser is unmoved. His meeting will proceed.

Howarth also points out that those clubs who will need to travel long distances for Saturday's games will be telegrammed earlier than the others, probably late on Thursday. But the rest will be telephoned on Friday to prevent the fixtures being printed in Friday's newspapers.

On Wednesday there are more protests from League clubs; from Brentford and Bristol Rovers, from Barrow – whose representative at the Manchester meeting admits to having voted, despite his club being an associate member – and from Charlton Athletic, whose manager Jimmy Seed says that advanced bookings for Saturday are well down, because no-one knows who the opposition will be, and that some supporters have threatened to boycott the game whoever the visitors are and as long as the Pools War lasts.

Meanwhile the PPA announces that it has a plan for Saturday. Instructions to 'investors' will appear in Friday's papers and no problems are envisaged whatsoever.

Alderman Masser announces that his protest meeting will be held on Monday, March 2, at Leeds Town Hall, on the same day as the Management Committee meets in London. Letters of invitation are sent to every First and Second Division club – forty-four in total – on behalf of Leeds, Manchester City, Sunderland, Stoke City, Blackburn Rovers and Newcastle United. Each club should send, if possible, two directors plus the manager.

'For all I care Leeds United and Manchester City can hold their protest meetings', says Charles Sutcliffe in another off-the-cuff remark.

Thursday, February 27. Sutcliffe says that the Management Committee's attitude to the 'growing menace' of pools is unchanged. The majority of clubs, he believes, are also opposed to the pools, but they are panicking in fear of low gates on Saturday.

Today alone fifteen clubs accept Masser's invitation. In addition to the five clubs who joined Leeds on Wednesday, they are Bradford Park Avenue, Bolton, Barnsley, Derby, Port Vale, Brentford, Birmingham, Charlton, Arsenal, West Ham, Plymouth, Huddersfield, Liverpool,

Tottenham and Everton. Yet Fred Howarth still insists there are no internal divisions in the League.

The vice-chairman of a Lancashire First Division club tells the newspapers, 'The League clubs realize that they have made a gigantic mistake (to allow the Management Committee to act as they did). Everybody knows that Saturday's interference with fixtures will be the last. We shall be back to normal next week. You cannot keep back the tide of public opinion. The League knows it must climb down, and will do so. Who are we to dictate the morals of the country? It is the Government's business, not ours.'

The PPA meet again and decide to delay the time of last postage for coupons until 3 p.m. on Saturday, for this week only. They deny that a truce has been agreed with the League for the week after.

It is now Thursday night, and in the offices of the Football League in Preston, Charles Sutcliffe, keeper of the fixtures, hands over his plans for Saturday to the Secretary, Fred Howarth. Those clubs who must travel a long way are to be notified immediately.

But will secrecy prevail? Are there spies about? Can the clubs be trusted to keep their affairs from the press?

Friday, February 28. There have been overnight leaks to the press, almost certainly by members of staff at the four clubs which received telegrams last night. So many club officials are angry with the League that the culprits could be anyone; directors or tea-boys, managers or ticket clerks. By morning it is known that Sunderland have to travel to Preston, Southampton to Bradford City, Swansea to Manchester United and Norwich to Newcastle. By mid-day it is common knowledge that these were the games originally scheduled for March 14 for the First Division and April 11 for the Second Division. The other games are thus simple to work out. Sutcliffe has merely brought forward whole sections of the original list.

But there are complications, because the FA Cup Sixth Round matches on Saturday are not subject to the League's jurisdiction. As a result, Bradford Park Avenue now have no game at all on Saturday because the League switched their original game against Manchester United with one against Barnsley, who are playing Arsenal in the Cup. Naturally, Park Avenue's chairman, Mr Ernest Waddilove, is furious.

'I consider the treatment meted out to us to be preposterous.' Perhaps, he suggests, it has something to do with the fact that in Manchester his club voted against the Pools War. He presumed the League would not be compensating Park Avenue for their loss of revenue.

There are disappointments all round. Wolves and Plymouth are among five other clubs with no matches on Saturday. Wolves are particularly upset because they originally had a potentially lucrative derby match against West Bromwich. The saddest upset is for 3000 Tranmere fans who had a whole trip arranged for the visit to Stockport County. All this has to be cancelled when Rovers find they must play Accrington Stanley instead. It was to have been the biggest supporters' trip in the club's history.

Despite the fact that half the nation already knows the fixtures for Saturday by Friday lunchtime, the League sticks doggedly to its position by refusing to announce the official fixture list until Friday evening. But in the meantime the clubs have been making frantic efforts to complete arrangements for tomorrow.

Fred Howarth issues a circular to all League clubs reminding them of the decisions made at Manchester on February 20. It was the clubs who agreed that pools betting was a menace and must be suppressed. It was they who empowered the Management Committee to 'take such steps as it may deem expedient'. And the clubs were fully aware that such steps included Charles Sutcliffe's scheme to scrap the fixture.

As a result of a 'breach of confidence' by some members, writes Howarth, this secret plan was leaked to the press (just as the new fixtures had been divulged the night before), so another meeting of all the clubs is felt to be necessary. It will be held at the Grand Hotel, Manchester, on Monday, March 9.

Alderman Masser's rebel meeting for Monday, March 2 continues to gather support. Norwich, West Bromwich, Doncaster, Southampton, Aston Villa and Bradford City accept the invitation, so there are now twenty-seven out of forty-four definitely attending. Fulham are the only ones so far to decline, but even they change their mind a few days later.

The PPA meets again, and decides to carry on as planned. There are branch meetings in five major cities, and in Leeds the newly-formed Northern Pools Promoters Association (consisting of those companies not centred on Liverpool) urges fans not to boycott tomorrow's games. 'In our opinion football pools, far from being a menace as suggested, give an added interest to the game.'

The Public Morality Council does not agree and offers its full support to Richard Russell's forthcoming Bill. So does the Bishop of London and his executive committee. They urge all church members to support a ban on the pools.

Saturday, 29 February 1936: a day when women may pop the question, while footballing men ask what all the fuss is about.

'After all the astonishing meetings and counter-meetings, denials and counter-denials, speeches, allegations and abuse', writes The Times, 'the public is not after all, to turn up to its various grounds today

Top Eight of this 1905 team group were suspended in 1906 and forbidden to play for Manchester City again as a result of illegal payments. Back row, left to right: Broad, McMahon (suspended six months), Moffat, Forrest (chairman, banned for life), Hillman (six months), Davies (director, suspended one year), Pearson, Booth (six months), Maley (manager, banned for life). Front row, left to right: Turnbull and Burgess (each six months), Jones, and Meredith, Frost, Hynds (each six months). Hillman and Meredith had already served one year suspensions for attempted bribery.

Bottom left Tom Hindle, the FA's auditor sent to keep an eye on City's affairs.

Bottom middle Lt. Col. Gibson Poole, Middlesbrough's chairman, had one eye on Westminster and the other on unusual accounting procedures. (Sport and General)

Bottom right Alec Mackie, Middlesbrough's manager, gave up football but was banned for life by the FA anyway.

Top Six of this Manchester United team were involved in the infamous rigged game against Liverpool on Good Friday 1915. Whalley (far right, back) and 'Knocker' West (second from right, front) were banned for life. Also playing in the game were Hodge (extreme left, back), Beale (goalkeeper), Meredith (extreme left, front) and Anderson (centre, front), each of whom gave evidence in West's court battle. (*Manchester Evening News*)

Bottom left Robert Jack, Argyle's long serving manager, was ordered by the League not to play Corinthians.

Bottom middle In letters to *The Times* Dean Welldon, later Bishop of Durham, was outraged with the League, and with football on Good Fridays. (Sport and General)

Bottom right G.N. Foster wanted his Corinthians to play Argyle. The League stepped in but *The Times* backed Foster.

Top left George Parsonage, in his Brentford colours — banned for life in 1908 while at Fulham for asking above the £10 maximum signing-on fee.

Top left middle Archibald Kyle, formerly of Rangers — caught in the act of bribery at a Glasgow pub in 1924.

Top right middle Barney Travers of Fulham — banned for life after a bribery attempt. But who put him up to it?

Top right Soccer's 'Happy Wanderer' of the 1950s, Ken Chisholm, pictured with Leicester only 18 days before he saw a fixed game which kept his team in the Second Division. (Photo Source)

Bottom Most sporting newspapers, like the *Birmingham Sports Argus*, viewed cynically the FA rules on bonuses and wages. On several occasions the *Argus* openly satirised Aston Villa's circumvention of the rules.

Mutiny In The Camp.

" The strain has become so great that I have heard a rumour of a combine to openly evade the F.A. rule as to bonuses to players."—Mr. W. McGregor, in the " Sports Argus."

POLICEMAN F.A.: "I must say I don't like the look of this. I don't care for that Aston Villa smile.

THE PROFESSOR: "No, your baton doesn't seem to scare 'em much! Don't you think you had better give up this bonus business.?"

Top In the net — Dixie Dean puts the controversial Cup Final ball in the net for Everton's second goal in April 1933, as referee Wood looks on. In the Royal Box — Arthur Kingscott, the man who thought up the idea of numbering the players, but who clashed with Wood before the game. (Photo Source)

Left Kingscott's ally — Sir Charles Clegg, former scourge of Middlesbrough and scrupulous President of the FA, but by 1933 old and weak.

Bottom Calm before the storm — Arthur Kingscott (centre) is joined by Sir Frederick Wall (right) and Lady Agnes (left) at Victoria Station at the start of England's continental tour, ten days after the 1933 Final. Moves to discredit Kingscott were soon to begin, and Lady Wall was called 'the mysterious woman' who dominated FA officials. (Associated Press)

Top The League's top three generals in the Pools War — Fred Rinder (left) of Aston Villa, Charles Sutcliffe (centre), the President who drew up the fixtures, and Will Cuff of Everton, who claimed to abhor the pools.
Littlewood's John Moores swore on a bible that these men had originally asked him for a 'substantial sum' of pools money.

Right 'Honest John' McKenna — the League President and former Liverpool chairman died two weeks after the Pools War ended.

Bottom Arsenal v. ?? posters like this appeared all over England and Wales as the League kept its fixtures from the pools companies. (Daily Mail)

Top left Sunderland's heartbroken chairman Bill Ditchburn leaves Roker Park for the last time before his lifetime ban — he had just bade his players a tearful farewell. *(Sunderland Echo)*

Top right Jack and Charles Steedman in 1963 — they saved East Stirlingshire Football Club but could not take it away from Falkirk. (E.S.F.C.)

Bottom Going home — members of the Shire SPA gather outside Clydebank Burgh Hall on 13 May 1964 following the crucial AGM. In the foreground are William Moffat (left) and Jimmy Middlemass, who as a precaution against possible trouble had asked SPA member Tom Baird (back right) to act as his 'minder'. But despite the fierce controversy there was never any violence throughout the year-long struggle. *(Glasgow Herald)*

Top left Ken Thomson (Hartlepool) — his exposure by *The People* was one of the first chinks in the betting ring's armour. *(Middlesbrough Evening Gazette)*

Top right Jimmy Gauld in his prime — scoring for Plymouth against Gillingham in November 1958. (Photo Source)

Bottom left Peter Swan in happier days — as an England star waiting for a flight to Lisbon in 1961. With him is Bobby Robson, later to manage Ipswich, the team Swan faced on that fateful afternoon in 1962. (Photo Source)

Bottom right Tony Kay (left) and David 'Bronco' Layne on their way to Mansfield Magistrate's court in October 1964. Neither of them expected prison. (Sheffield Newspapers)

Frank, fearless and free — another 'shattering exposure' for *The People*. But although Swan, Kay and Layne were barely involved in the betting ring, theirs would be the names associated with the scandal for years to come. Even the ringleader's name was forgotten. This edition of the paper was being exchanged for £5 a copy in some parts of Britain on Sunday, 12 April 1964.

Inset Michael Gabbert — the *People*'s reporter who worked with Gauld to expose the conspiracy, and was tailed by private detectives as a result. *(Daily Herald Archive)* ignorant of the team its heroes are to play.' That this is so is thanks to the clubs themselves.

The Times editorial takes great pains to explain to its noble readers what pools betting is all about and why they should be extremely suspicious of it. The PPA, it says dryly, is not a group of 'trustees' acting on behalf of 'investors' – as the PPA likes to think of itself – nor is it 'a society formed to secure integrity on the Stock Exchange'. It is in reality, says *The Times*, 'a combination of bookmakers'.

The Football League and Football Association are, on the other hand, 'actuated by the loftiest ideals'. They have the purity of sport in mind.

The PPA appears to be 'obsessed with anxiety for a gentleman called "the little man", to whom it seems the pools companies stand *in loco parentis*. The little man looks to his trustee for the endowment of his declining years' and thus does not begrudge his weekly postal order. The League calls it betting, the PPA calls it 'investment'.

Continuing its lofty tirade, *The Times* estimates that between 'six and seven million of the King's lieges exercise their minds weekly' in pools betting – the manifest assumption being that surely no *Times* reader would stoop so low. It reveals the existence of a vast industry whose leading companies have offices rivalling Somerset House in intricacy. Added to this is a proliferation of activities dependent on the pools – newspaper columns which devote more space to coupon betting than to football itself, plus myriad books and periodicals giving out advice to 'investors'.

Thus the PPA defends itself as the provider of much employment. But what of the purity of sport, asks *The Times*. One team might spend a lot of money on a centre-forward while another spends even more on 'fixing' their goalkeeper, says the newspaper.

This is an erroneous comment. The FA has denied all along that its opposition to the pools has anything to do with allegations of fixed matches, and it is fairly obvious that pools companies stand to gain nothing by arranging particular matches. Fixed Odds betting is far more likely to be the cause of match rigging, but very few instances have been proved in the period since the Great War (although see Chapter Five). *The Times* comment is ironic also, because the newspaper has often railed against the transfer system as a very negation of the purity of sport. But back to the editorial . . .

Lamenting the fact that the 1934 Betting and Lotteries Act left football virtually untouched, *The Times* calls for Parliament to intervene, 'to grasp the nettle . . .' now that football, '. . . the more popular of all open-air entertainments' has been reduced to 'chaos and public ridicule'.

'The crucial question is', concludes *The Times*, 'not whether commercially stimulated betting is bad for football, but whether it demoralizes the people.'

Is *The Times* right? Is football reduced to chaos and public ridicule? Certainly there has been chaos during the week, when no one quite knew what was going to happen on Saturday, and for sure the League is widely believed to have acted wrongly. But the actual game of football, is that in jeopardy? Surely not.

Saturday afternoon comes . . . the War enters its most crucial stage. Will the public show its annoyance by staying away from games? Frustratingly, it becomes impossible to judge, as a blanket of snow, sleet and rain sweeps across the North and Midlands. Attendances total only 193,000, compared with 318,000 for the same week last year. Comparing the same fixtures with last season, in the First Division gates are down from 129,000 to 70,000. But the Cup attendances are down also, so weather must surely be the most crucial factor.

At Sheffield Wednesday, where the crowd is the smallest of the season, a poll is conducted to discover if fans support the League's battle against the pools. Only one in ten voters answers in the affirmative.

On Sunday, opinion is divided. Alderman Masser declares that the low attendances were partly due to people objecting 'to interference with their liberties'. But most commentators blame the weather. At Newcastle for example there were only 4000, whereas the average is 22,000. At Aston Villa only 12,000 attend, instead of the usual 35,000. Several other clubs suffer their lowest gates of the season, but in the South, where the weather was much less severe, attendances are hardly down at all.

The *News Chronicle* shows a photograph of deserted terraces at Goodison Park, where Manchester City are the visitors. The pools boycott has produced 'an amazing slump' it reports. And whereas Friday is the usual day for a rush at the Post Office – when demand for postal orders trebles and extra staff are brought in to cater for the pools craze – this week the rush is on Saturday, right up until kick off time.

Crucially, the PPA reports that there have been no adverse affects on the pools this week. Is that just bravado on their part or has the League's plan really backfired?

On Sunday evening the League Management Committee meets to assess just that. It sits all night, leaving its mainly elderly members exhausted by morning. But the mood is entrenched and there is greater resolve to ensure no leakage of fixtures for the following Saturday, as all committee members swear to secrecy.

It is, however, implied that the Management Committee will act as the clubs instruct – if such is the case after the rebel meeting in Leeds tomorrow – although even if the Pools War is called to an end, nothing can be done until the official meeting of the clubs called for March 9. Therefore, next Saturday's fixtures are still scrapped. 'If you are told anything else during the week', says a weary Charles Sutcliffe after the meeting, 'you can take it you are having your leg pulled.'

Peace may loom on the horizon, but meanwhile the war must go on.

Monday, March 2. The FA joins in the battle, albeit only from a distance, by writing to the Home Secretary urging the Government to make pools betting illegal by passing Russell's forthcoming Bill.

At the same time representatives from thirty-six League clubs are gathering at Leeds Town Hall for Alderman Masser's rebel meeting. Some of the biggest names in football management are there, including, from the First Division's four leading clubs of the day, George Allison of Arsenal, Johnny Cochrane of Sunderland, George Jobey of Derby County and Clem Stephenson of Huddersfield Town. Only eight clubs have decided not to attend. They are Blackpool, Burnley, Bury, Manchester United, Nottingham Forest, Sheffield United, Swansea Town and Wolverhampton Wanderers.

The meeting lasts two hours, during which Masser and his supporters are at pains to emphasize that they remain entirely loyal to the Football League and the Management Committee, and fully appreciate 'the great services rendered by them'.

Finally a resolution is passed that while the clubs recognize the Management Committee has a mandate from them to scrap the fixtures, they now urge the restoration of the fixture list and a return to the *status quo ante bellum*. There are no votes against the resolution, but ten clubs abstain, wishing to reserve judgement until their boards of directors meet.

On hearing this, the following day John McKenna announces that if the Leeds resolution is confirmed by the clubs at the official League meeting on March 9, then the fixtures will revert to normal on March 14. Again he defends the Management Committee by repeating that it was given a mandate from the clubs. Fred Rinder says that some clubs were complaining that they had been rushed into a decision at the original Manchester meeting but were still not in principle against the action. It was just that they wanted to know who their opponents would be on Saturday.

But the League officials continue to create a confusing impression on the public. On one hand there is a desire for peace, on the other a determination to carry on the crusade. Fred Howarth confirms that next Saturday's fixtures are still scrapped, and that this week there will be even greater secrecy.

Alderman Masser is disappointed. In a statement to the press he reaffirms that the clubs have no desire to either encourage or discourage the pools companies. In fact they want nothing to do with them. If pools betting is wrong, he says, then the public should have an opportunity to express their opinion at the polls.

'For heavens sake, let us forget all about this trouble, and get on with the game . . . I think the sooner we get rid of all this cant and hypocrisy the better.'

Will Cuff puts a brave face on the situation. He has no doubt the clubs will wish to return to normal, and that the Management Committee will be forced to adhere to such a wish. His fighting spirit is ebbing away.

Thursday evening, 5 March 1936. Saturday's revised fixture list is ready, only this time the League is confident secrecy will be maintained until late Friday. Fred Howarth telegrams seven clubs who have long distances to travel.

All seven leak details to the press. By Friday morning it is clear that Saturday's matches are those originally scheduled for April 4 in the First Division, March 21 in the Second Division, April 18 for the Third Division South, with the Northern section keeping to its March 7 programme. The morning dailies carry a complete fixture list, so the pools are safe again and the Management Committee's plans are in tatters.

Nevertheless Saturday's attendances are down again, although not as much as expected. Altogether 500,000 spectators attend the 44 League matches. In the pools strongholds of Leeds and Liverpool, Anfield and Elland Road suffer their lowest gates of the season. Alderman Masser addresses the Leeds crowd of 10,500 over the loudspeaker system. 'Are you in favour of restoring the fixture list?' he bellows.

'Yes!' comes back a huge roar.

When the fans return home some of them hear unexpected news over the wireless. German troops have just re-entered the demilitarized Rhineland, and on Sunday it is not the Football League's battle which dominates the headlines, but the League of Nations'.

There is, however, a story in the *News of the World* alleging that a famous goalkeeper has received a letter from Ireland offering him shared spoils if he lets one or two soft goals in. The player reports the letter immediately. It is probably a hoax, but it adds more weight to the anti-pools lobby.

On Monday morning L. V. Manning of the *Daily Sketch* predicts the demise of the League's plan at that day's Management Committee meeting. He writes, 'The puir wee bairn will die unloved, unmourned. A short life and a stormy one. I hope to be at the funeral.' In a less poetic mood, adds Manning, 'No other sporting body in the world has dreamed of turning its fixture list into capital.'

But surely the League has never wanted to do such a thing. The pools, are, it keeps telling us, 'a menace'. Perhaps not, because also on Monday morning there is a fascinating report in the *Daily Mail* of an extraordinary event which took place at Great George Street Congregational Church in Liverpool the night before. Allegedly, as part of an after-service discussion on pools betting, Mr John Moores, co-founder of the Littlewoods pools company, lifelong Everton follower and a prominent member of the PPA, stood up in the church's pulpit, bible in hand, and gave precise details of the alleged discussions which took place on January 3 between the League and the PPA.

Moores told the gathering how he and Cecil Moores, Mr V. Sangster of Vernons and their legal officer Mr E. Holland-Hughes had met with Messrs McKenna, Cuff and Sutcliffe on 3 January 1936. (It should be noted that the major difference between these men was their ages. The PPA representatives were each about twenty to thirty years younger than the League's trio.) During this meeting the League officials referred to Watson Hartley's scheme and so Cecil Moores questioned them outright. Were they asking for money?

Yes, replied the League representatives, according to John Moores, and although they did not specifically ask for a sum of money, the figure of £100,000 had been mentioned in relation to Watson Hartley. The ensuing negotiations were based on that figure. After the meeting, John Moores said, he wrote to the Football League offering them an ex gratia payment. It was then that the League had opened their campaign.

Monday afternoon, 9 March 1936. Before the League's meeting at the Grand Hotel, Manchester, can proceed, there is widespread annoyance among delegates from the eighty-four clubs attending, when they discover the Management Committee will permit entrance to only one representative per club – not two as expected. Dozens of irate men jostle in an adjoining room and pass a resolution demanding entry. They are denied once more.

Next door in the crowded hall, the meeting gets under way under a cloak of secrecy. For the sake of League unity no one should ever know what acrimonious exchanges might take place, what accusations may be hurled, what demands made. As the debate develops however, there is a sudden commotion.

Charles Sutcliffe, describing it afterwards, writes, 'During the proceedings ... behind what purported to be closed doors ... a shadow was seen to pass across the glass lights on a floor above, where a window was discovered to be open, and investigation resulted in the discovery of a photographer and reporter from a prominent newspaper, who had succeeded in getting shots and making notes of what had been transpiring. These gentlemen afterwards appeared in the meeting, apologized for their action and surrendered their notes and plates.'

'Newspaper sleuths caught red-handed', reports the *Daily Sketch* on Tuesday. 'Two irresponsible youths', says the *Daily Mail*. No paper owns up, however.

What stories these two men could tell – and no doubt will among their press friends – of the real goings on at the Grand Hotel! All the public will ever know, however, is that Alderman Masser's resolution, seconded by Messrs Waddilove of Bradford and Woolfe of Sunderland, is passed unanimously. The fixtures are to be restored.

The Pools War is over.

More than that, another resolution is passed, this time by seventy-nine votes, to expunge from the League minutes the original statements which described pools as a menace to football. Thus a little bit of football history is rewritten, and as the furore dies down, so it becomes apparent that the pools, far from being a menace to football, could actually be rather useful to the game.

There are more reports of how a group, apparently in attendance at the Grand, has repeated its offer of £50,000 for exclusive rights to reproduce the fixtures. The group is believed to be composed of turf accountants, but they are never heard of again.

Charles Sutcliffe meanwhile is defiant. Monday was not a defeat. He tells journalist Ivan Sharpe that the fixtures are indeed his own, personal copyright, because he owns the charts from which they are composed every season. It has been reported that Sutcliffe threatened to refuse to let the League have the fixtures if copyright is not observed, but he reassures Sharpe that this is not true. He is happy to hand over the copyright free of charge.

'The fixtures are what are described as a literary work, and in the Act come under charts and compilations', he says. We can expect, no doubt therefore, that the League will be pursuing its copyright as soon as possible.

The Pools War has had one major effect. Opinion within football has changed dramatically over the past fortnight, as officials and administrators have veered away from the Management Committee's outwardly expressed view and towards some kind of financial deal with the PPA. Apparently only two league chairmen are now known to be dead set against the idea. Will Cuff of Everton is one of them.

But if what John Moores has said is true, then such a deal seems to have been the Management Committee's policy all along. The Pools War was thus a futile gesture, and for a short time a damaging one also. The following Saturday gates are back to their normal level.

The fight is not quite over yet, however, because Mr Richard Russell has yet to have his Bill debated in Parliament. Two weeks pass, but the signs do not appear to favour him. Conservative private members remind Russell of the public outcry which occurred when the 1934 Act threatened to affect pools betting.

Friday, 28 March 1936. Russell introduces his Bill to make illegal pari-mutuel or pools betting. He is supported initially by four Tories, two Liberals, one Liberal National, one National Labour and three Labour members. He also has the backing of the Church and the FA.

The church's support comes in the form of a letter addressed to all Members of Parliament and signed by nine bishops and other leaders. The letter states that, in addition to the serious moral, social and economic consequences of the pools 'there is imminent danger of the permanent establishment of a new vested interest claiming an unconditional right to make money by inciting others to gamble'.

The FA also sends to every member a letter signed by the president, Sir Charles Clegg. It contains an ill-concealed *volte-face* in which the FA suddenly adopts the Scottish argument. For example, Clegg mentions crowds barracking home teams when, contrary to all the pools predictions, they unexpectedly lose. 'This tends to discredit the honesty and fairness of the game, and is bound to have an unhappy effect upon the players . . .' (A very tenuous argument. Were crowds supposed to cheer when their team lost at home?) Clegg also gives the statistics relating to pools betting, the most significant being that over sixteen times more people enter the pools than the turnstiles, with the consequent danger that football's importance will become gambling, not sport.

'Football . . . should be protected from the parasitical outside organizations that fasten upon it for the sake of profit', concludes Sir Charles, the elder statesman of English football, who is, sadly, now close to death.

Tuesday, April 1. In anticipation of the debate in the House there are three motions to reject it and Mr A. P. Herbert, the witty author and extremely Independent member for Oxford University – a constituency which no longer exists as a separate entity – hands in an amendment. Accusing Russell's Bill of being restrictive but not constructive, Herbert says that betting is harmful only in excess, and should be licensed, controlled and taxed. Ending pools betting would only force the public to adopt other forms of gambling.

The bill finally comes up for debate, as scheduled, on Friday, April 3. Opening the discussion, Russell says that in 1934 £9 million had been spent on pools betting, but that this figure had more than doubled to £20 million in 1935. The national total spent on all forms of gambling is currently around £500 million. Every Saturday some five million coupons have to be checked in a great hurry, and surely no system can be entirely efficient.

But Russell prefers to dwell on the 'internal dangers' of pools betting, the 'deterioration of character' which it advances. No doubt the House would hear from other speakers about the liberty of the individual, but what about the liberty of pools companies to exploit young people?

Mr Russell's own personal liberty was also in peril. Since introducing his Bill he had received many poisonous letters and death threats.

Seconding the Bill, Mr Barr, the Labour member for Coatbridge, Scotland, argues that there should not be one law for the rich and one for the poor, but Parliament did nevertheless have a duty to see that working people spent their surplus money in 'pure, noble and innocuous ways'. He is not a killjoy, says Barr, but he did seek to kill the sorrows that betting brought in its train.

This is an issue which apparently cuts right across party lines. The Conservative member for Mid-Bedfordshire, Mr Lennox-Boyd, calls for the rejection of the Bill as an 'unjustifiable interference with private liberty'. Gaming, he claims, is inherent in human nature. To suppress it would be to lead it underground and thus result in greater exploitation. To him, the reaction of the League is 'amazing and unsavoury'. The passage of the 1934 Act on betting, which did not affect football, had been 'a day out and a night out for the cranks in the House'.

Another Conservative, Mr G. Lloyd, representing Ladywood, Birmingham, brings a note of levity into the debate by announcing that he has had a letter from a constituent who dislikes betting but asks his MP to oppose the Bill nevertheless, because the pools keep his 'old woman quiet for at least two hours every week'.

Mr T. Williams, the Labour MP for Don Valley, speaks movingly of the great difficulty he has encountered in supporting this Bill. He too has received hate mail, much of it from people threatening never to vote for him again – a threat readily appreciated by fellow members – but support Russell he would. Promoters made such easy money, promising £100 for a halfpenny. Instead of buying humbugs kids were betting, and the profits were even greater now than coal-mining.

So the debate continues, it becoming clear that the Labour Party is broadly opposed to the Bill. Mr McGovern of Glasgow, for example, resents the sinful insinuations about workers gambling. Although he is a non-smoking, non-gambling teetotaller, he insists that the working man is as much entitled to his beer and cigarettes as McGovern is to tea and lemonade. Had not the churches indulged in lotteries to raise money? Certainly the Trade Unions had.

But another Labour man, Mr R. J. Davies of Westhoughton, suggests that often the money for pools betting came from families' social services and pensions benefits. He derides A. P. Herbert for opposing the Bill.

Herbert himself makes one of the longest and most vehement speeches of the debate. He is comparatively young, much admired, and has only been in the House for a matter of months.

Even if the pools were abolished, he says, Fixed Odds betting through bookmakers was still possible. He opposes the Bill because it is rotten; it is an attempt to cosset people.

'Temptation was sent into this life to try to strengthen character', Herbert tells the House. Parliament should not wipe out all 'the ancient and virile pleasures' just because a few people fell by the way. If it did we would be left with 'a Namby-pamby anaemic race', such as all those H. G. Wells-Utopian-arty-crafty types who sit around all day discussing science. Are Members of Parliament gods, supermen or dictators to say how a poor man should spend his money?

'Let's leave a bit of folly in the world', says Herbert, reaching a crescendo. And leave it they do, for when the votes are counted the Bill has been roundly defeated, by 287 votes to 24.

The pools survive.

So it was that as the 1935–36 season drew to a close the Pools War was rapidly forgotten, treated as an aberration and nothing more. The real war was only just beginning, in Spain, China and closer to home in central Europe.

'Honest John' McKenna did not witness any of this, or indeed the end of the season. Only two weeks after the Pools War was settled the Liverpool chairman died, aged eighty-two. (A plaque commemorating his achievements went up at Anfield, but is no longer displayed.) 'He lived for football. He was football', wrote his old friend Charles Sutcliffe, who, predictably enough, was elected President of the Football League in McKenna's place at the AGM in June 1936.

In another election, to fill the vacant spot on the Management Committee, Alderman Masser failed by just a few votes to join those he had challenged only weeks earlier. Masser remained chairman of Leeds United for another year only and thereafter concentrated his efforts on the local parks and golf-courses belonging to the City Council, for whom he eventually became the longest ever serving member.

(Just before he died in October 1950 Masser requested that one third of his ashes be scattered over Temple Newsam Municipal Golf Course, one third should go to his widow and the remainder be sent to the curling field at Arosa in Switzerland. This last request proved impossible to implement, so the ashes were scattered instead over Roundhay Park in Leeds).

Charles Sutcliffe maintained his dislike for the pools, as was shown in August 1938 when the League rejected an offer from the PPA of £5000 a year to help with the League's £100,000 Jubilee Fund.

Will Cuff also remained bitterly opposed to the pools, as he proved when he too became President of the League in succession to Sutcliffe, who died in January 1939. Almost as soon as the Second World War ended, the PPA offered the League a sum of £300,000 to be paid over the course of three seasons. How easily they could afford such an offer became apparent as the post-war soccer boom boosted the pools profit so greatly that in 1948 the promoters paid £12.5 million in tax alone. Nevertheless the money was again refused, and this time no further offers were made.

Cuff died in February 1949. It was perhaps as well that this stern man, who had watched Everton when they were still St Domingo's Sunday School Club at Stanley Park in the late 1870s and had been on the Everton board since 1895, should not survive to experience the ultimate irony of this story. His old pools adversary, John Moores, later Sir John, joined the Everton board in the late 1950s and in 1960 became chairman, Cuff's former position from 1921–38. Indeed it was money derived from the great Littlewoods pools empire which helped revive Everton's fortunes during the next decade. How Cuff would have fumed. He would also have been somewhat shocked to see who was acting as Everton's solicitor at that time. It was Mr E. Holland-Hughes, former legal officer of the PPA and in the 1960s a director and later chairman of his beloved Everton.

By that time, however, the often difficult relationship between the PPA and the League had been settled.

Opinion during the 1950s moved increasingly towards the view that the pools ought to contribute towards the general welfare of football. In January 1955 the Southern Section League clubs proposed a motion asking the PPA to contribute £400,000 per season for the use of the fixtures, this money to be shared among the ninety-two clubs for ground improvements, but the League rejected the motion on the grounds that it was against FA rules to be a party to the promotion of pools.

How is it, asked Ralph Hewins in the *Daily Express*, that Hungary had beaten England so convincingly? Was it perhaps because they had a Ministry of Sport, that since 1946 they had built 6215 new stadia, that thousands of sportsmen and women had been given free training and free equipment and that Hungary had a free Medical Institute for sports injuries? And who had paid for all this? The state-run pools company, wrote Hewins (before he is accused of spreading socialist principles in the *Express*, of all newspapers, we should add that in Western Europe it is also common for pools competitions to devote their profits to the creation of sporting facilities).

And what did British sport get from its private pools companies? Nothing, even though together they now constituted the seventh largest industry in Britain, employing around 100,000 people.

There was a further irony in the fact that while the Football League refused to accept money from the pools, several clubs were accepting money which had been raised by their supporters' clubs own pools competitions.

It was time once again for action, only on this occasion the Football League prepared itself properly, and the second pools war was a much more civilized event. Rather than conduct secret meetings or try to scrap the fixture list the League took the matter to court, exactly as it should have done in 1936.

In October 1958 the League issued a writ against Littlewoods (chosen only because it was the largest company), claiming that the League held the copyright for the 1958–59 fixtures. There was to be a test case, to determine in law whether Charles Sutcliffe had been correct in his claim all those years before. Cecil and John Moores were still at the Littlewoods helm, and to give evidence for the League was the man who had inherited Sutcliffe's task of compiling the fixtures. He was Harold Sutcliffe, son of Charles, and heir to the mysterious mathematical charts. Neither the names nor the principle at stake had changed, twenty-two years on.

But the PPA was also prepared. Aware that the case might be coming up, Littlewoods had tried to avoid printing an exact copy of the League fixtures by changing the order of matches very slightly. Thus the Judge, Justice Upjohn commented at the court hearing in May 1959, that it could be argued that the PPA was only using the information, rather than simply reproducing a list. On the other hand he agreed that the League, not unreasonably, thought they should receive some contribution.

Ultimately the case rested on the question of whether the League fixture list represented a literary work. Facts alone were not subject to copyright, it was the skill which went into presenting the facts which counted. The PPA argued that the skill which went into its compilation was not relevant, because otherwise every skilled selection – the choice of an MCC XI for example – would become subject to copyright.

For the League, Sir Milner Holland replied by suggesting that if the fixtures were not copyright, why did Littlewoods not publish the daily Cause List, which gave details of cases to be heard in the High Court? Perhaps they could take forecasts on whether each case would be won, lost or drawn. 'Surely nobody would be entitled to use such a document by just copying it', said Sir Milner.

Harold Sutcliffe, giving evidence, said that anyone could draw up the list, but his job was to do this to the satisfaction of ninety-two clubs, all with specific interests. He had to avoid neighbouring clubs having home games on the same day, he had to prevent whenever possible teams having long distances to travel over Christmas and Easter. Each town had its own holidays which begged for a local derby, and special events, like the Grand National, which affected attendances, transport and policing arrangements. Mid-week matches at grounds where there were no floodlights had also to fit in with early closing days. To accommodate all these separate criteria required 'skill, hard work and ingenuity' commented the judge.

Every attempt at drawing up the season's full list of 2028 matches took Sutcliffe nine hours to complete, but he then needed nine or ten further attempts to finalize it according to various requests from clubs. He did not do this for the sake of it, said Sutcliffe. He did it to enable the League to function.

After weeks of waiting and sifting the evidence the final judgement came on 13 May 1959. The League had won its case, and considering all the fuss and niggling memories from 1936, agreement for the use of the 1959–60 fixtures was reached fairly quickly. In July 1959 four members of the PPA signed a ten-year agreement to pay the Football League and the Scottish League a royalty of one half a per cent of their gross stakes, with a minimum of £245,000 per annum. Agreements with other firms not in the PPA brought this promised amount up to around £400,000.

'This is the greatest happening in football since the League was formed in 1888', said the elated League president Joe Richards, as the clubs rubbed their hands with glee at this long-awaited bonus. But The Times sounded a warning note in its leader comment the following day.

This money should be spent wisely, The Times advised, not on the undermining of the FA – who at that stage were not part of the agreement – or on projects like a northern rival to Wembley stadium or a League knock-out competition. Instead, the pools money should be spent on ground improvements, supplementing FA coaching schemes, easing small clubs' overdrafts and perhaps most important of all, building new League headquarters away from 'distant Preston'. The new location should be Dover, said The Times sarcastically, 'nearest to the Continent, where most progressive ideas are to be found'.

Since that major breakthrough the League have negotiated several new deals with the PPA, as have the FA for the use of FA Cup matches on pools coupons. 'Spot the Ball' competitions also provide vital monies for the Football Trust, from which the Football Grounds Improvement Trust is entirely funded. Prominent in that work has been the Littlewoods company.

The latest agreement with the PPA is for twelve years, signed in December 1984, by which the League stands to gain £5.5 million a year, a twenty-five per cent improvement on the previous agreement.

It still represents only a fraction of the PPA's income, and there perhaps remains a case for setting up a pools company run by the football authorities themselves, independently of the PPA, with the specific aim of ploughing money back into football. The idea has been mooted on several occasions since 1960, though never carried further. Since then the government tax on pools betting has also risen, to a staggering 42.5 per cent. In comparison, horse racing pays only an eight per cent levy. It is a staggering inequality.

But at least football now derives some benefit from pools betting, even if those who waged the first Pools War of 1936 would have publicly shuddered at the prospect. Behind closed doors, however, who knows how Messrs Cuff, Rinder, McKenna, and Sutcliffe would have reacted to this windfall from 'the menace of the pools.'

From my secret vantage point on the glass roof of history, notebook in hand, I would venture to say; tentatively at first, but checking there was no one at the door, gleefully thereafter.

8
The Last Straw

IF indeed 'Laws were made to be broken', as Christopher North said, might it not follow that law-makers are subject to breakage also?

Between 1901 and 1961 the Football League had a rule which placed a limit on the wages professional footballers could earn. It was also stated that no more than £10 be paid to a player signing on for a new club.

We have already seen how enquiries proved that these rules were broken throughout the Edwardian era, notably by Manchester City and Middlesbrough; in the 1950s there were two major investigations into similar breaches, involving Leyton Orient and Sunderland. But the enquiry into Sunderland's affairs went badly wrong, and for the first time in the history of the game the FA found itself in the dock ... on the losing side. This is the story of how football's law-makers were found to be their own law-breakers, and how professional football has never quite been the same since.

Before we find out why, we must restate the effect the maximum wage rule had on players and their clubs. Primarily, because of the need to keep extra payments out of club accounts, 'illegal' wages and bonuses usually changed hands in a variety of ways, often more subtle than the simple brown envelope full of bank-notes slipped into the jacket pocket. For example, the payments might be presented to the player's wife in the form of jewellery, which she could never wear in public because players were not supposed to earn enough to afford such luxuries. Instead the player would resell the jewellery for his 'bonus'. Occasionally extra money would be handed over by the conclusion of quite ridiculous transactions, such as in a couple of apocryphal cases from the 1950s when two players were 'rewarded' by the sale of a worthless old car for over £1000 and a mongrel dog for £500.

Cheap or even free accommodation was another hidden benefit which allowed the club to keep officially to the maximum wage. One player after the Second World War was reputed to have rented his semi-detached house for one shilling (5p) a year. Another ploy was to let the player buy his club house for a pittance, then a few years later he would sell it at the true market value for an enormous profit. That way none of the bonus entered the club's books.

Much depended on the player's bargaining ability. One former professional had a system whereby he would demand twice the amount he thought his new club could afford, then split the difference. (For a more detailed account of how players and clubs circumvented the rules and their differing reactions to the maximum wage see *The Football World* by Stephen Wagg, Harvester Press 1984.)

But no club would offer illegal payments unless asked, and not every player asked, perhaps out of shyness, perhaps because he genuinely accepted the wage level. Jimmy Hill, the former Brentford and Fulham player who went on to become manager of Coventry and a leading television sports presenter, remembers that when he left Griffin Park for Craven Cottage he did not ask Fulham for any extras. 'I just did not have the nerve', he said. Almost certainly a few young players were not even aware of any under-the-counter payments, while older, more established players with outside business interests were known to publicly defend the maximum wage. Stanley Matthews, Jack Milburn, Billy Wright and Ronnie Clayton were among them.

The essential point however, as both Jimmy Guthrie and Jimmy Hill each stressed as chairmen of the Players' Union, was that it was degrading for players to have to earn their due in such an underhand, unsavoury manner. Players' wages were already slipping behind the general rise in wage levels during the 1950s and it was humiliating for them to have to maintain and improve their standard of living by accepting 'illegal' extras.

Furthermore, in doing this they were constantly putting themselves at risk, in what was always an uncertain business; a player might be refused by one director but accommodated by another. There were different levels of awareness both within the boardroom and the dressing room. One ill-phrased demand to the wrong director and a player might find himself reported to the FA, and like George Parsonage of Fulham in 1908, banned for life (see Chapter Two). In practice this happened very rarely, but it was always a danger, as Trevor Ford discovered when he was reported by the Chelsea chairman after asking about the chances of a part-time job should he sign for Chelsea in 1950. Ford was fined £100 for putting the question.

The most bizarre aspect of this situation, as Billy Meredith once pointed out (see Chapter Two), was that some of the directors who went to London every year to vote in favour of the maximum wage were the very ones who returned to their clubs to sanction illegal payments.

Briefly stated, these were the main reasons for the continuance of this curious behaviour. Firstly the maximum wage supposedly ensured that poorer clubs were not priced out of the market, and that team spirit was not affected by some players earning a lot more than others. However, it could be argued that because the maximum rule kept wages artificially low, richer clubs could better channel their own funds to suit the star players. Certainly the bigger clubs could afford higher wages, otherwise they would never have been able to finance their 'illegal' payments. The smaller clubs clung to the maximum because they knew they could not afford more.

That the maximum wage suited the majority was amply illustrated every time the matter came up for a vote. Indeed it was the League chairmen, rather than the FA Council, who originally supported the regulation at the turn of the century, and although several senior officials in the FA vociferously opposed it, democratically they had to enforce the maximum once it was adopted.

But the single most important reason why the maximum wage remained in force until 1961 was that no-one challenged it in a court of law. It was as simple as that, and one of the reasons why it took so long to be scrutinized was that very few individuals were prepared to expose the situation for the sham that it undoubtedly was. As Jimmy Guthrie argued, public opinion would never be won over as long as footballers and officials concealed the true state of affairs in a conspiracy of fear, self-interest and obedience to their masters at Preston and Lancaster Gate. For their part, without concrete evidence of irregularities, the League and FA were powerless to act also.

In fact apart from the investigations at Manchester City and Middlesbrough (see Chapter Two) plus sundry fines in the 1920s, the authorities received only a few isolated complaints and tip-offs from interested parties, and not all of those could be investigated. Everyone knew the rule was being broken constantly, yet finding evidence was always the biggest obstacle. In many cases the players themselves were loath to change the system because it meant that they were receiving substantial under-the-counter payments tax free, and who wanted to be branded as a criminal? For the majority it was best to leave well alone and either milk the system or suffer it while it lasted.

Fortunately a sufficient number of people, albeit small, did want to blow the lid off the whole system. The Players' Union was developing the muscle but needed the publicity. Trevor Ford tried to expose the hypocrisy within football in his frank autobiography *I Lead the Attack* (Stanley Paul) which first came to the authorities' attention in 1956. But when questioned, as we shall discover later, the Welsh centre-forward was not surprisingly unwilling to give further proof without some guarantee of immunity. It was thus convenient for officialdom to brand his 'revelations' as the sensational outpourings of a troublemaker.

What the situation really required was a person other than a player, someone of substance, literally to 'inform', to provide a lead for the Football League and the FA to investigate. If one club could be found guilty of breaking the rules then surely, with an orchestrated campaign, it would be relatively simple to involve all the others and eliminate the rule itself.

In 1950 Manchester City's chairman Bob Smith tried to persuade the League to vote for an amnesty for every club that had broken the rules. He even compiled a dossier of clubs who had secretly admitted their actions. But the vote at the AGM went against him and the matter faded into the background. He tried once more in 1953, but failed again.

There was also the possibility that even if an informer did come along, unlike Bob Smith his true motive might not be to reform the wage and bonus structure but to clamp down on the law-breakers, to make an example of them. In January 1957 that person came forward.

To this day only a handful of people know his true identity, because in writing to the Football League he would only sign himself 'Mr Smith'. But so closely did 'Mr Smith' relate Sunderland's affairs to the League that it was strongly suspected that he was either one of the directors himself or was at least being fed information by one of the board. But why would a club director wish to inform on his colleagues?

More than most newspapers the *Daily Express* and the *People* came closest to the real heart of the story. In fact the sports editor of the *Express* actually saw the two anonymous letters and commented on 7 January 1957, when the story first appeared, that '"Smith" gives enough facts to show he is well acquainted with the Sunderland club and that his object is the punishment of individuals.'

But were these letters simply the act of a man outraged by the transgressions of others? Did 'Mr Smith' want only to clean up football? One of his letters, reported the *Express*, contained a statement that two of the Sunderland directors had threatened to demand an inquiry unless two of the others resigned. So was there also a power struggle going on within the board?

In Alan Hardaker's autobiography (*Hardaker of the League*, Pelham Books, 1977) the late Secretary of the League wrote of the mysterious letters, 'I am very sure I know who sent them. I compared type-faces and style with one or two other letters I had received and there was no doubt in my mind that they tallied. His name, if I revealed it, would cause enormous surprise even now . . .' But Alan Hardaker remained silent.

Without proof we cannot put in print the suspicions of several people who were close to the affair. Suffice it to say that they are still personally convinced of 'Mr Smith's' true identity and allege that he was in fact a member of the Sunderland board as it existed in early 1957.

But we must return to Alan Hardaker at the League's headquarters in Preston. Hardaker had only been in the post of Secretary for a matter of days when the letters from 'Mr Smith' began to make sense. According to him, this is how the trail began.

When the FA and the League first responded to 'Mr Smith' by examining Sunderland's books they could find nothing incriminating, and Hardaker was just about to write off his anonymous informer as a crank when he noticed a lightly pencilled question next to one of the figures. It read 'Where do I post this?'

The figure, which was for about £3000, related to the purchase of straw. Sunderland were one of the few clubs who still used straw as a means of protecting their pitch from snow and frost. It was an old-fashioned and unwieldy method but it usually worked. Hardaker's suspicions were now aroused, so he telephoned his brother Ernest, who was chairman of Hull Rugby League Club, and as the late Secretary's autobiography relates, the conversation went as follows:

'How much does it cost you to cover your ground with straw in a normal sort of winter?'

'It would depend on how many Saturdays were involved', he replied.

'Well', I said, 'if I gave you £3000 would you be able to manage for a season?'

'Blow me', Ernest answered, 'for that we'd manage for twenty-five seasons!'

Sunderland's straw cover was blown.

Coincidentally, on the same day that 'Mr Smith' was introduced to the public, it was reported that Trevor Ford was refusing to 'substantiate or withdraw' any of the comments he had made in his book, as ordered by the Football League Management Committee.

'I cannot retract a single syllable without being dishonest to myself', he wrote in the *Daily Express*. 'I refuse to substantiate it without an amnesty for the guilty ones. I will not rat on my friends.'

Ford's determination was in stark contrast to that of the anonymous 'Mr Smith'. One would not give the names of the guilty in order to protect them, the other would not give his own name to protect himself in the act of implicating others. Although it was not known then, to add irony to the situation, one of the very people who Ford refused to name was destined to be the chief victim of 'Mr Smith's' letters.

Three weeks later Ford shared the headlines with 'Mr Smith' once again. As the FA announced the setting up of a joint commission to investigate Sunderland's affairs, Ford, who was then thirty-one and playing out his often stormy career in Cardiff City reserves, was suspended *sine die* by the League for his reticence over the revelations.

The player was furious. He claimed that no charges had been made against him. 'This is Britain', he complained to the press, 'not an Iron Curtain country.' It was the same 'Russian darkness' we heard about in the Meredith affair.

For a couple of months Ford's appeal against his ban created more interest than the investigation at Roker Park, though the two were linked by a common thread; Ford had been a Sunderland player for three years and had claimed in his autobiography that when he signed for the club in 1950 manager Bill Murray had promised him a part-time job worth £1000, plus the house of his choice to be decorated to his satisfaction at Sunderland's expense. So Ford's case only served to increase the glare of attention already dazzling the Wearside club.

Meanwhile, as the footballing public awaited the outcome of Ford's appeal and Sunderland's examination, there was one other noteworthy event.

This occurred on January 28, when Jimmy Guthrie, the controversial chairman of the Players' Union, was sacked in Manchester after eleven years in the post. Opinions differ sharply as to whether Guthrie deserved this treatment after all he had achieved, but there can be little doubt that the man who took his place made a considerable impact. He was Jimmy Hill, the bearded Fulham player whose middle class up-bringing had not given him the nerve to ask for illegal extras. But Hill had other advantages; experience in business, youth, and a willingness to work for the Union without pay.

Hill never forgot that Jimmy Guthrie had once been advised by a sympathetic lawyer that the only way the players could break the grip of the football authorities on wages and bonuses was by whipping up public indignation. The Sunderland case would certainly do that.

On March 3 Ford was allowed to return to football when his appeal was successful, and three weeks later he left Wales to sign for a Dutch club. Attention now focused upon Roker Park, where a report was anxiously awaited from the joint FA and Football League commission.

What had its members made of this £3000 for straw? After enquiries conducted at York and Sheffield the commission found Sunderland's methods to be subtle but simple. In order to finance illegal payments the club had apparently placed orders with two contractors – for straw and for tarmac – far in excess of their actual requirements. When the suppliers then delivered only the required amounts Sunderland were given credit notes. These notes were cashed at a later date and the extra money, which never appeared in the accounts, was paid over to the players. This had been going on for five years, and although the total amount was £5427 14s 2d, once this had been divided among a number of players it hardly represented a windfall for any individual.

The sixty-nine-year-old Sunderland chairman, Bill Ditchburn (also

121

known formally as Edward), always insisted that the responsibility for this system was his alone. In fact, until 'Mr Smith' spilled the beans Ditchburn thought that of the eight board members only he and his close friend Bill Martin knew anything about the irregular practices. Later Ditchburn was to say that he always told the board 'I'll do the worrying.' He also added, 'But I didn't worry, because I knew every other club was doing the same.' Even so, at one point when he did fear being found out Ditchburn paid £2700 into the club's accounts in order to hide some of the illegal payments.

Ditchburn was a typical football club chairman in many respects. A Sunderland devotee almost from birth, he had started in his father's basement shop at the age of twelve and built up one of the three most successful furniture businesses in the country. In 1930 he joined the Sunderland board and in 1934 he was elected Mayor of the town. He was the kind of man the founder of the Football League, William McGregor, was referring to in 1905 after one of Middlesbrough's brushes with the FA. 'It strikes me as unaccountably strange', wrote McGregor, 'how men, socially and in business the essence of integrity, should descend to malpractice in football matters.'

But Ditchburn was different in other ways. Bob Pennington in the *Daily Express* described him thus: 'This bow-tied, wing-collared little man looks like a character from Dickens. His approach to football is a strange mixture of the business tycoon's "Money talks" and the naive enthusiasm of a soccer bobbysoxer.' Pennington's next sentence was perhaps the key to 'Mr Smith's' behaviour. 'His bluntness has upset everyone, including his fellow directors.'

Yet otherwise Ditchburn was extremely popular, with his workmen at the furniture factory and with his players at Roker Park. For example, every new player he signed was immediately fixed up with a part-time job or commercial interest to secure his future. 'He is the kindest hearted man I have ever met', said one of his fellow business directors.

He also had what the *Daily Express* called 'the common touch'. One of the players from the 1950s, Len Shackleton, recalls how Ditchburn used to go out in his distinctive pink and mauve Rolls Royce to buy fish and chips. The chairman also foresaw the growing influence of broadcasting on football, and refused to allow any radio commentators into Roker Park.

Football was Ditchburn's only passion in life. 'He had red and white eyes', said Bill Martin. He also wanted the very best for Sunderland and was always prepared to pay for it. But since the heady days of the mid-1930s, when Sunderland briefly stole the First Division limelight from mighty Arsenal, the club had endured a patchy existence. Apart from finishing third in 1949–50 their greatest claim was to have had the longest unbroken spell in the First Division, having been members since 1890 – hardly enough for a club of Sunderland's great tradition.

So, under Ditchburn's chairmanship, Sunderland spent more heavily on players in the post-war period than any other club in Britain, beginning in 1948 with a record £20,050 for Len Shackleton from Newcastle, followed by another record £30,000 for Trevor Ford from Aston Villa in 1950 (Ford made a sensational debut, inadvertently breaking the opposing centre-half's jaw, scoring a hat-trick and splitting one of the goalposts at Roker Park).

Even though money failed to win the club success Ditchburn continued to buy. In the 1953 close season alone he spent the then prodigious amount of £70,000 on three international players; Billy Elliott, the England outside-right, who cost £27,000 from Burnley, Ray Daniel, the Welsh centre-half who cost a similar amount from Arsenal, and Jimmy Cowan, the Scottish goalkeeper from Morton.

A few months later Ken Chisholm, the well-travelled Scottish inside-forward (whom we met in Chapter Five) arrived at Roker for £15,000 from Cardiff, and among several other signings in the next two seasons came another Scottish goalkeeper, Willie Fraser from Airdrie, for £5000, and from Morton, the winger Johnny Hannigan for £6000.

No wonder Sunderland were called 'the Bank of England club', though apart from reaching two Cup semi-finals between 1954–56 and finishing in fourth place in the League in 1955, the investments were still hardly a success on the pitch. Off the pitch of course, these new signings cost the club dearly in 'extras'. Rules or no rules, it was almost inconceivable to pay nearly £30,000 for a player to perform in front of packed grounds and yet compensate him for his move to the tune of only £10, a figure which had been agreed upon in 1891.

Ditchburn knew the rules were farcical, and did his best to pay the players as he saw fit. But now, thanks to the anonymous 'Mr Smith', the Sunderland chairman faced the consequences of his actions. He knew, and most of the other clubs knew that it could have been anyone facing the commission of enquiry. (It was in many ways a situation parallel to that of Leeds City in 1919).

Even so, there was by no means universal sympathy. Many clubs were hostile towards Sunderland because of their big spending, just as many clubs had reacted against neighbours Middlesbrough in 1905 after the signing of Alf Common (see Chapter Two). The former chairman of Manchester City, Bob Smith, also pointed out that when he had called for an amnesty for clubs breaking the rules in 1950, Sunderland had been one of the clubs who voted against him.

Nevertheless, the FA's judgement, when it did come on April 10 was still an enormous shock to everyone in football.

Firstly Sunderland were to be fined £5000, by far the largest sum ever imposed by the FA (until then the highest figure had been £750 when Newcastle United were fined for fielding weak teams before their Cup Final in 1924). This punishment alone was sufficient to put Sunderland in the headlines and bring BBC news cameras to Roker Park for the first time.

Each director was also punished. *Sine die* bans were placed on the Sunderland vice-chairman Stanley Ritson and Lawrence Evans. Evans, the managing director of a building company, received the news as he lay in bed on the morning of his birthday. Ritson was a well known surgeon and magistrate.

The remaining board members, Colonel John Turnbull, John Reed, Jack Parker and Sidney Collings were severely censured for failing to report their suspicions to the FA. Collings, a businessman, only found out about the decision from a newspaper while on holiday in France and he immediately flew back. Only a few months before he had been elected to the FA Council (but he survived the censure so well that he went on to become a prominent member of the FA and Football League Management Committee. Collings was partly instrumental in the appointment of Alf Ramsey as England manager). The censure was also potentially embarrassing for John Reed, an accountant who was naturally concerned about his own professional reputation.

Sunderland's manager Bill Murray, and the secretary George Crow, both of whom had been in their jobs since 1939, were exonerated for the time being, the FA recognizing that although they took part in making the illegal payments they were in a difficult situation as servants of the club.

The worst to suffer, as expected, were Bill Ditchburn and Bill Martin. The latter, a fifty-three-year-old accountant, local councillor and managing director of a chain store, was Ditchburn's main associate in the financial dealings.

Their punishments were the harshest possible – permanent bans from football.

Not surprisingly, one of Bill Ditchburn's first public utterances was dedicated to 'Mr Smith'. 'I hope he's satisfied with his work', said the shattered chairman, and he promised to hit back. 'We have enough ammunition to hit really hard', he told the press, outlining his intention to collect sufficient evidence to show how almost every major club in the League was no less guilty than Sunderland. 'Anyone who thinks I won't have the guts or the money doesn't know Billy', he added. Bill Martin was going to join him on this crusade. 'Neither of us need count the funds', said Ditchburn.

The Sunderland chairman later revealed that Bill Martin had actually offered to volunteer his part in the irregular payments in front of the commission, resign his seat on the board and take all the blame. It was suggested that Martin had been involved in a business feud with a director of one of the firms which had supplied the overpriced invoices and that 'Mr Smith' as a result wanted him off the board. But the Sunderland directors had refused to let Martin make this personal sacrifice. Could it have been that some of them wanted more than just Martin's resignation? Ditchburn then exonerated Stanley Ritson from any blame. The surgeon had not even known the illegal payments were being made, he said. Whoever 'Mr Smith' was, it was not Ritson, Ditchburn implied.

However, Bill Ditchburn's most significant comments were these, reported in the *Daily Express*. Recalling the enquiry he said, 'At Sheffield we were told this was only an enquiry. At York we were told the same people would be acting as jury and later as judges. We asked for legal representation and were refused. Sir Leslie Bowker is a barrister. He was dealing with laymen.'

Sir Leslie was the leading member of the Sunderland enquiry, and although he and almost everyone else did not appear to realize it at the time, the commission had broken the FA's own rules. How it did this was not discovered until weeks later, but as we shall see, the oversight was to have disastrous consequences for the football authorities.

In the meantime, Bill Ditchburn's son Jack, a solicitor, at first thought to seek legal redress for his father and Bill Martin on the grounds that the FA did not have the power to suspend a company director, because company law came above that of the FA. But in the immediate aftermath of the judgement that was little consolation for Ditchburn. For him the shock was almost too much.

The following day he broke down in the dressing room while bidding a tearful farewell to the players. He told them to keep their peckers up and reminded them how he had always 'put the man on the ball first'. One of the players, Don Revie, wished him well and was told by Ditchburn, 'You have no idea what this parting means to me.'

As he left the ground in a highly emotional state he told reporters that if the full story were known very few clubs in the League would escape punishment. Corruption was so widespread in the game that only in the past twenty-four hours had he heard of yet another attempt to fix a match. Then with some irony, Ditchburn, the football fanatic who had banned the broadcasters from Roker Park, told the gathering, 'I won't be seeing you Saturday. No, I'll be staying away. There'll be a football match on the wireless.'

But Bill Ditchburn was determined not to give in so easily, even though the FA had told him there could be no appeal. 'I shall carry on fighting', he told the press. He also gave an interview on BBC's *Panorama* programme, and was approached by a number of players, both past and present, willing to contribute evidence to a secret dossier of information with which he planned, one day, to confront the authorities. Among those who came forward were the former Sunderland players Trevor Ford and Ken Chisholm, and Hughie Gallacher, the former Scottish idol of the pre-war period who was then working in a Gateshead factory.

Ditchburn's main aim was to find out about irregularities at clubs represented by members on the FA Council and League Management Committee. He also asked the former Manchester City chairman, Bob Smith, for material from his own dossier which dated back to 1950. But Smith refused, saying, 'I have no wish to be known as the sneak of the football world.'

Meanwhile, the FA had not finished with Sunderland. The players had yet to be examined, and on April 25 five of them faced another joint FA–Football League commission at the Midland Hotel, Manchester. They were Ray Daniel, Billy Elliott, Willie Fraser, Johnny Hannigan, and Ken Chisholm, who was now at Workington.

These five were the men named as having received illegal signing-on bonuses by manager Bill Murray, under questioning during the earlier commission proceedings. At first Murray had been reluctant to give any information but after long periods of silence Sir Leslie Bowker had demanded to know some names. There was no ill-feeling between Murray and the five – they knew he had no choice. In fact Murray attended the players' hearing. Sunderland's captain, George Aitken, was also in attendance and Trevor Ford flew in from Amsterdam.

It was probably the single most important confrontation between players and the authorities for a disciplinary action, as opposed to wage negotiations, since before the First World War, and recognizing how the affair might at last be a lever with which to overturn the archaic wage and bonus restrictions, Jimmy Hill of the Players' Union was on hand to advise the players. A Manchester firm of solicitors, George Davies and Co., provided crucial legal advice and back-up (it was this firm which steered the union through the Eastham case in 1963).

Jimmy Hill had already made an impact in his first few weeks as chairman of the union, and prompted Maurice Smith of the *The People* to comment that he was the one man who could 'blow the Football League's stubborn, stupid defence of a rotten system sky high'.

But equally important was the presence with Hill of the well-respected union secretary Cliff Lloyd, a determined but affable man who had also played for Fulham in his own, less distinguished football career. One of the solicitors who acted for the union described Lloyd as 'A gift from the gods for the Players' Union. He was a joy to work with and was a methodical, dogged and patient negotiator.'

The very fact that Hill and Lloyd were allowed to attend the enquiry was in itself something of a minor breakthrough, because until that point players had always been denied any form of representation at official hearings. Remember how men like Hillman and Travers were left to face the FA alone? The Players' Union desired that members should also have legal representation, but this was refused by the FA, despite recommendations by a 1952 Ministry of Labour report that they should have such a right.

So, without solicitors, the players entered room 104 at the Midland Hotel to face the six man commission. Its members were Arthur Drewery, chairman of the FA, Sir Leslie Bowker, the vice-chairman and Fred Barrett, with Arthur Oakley, Joe Richards and Harold Shentall from the Football League. Also in attendance as observers were Sir Stanley Rous and Alan Hardaker, secretaries of the FA and League respectively.

To begin with, the commission asked each player to give details of how he had received illegal payments. According to English law however, no man should ever be forced to give evidence against himself. On the instructions of the union's lawyers therefore the players remained completely silent (this was particularly difficult for one of the five, who claimed later that he knew for sure that one of the commission members facing him had once offered an illegal bonus to a friend of his).

Faced unexpectedly with five silent men the members of the commission were flummoxed, and almost certainly as a result of their confusion it was at this point that they made a surprising decision, despite the presence once again of barrister Sir Leslie Bowker. When the players refused to incriminate themselves, as was their right, the commission decided to suspend the five players *sine die*. As this was announced to a surprised gathering there was a sudden, momentary hush. For Cliff Lloyd that was the worst moment of the whole episode.

Soon after, however, the union was given an unexpected glimmer of hope. A young articled clerk at George Davies and Co. went through the rule books of the League and the FA, knowing that in order to challenge the commission's decision he would have to prove that either the laws of natural justice or the rules of either body had been broken.

As the clerk discovered, the conduct of the commission twice contravened FA and Football League rules as they then existed. Firstly, according to these rules the FA and League – and therefore any commission wholly or partly appointed by them – did not possess the power to suspend a player or official *sine die*. Only member clubs had this power. Secondly, the commission was appointed only to enquire into the allegations concerning Sunderland. It had been given no powers to adjudicate. In other words, the commission could investigate like a detective but not pass sentences like a judge. FA rules said that judgement had to be in the hands of a newly-appointed commission composed of different individuals.

Thus, perhaps in its panic, perhaps through lack of knowledge or planning, the commission had broken the rules of the very bodies which set it up.

These transgressions were only technicalities, but they formed just the breakthrough the union was seeking, and one which was seized upon by Bill Ditchburn and Bill Martin's solicitors soon afterwards. If the commission had acted *ultra vires* in the players' case it had done the same in the directors' case also.

Not that the players were particularly happy about their situation. Although Daniel and Chisholm were resilient, carefree characters, a couple of the players were clearly finding the attention thrust upon them hard to cope with. It was especially difficult for their families, since it appeared that the men had somehow done something 'illegal' by accepting bonuses.

Indeed, however confident Cliff Lloyd and Jimmy Hill seemed, the situation was extremely worrying. They knew that if the union failed it might indirectly be responsible for at least depriving the players of their income for some time, at worst ending their careers in England. But if the union succeeded, the victory would be a major step forward in the struggle for players' rights.

Recalling those difficult days in April and May 1957, Cliff Lloyd said, 'I felt sorry for the players involved, but it had to happen. We were relieved to get it into the open. The players were worried at the time, knowing how harsh the penalties could be. I was very worried also, but there was no resentment from the players towards the union. We prided ourselves on our legal advice.'

Somehow relations between the union and the League did not greatly suffer from the April 25 confrontation. Indeed the following day both parties held a routine meeting at which the union put forward various matters for the League's AGM to consider. Apart from the Sunderland affair there had been two other events which put the players' situation into a wholly different perspective.

The first was the Government's Budget decision to abolish entertainment tax, a burden on football clubs since the First World War but particularly so since 1945, when it had risen to cover a fifth of all gate receipts. Its disappearance meant that potentially clubs had twenty per cent greater incomes overnight.

· The second was John Charles' much publicized transfer from Leeds to Juventus of Italy. It was reported that Charles had negotiated a massive £10,000 signing-on bonus, a figure which astounded League professionals, who were only legally entitled to £10. As the union no doubt pointed out to the League, many more top British players would follow Charles abroad unless the petty restrictions were lifted.

During the following days the union had also to consider ways of helping both financially and morally the five suspended players (a decision on Ford had been deferred). There were three main ideas; a levy on fellow union members, an appeal to the public, and the one which the union pursued immediately, a suggestion which Maurice Smith of the *People* newspaper claimed was his own. This was that Hill should draft a document in which players admit to having received under-the-counter payments. Such a document would then be signed by as many players as was possible.

'This is the most sensational move so far in the war between the League and the union', wrote Maurice Smith in the *People* (well he would, wouldn't he?). One player told him, 'If they threw out everyone who signs our admission of guilt they won't be able to find a couple of teams.' For once, added Smith, 'the union has got the ball at its feet. If its members now rally round and sign the confession the Football League bosses will be given a trouncing on their own ground.'

On April 28 Hill announced that the Players' Union was calling for the League and FA to hold an enquiry into the whole question of improper payments. He pledged the Union's co-operation for this on three conditions. They were:

1. no action be taken against players on evidence freely pro-vided (i.e. those who had signed the document)

2. the current suspensions of the five players be lifted and reviewed if necessary later

3. if a change of rules was agreed upon, this be implemented speedily

Thus, backed by a surprisingly solid executive and in a mood of great determination Hill prepared for the commission's next hearing, due on May 8. He was already driving up and down the country in his Morris Minor collecting signatures from players who admitted receiving payments, however small, and reckoned he would get as many as 1000 players to sign, out of a total Union membership of 2500. Some of the signatories were internationals.

The League's response to this unexpected rush of fervour among the players came from Alan Hardaker. If the union gave him a list of the signatories he said he might be forced to hand it over to the tax authorities. Of course technically Hardaker was right – the players had received tax free payments – but his attitude hardly helped to narrow the gap between the League and the players.

Cliff Lloyd's response was equally direct. 'Such a disclosure would result in a tax probe into every club in the country.' Touché!

The spotlight was now well and truly on the five players and the campaign to abolish the maximum wage. Unwittingly, 'Mr Smith' had stirred up a hornet's nest which hummed far beyond the confines of Roker Park.

Speaking to the *Sunderland Echo*, Bill Ditchburn stayed loyal to his former players by saying that it was contrary to British justice for a man to be penalized for refusing to convict himself. It was victimization. Since his own suspension the former chairman had been collecting his own evidence 'to blow the lid off the game'. He said, 'Some of the information I have received shows me that I am just an infant in this business.'

In fact Ditchburn was conducting his very own private investigation, with hired 'detectives' going around the country collecting information. He claimed at one stage to have gathered an entire team of international players, all of whom had admitted accepting illegal payments. This information, reported the *People*, was filed away in the 'millionaire Soccer man's luxury home'.

And there it was destined to stay, despite Ditchburn's dramatic announcement on April 30 that unless the League began to discuss the question of payments in the next ten days he would reveal the names of club's he had evidence against, '. . . starting with the big ones first'. Sadly we will never know what the dossier contained. It was accidentally destroyed some years later.

Another person ready to 'tell all', as we learnt earlier, was Trevor Ford. In his autobiography Ford wrote of the 'fiddles of football'; the money left in envelopes, the £5000 backhander once reputed to have been offered to a top player, and the £5000 backhander also reputed to have been refused by another. It was racy stuff, the basic theme of which was his statement that 'It is well nigh impossible for a player to reach the top without breaking almost every law in the book.'

Ford's writing, the Players' Union campaign and Sunderland's plight all contributed to the growing support for the abolition of the maximum wage. The players also won limited support in Parliament. Hugh Delargy, the Labour MP for Thurrock, asked for legislation to allow individuals the right of appeal in matters decided by non-statutory, informal tribunals, such as an FA–Football League commission. Sir Edward Boyle, for the Government, refused.

One of football's most eloquent and passionate supporters in the House of Commons was the Labour member for Huddersfield East, J. P.

W. 'Curly' Mallalieu, who also happened to be married to the daughter of the famous manager Jack Tinn. Through Tinn the MP had a close association with Jimmy Guthrie. Mallalieu suggested the formation of a Royal Commission 'to examine the affairs of the football industry', an idea also rejected by the Government. Mallalieu asked again if 'the Lord Privy Seal was aware of considerable evidence of corruption in this industry and some evidence of tax evasion?' But even this failed to move the Conservative administration. R. A. Butler declared that he preferred to leave the affairs of the football industry alone.

The Times agreed. In a leader comment on May 2 it described Mallalieu's suggestion as ridiculous. Parliamentary intervention would not, said the newspaper, solve football's problems, and nor should Mr Harold Wilson (then a shadow cabinet minister) attempt to make political capital out of football by endeavouring 'to win his battles on the playing fields of England'.

Mallalieu would not be deterred, however. As feelings rose steadily against the concept of a maximum wage, largely thanks to the efforts of the Players' Union, he and fellow MP Eric Fletcher tabled an amendment to a section of the Finance Bill (the budget) which dealt with the abolition of entertainment tax. Mallalieu proposed that the tax should remain in force at all matches where players were bound by the maximum wage. Again the suggestion was not adopted.

On May 3 Hill received a letter from the League saying that it would only accept the union's evidence unconditionally, not 'under threats or impossible conditions'. Faced with this response the players then held a rally at the Wembley Pool, a few hours after the 1957 Cup Final (in which Aston Villa beat Manchester United in controversial circumstances). The idea of collecting signatures, it was announced, was 'to make it so big they cannot persecute individuals'.

In later years Hill claimed that every club he visited co-operated fully and that almost every player did sign the document, but with the close season just beginning and the players dispersing for their holidays the figure of 1000 was beginning to look impossible. Furthermore, not all the union's committee members who were out collecting signatures were as persuasive as their chairman.

Newspaper reports suggested that many players had in fact refused to sign. Even Maurice Smith of the People had to report on May 12 that despite Hill and Lloyd's assurance that all was going to plan, the drive to collect signatures was in reality a mess. Smith wrote of a 'widening split' in the union executive, a growing divide between Northern and Southern players, and of accusations by some players that certain union members were trying to cash in on the publicity. One committee member told Smith, 'When I asked the players of one Second Division club to sign they just laughed at me.' They had apparently told him, 'All we've had in the way of illegal payments is £15 for three floodlit matches.' (This was just before the League sanctioned additional payments for floodlit games.)

Some lower paid players were, in effect, loath to sign a document which put themselves at risk for the sake of those better paid players who wanted more. Or so it seemed. 'Sometimes I feel professional footballers are their own worst enemy', wrote a disappointed Smith.

Roy Peskett portrayed an even more dismal scenario in the following day's *Daily Mail*. He called the drive for signatures 'a flop' and reported that only forty professionals had signed the document. In reply, Hill was reported to have said, putting on a brave face, 'The number is considerably more than twenty and twenty is a serious matter anyway, isn't it?'

But because of the document's actual wording it was important for the union to obtain those promised signatures. This is what the document said:

'We the undersigned are prepared to swear on oath that we have received illegal payments (however small) in contravention of the rules of the FA and the Football League. It is understood that this document we have signed will not be produced to any person or body other than the Association Football Players' and Trainers' Union without prior consent of the signatories unless

1. it is produced in order to benefit professional footballers generally and

2. it (or copies of it) have been signed by not less than 1000 persons.

To add to Hill's task, two of the five suspended players were also reported to have been unhappy about the lack of financial support they were getting from the union. 'Pay us some compensation or we tell all', Billy Elliott and Willie Fraser were alleged to have told the union. 'Why should we go on carrying the can for other players who may have done worse than us?' one of them told the *Daily Mail*.

Even greater publicity was given to the fact that one of the Sunderland players had refused to sign the document and that there was a rift in the dressing room. 'This player will have to go', said one of the eighteen signatories at Roker Park. 'The boys just don't want him in the ground after his refusal to sign the union's confession.'

A few days later his identity was revealed. It was Len Shackleton, one of the most enigmatic and popular footballers of his time who was known as 'the Clown Prince of Soccer'. Then aged thirty-five and within a couple of months of retirement, Shackleton replied to his critics by saying that he believed the best way to change the wage and bonus structure was for the players to strike. Signing confessions would not, he said, help anyone. 'I am a union member, but I still have the right to form my own opinion.'

The union's leadership remained determined. Five days after the Cup Final they held a seven-hour meeting and reaffirmed their insistence that no evidence would be handed over to the League without a guarantee of immunity against punishment.

The collection of signatures had by this time almost ground to a halt – most players were on holiday – but in the end Hill claimed to have collected 250 signatures. Undoubtedly, however, the number was far less significant than the point he was trying to make. It was exactly Jimmy Guthrie's argument of a few years before. Why should footballers, as top entertainers, be degraded in their efforts to seek a decent reward for their skills? Why could a footballer not become like any other professional entertainer, or indeed any other professional sportsman? If nothing else, the union's campaign roused public opinion to an awareness of this argument, even if not everyone agreed with it. Gates were dropping and so, according to some reports at the time, was the standard of entertainment. It was all too easy therefore for the sceptics to argue that footballers did not deserve higher rewards.

On May 17 the second meeting of the commission took place. At this stage the union's solicitors were still drawing up their case against the FA and the League, and the law being a slow process at the best of times no challenge was made for the time being. (The solicitors also knew that if the authorities were made aware of their mistakes they could easily reappoint a new commission, start the whole process again from scratch, conduct the enquiry properly and still reach the same conclusion. Some delay was vital to the union's cause, therefore). But the solicitors did advise the players to answer the commission's questions this time. There was no longer any purpose to be served by the player's silence; the union had made its point and knew that it had another way to fight back.

Accordingly the five players owned up to having received illegal payments and the suspensions were immediately lifted. There was, however, one tense moment when the commission came to Ken Chisholm. In common with the other players he was asked if he had received a certain sum for signing on at Sunderland. Chisholm denied it, and for a few seconds the commission must have thought there was going to be more trouble. But Chisholm countered quickly by telling the officials, 'You don't think I would sign on for that amount do you? I got much more than that!'

Now that the suspensions were lifted and the players had admitted their guilt, all that remained was for the FA and the League to pass a sentence, if any, The players waited a week, but when the announcement came the judgement appeared to be so oddly formulated that it invited a response mixed with derision from one side and confusion on the other.

In brief, the FA decided to penalize the players by stripping them of part of their qualification to benefits. This meant that the players were not so much fined in cash but prohibited for a certain period from receiving payments they were due.

Three of the players, Chisholm, Daniel and Elliott, were to forfeit two years of their qualification for benefit, or the equivalent accrued share of benefit. In real terms this meant that Daniel and Elliott, who were promised benefits the following season (because they had been at Sunderland for the minimum qualification period of five years) would not receive £300 due to them, unless of course they remained at Roker for another two years. In addition they had lost twenty-two days pay during the suspension period.

Clubs were not, however, forced to pay benefits; it was a purely voluntary agreement. Thus Ken Chisholm stood to lose nothing, because his present club Workington could not have afforded to pay out benefits anyway, even if he had stayed there long enough.

The other two players, Fraser and Hannigan each forfeited only six months of their qualification for benefit – equivalent to £75 – because they had received only small illegal payments. No decision was taken on Trevor Frod, who was still in Holland, and the commission took no further action against George Crow, the Sunderland secretary. But Bill Murray received a £200 fine for his part in making under-the-counter payments, a fine which was said to have been lenient in view of his co-operation with the commission. A month later Murray resigned, after twenty-eight years at Roker Park as player and manager.

Like so many managers of his time, Murray had never been one to grab the headlines. He was one of 'the old school' who let players get on with the game, giving them the same, basic team talk before every match. Nevertheless he had no enemies, and was widely mourned on his death a couple of years later.

The legacy of 'Mr Smith' was still not complete. There was more, because it transpired that Sunderland had paid all the first team players illegal bonuses during the successful FA Cup runs between 1954 and 1956. Therefore the commission's net widened its sweep and five weeks later bagged another eight former and current Sunderland players, who were all punished by forfeiting six months qualification or accrued share of benefit. The players were Len Shackleton, George Aitken, Stan Anderson, Billy Bingham, Joe McDonald, Bill Holden (then with Stockport), Sam Kemp (Sheffield United) and Ted Purdon (Workington). So obscure was the punishment that not all of the players even realized it had been imposed.

The Commission also made its final decision on Trevor Ford. For his part in receiving illegal payments, and no doubt for his general refusal to give evidence, Ford was banned from registering with the FA as a professional for three years. This in effect meant that Ford was able to carry on as before, playing in Holland.

Overall, the punishments were much less harsh than had been expected, and the new Sunderland board, chaired by Colonel Turnbull, could even have been forgiven for feeling somewhat amused, if not relieved. After all, the effect of the FA's judgement was to reduce the amount of benefit the club would have to pay to all the players.

Indeed it was calculated that Sunderland had been saved some £1650, a sizeable chunk of the £5000 fine they had had to pay earlier.

And so Sunderland faced the 1957–58 season with renewed hope and a new, strict young manager, Alan Brown from Burnley. The storm, apparently, had passed. At the League's AGM the newly-elected president Joe Richards looked forward to a period of adjustment and prosperity, while a letter to the meeting from a Mr Ditchburn of Sunderland, calling for an amnesty for players, was virtually ignored.

There was one consolation for the players. They might not have won the abolition issue, yet, but the League did decide to allow them to take part in authorized and registered pools competitions. That was one way of making them rich!

History now shows that in a wider context the storm had only just abated for Sunderland and the Football League. As the Players' Union and its legal advisers regrouped, within months of the new season starting the League and FA found themselves investigating another club for illegal payments. This time the FA had received letters from a former Leyton Orient official, a man perhaps emboldened by the example of 'Mr Smith', though at least this informer gave his real name.

In February 1958 as a result of the commission's enquiry Orient were fined £2000 for mismanaging their books and making an improper loan to a player. The problem of illegal payments would just not go away. Ken Chisholm, called by *The People* 'the stormy petrel of football', added to the authorities' dilemma by sending them full details of illegal extras he had received from three clubs, Partick Thistle, Leicester City and Leeds United. The last two had representatives on the League's Management Committee and therefore Chisholm's letters, backed up by bank statements, were highly embarrassing. In the end no action was taken, and we can only guess why.

Meanwhile the Professional Footballers Association (as the Union was renamed in 1958) and its solicitors were preparing to challenge the FA and the Football League on their conduct of the Sunderland investigation. 'Mr Smith's' legacy had yet to reach its most decisive outcome.

Although the union wanted to let things cool before they acted – for reasons we mentioned earlier – the lengthy process of the law meant that it was not until October 1959, over two years after the commission's original verdict, that the FA, Football League, and each individual member of the joint commission received their first summonses in the High Court.

The players' claim was that the *sine die* suspensions handed out on 25 April 1957 were 'illegal, *ultra vires*, invalid and void'. They also contended that the May 17 judgements concerning their benefits were illegal. As we have seen the grounds for these claims was simply that the commission, by suspending the players *sine die* and going beyond its brief to investigate the matter, had broken the rules of the FA and the Football League. Thus the use of the term *ultra vires*.

Mr Justice Vaisey agreed that they had a case, and soon after, Jack Ditchburn, on behalf of his father and Bill Martin made the same claim, also successfully.

So, for the first time in its history, the FA seemed to be in the dock itself . . . and guilty. Indeed by the time the case was finally heard in the High Court in April 1962 – by which time the maximum wage had been abolished – the FA and League had already recognized their mistakes and paid damages out of court to the five players, in return for a pledge that the charges of conspiracy against each individual member of the commission be dropped. This was agreed. The benefit money was also refunded, even though in some cases it was never likely to have been paid anyway.

The late Bill Murray was not forgotten. His £200 fine was returned to his widow, who no doubt asked herself whether her husband would have lived longer had he not been forced to resign from Roker Park.

Speaking for the players in 1962, Mr D. G. A. Lowe told the court, in a hearing that lasted a mere seven minutes, that 'The FA recognize that there were grave errors in the procedure in the appointment of the joint commission and the conduct of the personal defendants who constituted that joint commission.' Since one of these defendants was the barrister Sir Leslie Bowker, this was particularly embarrassing.

Of the other commission members, four still held various offices, except for Arthur Drewery, who had died, and Arthur Oakley, who had retired as President of the League for health reasons within a few weeks of the original Sunderland verdict.

The immediate result of this successful but long drawn out legal battle was that all five players' names were now withdrawn from a suspension list, and their right to benefits was restored. But apart from the fact that their costs were paid, this had almost no effect on the men because four of them were no longer playing in England. Billy Elliott had finished his career in 1958 (he later managed Darlington and for a short spell Sunderland), Ken Chisholm was playing in Los Angeles, Ray Daniel had stopped playing in 1959 at Swansea and Willie Fraser was also out of League football after a brief spell at Forest in 1958. The only one of the five still playing in the League was Johnny Hannigan, who went on to play for Derby and Bradford Park Avenue until 1963.

But that was not the point. The PFA had taken the action to make it quite clear that the authorities could not just act as they pleased in matters affecting peoples' livelihoods. True, the £10 signing-on bonus had been finally abolished in 1958. Players were now entitled to a share of the transfer fee. And in 1961, as a direct result of Hill and Lloyd's skilful negotiations and a threatened players' strike, the maximum wage was also deleted from the rule book, after sixty years. In some ways Len Shackleton was right – a strike threat had been the best ploy.

The whole question of how disciplinary commissions were conducted was also still a vital issue which could arise at any time. It was important therefore that the PFA had shown itself to be vigilant in its members' interests, and psychologically as well as legally it was also important that the players had been able to take their parent body to the courts and win. In this sense the 1957 affair was a crucial prelude to later cases, most notably George Eastham's in 1963.

Bill Ditchburn and Bill Martin followed the players to court in June 1962. Mr Lowe again told the High Court that the FA had already recognized its grave error, 'so serious that the defendants conceded that the decision of the joint commission could not, as a matter of law or equity, be sustained'.

In fact the two former Sunderland directors had already agreed to an out of court settlement with the FA for £650 compensation. But the money meant nothing to either man. Ditchburn in particular had been broken by the original suspension, which was now lifted, and he wanted only one thing – to return to the board at his beloved Roker Park.

'I have fought many battles in my life', he told the *Daily Mail* after the court hearing in 1962, 'but winning this case has given me greater satisfaction than anything else. All I want now is to get back into football.'

The fans apparently wanted him back too, or at least they did two years previously. Sunderland had been relegated to Division Two for the first time in their history just twelve months after the 1957 affair – which no doubt contributed to the club's decline – and in May 1960 the fans were calling for manager Alan Brown's resignation. In addition, some 30,000 supporters were said to have signed a petition pledging no confidence in the board and demanding the reinstatement of their favourite, Bill Ditchburn.

Full of hope that he would return, the first thing Ditchburn is said to have done after he left the court in 1962 was to drive off in his pink and mauve Rolls Royce and head straight for Roker Park, just for a glimpse of the pitch he had not seen since 1957.

The final tragedy of this long and legal tale was the Bill Ditchburn never managed to get back on the board. Since his departure there had been a shift in the balance of power in the Roker boardroom, and there was no longer a place for the seventy-four-year-old former chairman. Having gone through so much pain already, and sensing that final restitution was near, this rejection at the hands of some of his former directors knocked the heart out of Bill Ditchburn. Five months after having watched from the sidelines as his favourite team fought their way out of the Second Division in 1964, Bill Ditchburn, the players' and the fans' favourite, died.

His name lived on however, because seven years later Ditchburn's son Jack succeeded him by becoming a director of the club and later the vice-chairman. One of Jack's fellow directors was E. M. Evans, son of Lawrence Evans, one of the club directors suspended in 1957. Sidney Collings' son Keith also became a director and later chairman.

Like Bill Ditchburn, Bill Martin did not rejoin the board either. Although he was still a regular attender at Roker Park in 1985 he said of the 1957 affair, 'I was so disgusted by the treachery that I never made the slightest effort to get back on the board.'

Bill Martin knows very well who the mysterious 'Mr Smith' was, as do several other men close to Sunderland Football Club. But for us, looking back at those controversial and troubled episodes in the history of League football, the identity of 'Mr Smith' is less important than the subsequent impact of his letters.

Undoubtedly the days of the maximum wage were already numbered when the Football League began its enquiries into Sunderland's affairs, but we can be sure that the investigations speeded up the abolition issue, if only by giving men like Jimmy Hill the confidence and experience to make a final and successful challenge three years later. Indeed it could be argued that the Sunderland affair came at a perfect time for Hill, who had so much to prove when he took over from Jimmy Guthrie.

By 1961, however, Hill had turned to management and football was presented with an even greater problem, which would become, over the course of the next two or three years, the biggest scandal in the entire history of British football.

But before we look at these events, and others North of the border, it is time for a day of rest.

9
Dear Sir, I Must Protest Again . . .

'**F**IVE days shalt thou labour, as the Bible says. The seventh day is the Lord thy God's. The sixth day is for football . . .'

These were the words of Anthony Burgess in his novel *Inside Mr Enderby*, but for many years they could so easily have been those of the Football Association, because it was not until 1960 that the FA officially recognized the existence of Sunday football in England. Playing on Christmas Day or Good Friday was another matter which the FA had been forced to come to terms with much sooner.

That any of these possibilities should be considered at all was always a difficult matter for the authorities however, and more so because it was also a subject for lengthy correspondence in the newspapers.

In the early years of professional football fixtures on Christmas and Good Friday were rare; the former because there were insufficient teams to justify holding games on that day, the latter because the season was more or less over by Easter.

On 21 January 1891 the FA ordered Royal Arsenal to pay compensation of £5 to Rotherham Town for failing to play a match arranged for Christmas Day 1890 (neither club was in the Football League at that time). The fact that it was on Christmas Day was irrelevant to the FA. Arsenal were fined for failing to fulfil a fixture.

But it was not irrelevant to outsiders. Association football, and especially the professional sector, was in its infancy and desperately needed approval from all sections of the community. Furthermore, several clubs rented grounds from the church commissioners, while many more had their roots in church organizations, so it was hardly wise to alienate religious sentiment.

Perhaps it was such a consideration that led the FA to a change of heart when the matter was next raised eight years later at an FA Council meeting, on the morning of the 1899 Cup Final at Crystal Palace.

Secretary Frederick Wall reported that he had received letters from several clubs objecting to playing Cup ties on Good Friday. It was resolved therefore, 'That in the opinion of the Council a Club ought not to be compelled to play any match on Good Friday or Christmas Day.' Royal Arsenal did not, as far as we know, ask for a refund of their £5.

Although not specified, this decision must also have applied to individual players, since the FA took immediate action in 1904 when, contrary to the new ruling, the Stockport FA suspended Swindells of Chapel-en-le-Frith FC for refusing to play on Good Friday. The Stockport association was then forced to rescind the ban when its parent body, the Derbyshire FA, threatened to order all Derbyshire clubs out of the Stockport and District League.

It was a salutary warning for anyone tempted to penalize a footballer for his religious beliefs, and a couple of years later helped paved the way for two more famous players to exercise their rights. E. G. D. Wright of Cambridge University, who won one England cap in 1906, was one of the first, but the most often mentioned was Harold Fleming of Swindon.

Fleming was a popular and witty man who had taken up the game originally on the advice of his doctor, in order to get more fresh air. He signed for Swindon in 1907 and was capped for England while the club was still in the Southern League. Fleming opted out of his first match on Good Friday 1909, when Swindon were due to play Bristol Rovers, only a week after his first, but dramatic last-minute call-up to the England team.

Fleming played until 1924 and, to our knowledge, broke his rule only once, when Swindon toured South America in May 1912 and found one of the games scheduled for a Sunday.

Sundays were in fact far more troublesome for the football authorities than Good Fridays or Christmas. The FA's first ruling on the Sabbath was rather forced on them in 1905, when in February a representative team from the London League was invited to play a game in Paris on a Sunday. The FA refused permission, a decision heartily endorsed by *Athletic news*, which declared that 'we are sufficiently English and antiquated', to believe in keeping Sundays free from football.

A month later the FA Council passed another resolution saying that 'players shall not be required to play on Sundays'. (There was nothing, meanwhile, in the Football League rules either to contradict or concur with this ruling). The problem was, however, that working people would persist in playing the game on Sundays, no matter what the FA determined. Watch your team on Saturday and play on Sunday – what could be the harm in that? Besides, what else was there to do on an English Sunday?

Sunday sport was even something of a tradition in England. In Elizabethan times Sunday was regarded as a day for sport, fairs, athletics contests and many other forms of recreation and entertainment. In 1617 the *Book of Sports* was written specifically to lay down which sports were permissible on the Sabbath . . . after church of course. But the Puritans put a stop to all this and for the next two centuries Sunday football became a rarity, until at least the end of the eighteenth century.

The Industrial Revolution gradually changed the situation, however. Two historians of Victorian England, J. Lowerson and J. Myerscough, have even suggested that it was the very fact that British workers had, in addition to Sundays, Saturday afternoons free plus perhaps another half day during the week, which gave them their unrivalled capacity for developing new sports, at a time when the rest of industrial Europe worked a six-day week.

But you did not have to belong to the FA to play in the streets or parks on a Sunday, so what could the authorities do? Would they turn a blind eye to the steady stream of complaints from church-goers and others, such as J.W. of Preston, who wrote a typical letter to the *Preston Herald* in 1884 (quoted in *Association Football and English Society 1863–1915* by Tony Mason):

'On a Sunday the parks are visited by numerous gangs of young lads, who seem to vie with eath other in the use of obscene language whilst indulging in their wonderful game . . . I should almost imagine there is a match arranged for at this place each Sabbath afternoon, the contestants are so eager and noisy.'

Or would the FA simply admit that as an organization they were incapable of controlling every branch of English football?

This was almost the case in February 1908 when Frederick Wall wrote 'The FA does all it can to discourage Sunday Football' with its proviso that a 'match shall not be played on Sundays within the jurisdiction of this association'. If this was partly an admission that the FA could not control non-members, Wall countered by quoting another part of Rule 25, which stated that no player 'outside the jurisdiction' of the FA should be compelled to play on Sundays either. And to emphasize the seriousness of it all, the Secretary added severely that if any player with a member club played on a Sunday in England he would be 'at once suspended, probably for a long period'.

If this seems a little harsh to our more liberal sensibilities we should note just what the character of Sunday football often was at the turn of the century. While undoubtedly most of the participants were eager amateurs playing for fun, there were a considerable number of games organized by pub landlords, often on private grounds alongside the pubs, where the lure of a game and a wager was sufficient to attract large crowds of drinkers. The teams were subject to no official rules, the referees and linesmen were unqualified, and it was suspected that the players received payments of some sort from the grateful landlords.

Such activity was perfectly legal if on private ground, and as long as no admission money was charged. The law on this, which still applies in certain instances today, dates back to the reign of George III and states that anyone charging admission or being involved with such a Sunday event can be fined from £50 up to £200 (this was later amended in the nineteenth century to allow for pre-booking).

One area particularly affected by this brand of unruly football was Essex, where the local county FA took its own action, passing a by-law which stated that 'No person who takes part in Sunday football in the United Kingdom as player or official shall be recognized by this Association.'

Admirable stuff, said the FA, who approved the Essex decision in January 1909 and promised at the first available opportunity to strengthen, if necessary, the rules dealing with Sunday football.

So the die was cast. Instead of seizing a golden opportunity to embrace the entire footballing nation, the FA decided to cut off those players and clubs who through choice or necessity – usually the former – played on the Sabbath.

We are presented therefore with a fanciful image of disguised FA representatives patrolling parks on Sundays to note down the names of guilty players! They would no doubt be careful to omit the names of those promising youngsters who sharpened up their game on Sundays in the hope of signing for bona fide clubs on Saturdays, for surely it is beyond the bounds of reality that a club should have asked a prospective player, 'Well son, tell the truth. Have you ever played soccer on a Sunday?'

Yet perhaps this did happen in certain circles, for in December 1911 the FA Council was asked to define exactly what it did mean by refusing recognition to any person who had taken part in Sunday football. Mr G. W. Simmons suggested that it would be preferable to rule that former Sunday footballers could not play under FA jurisdiction unless and until given permission. This implied at least the possibility of redemption and forgiveness.

The amendment was defeated, however. Instead the Council voted to add on to rule 25 a clause which said 'that the rule has no application to players who are not under our jurisdiction'.

And there it was – confirmation that the FA Council did not hold sway over the entire footballing population. Either it would not take in the Sunday clubs, by conviction, or it could not, perhaps on principle, perhaps through distaste. Whatever the reason, in future years the 1911 decision gave opponents the perfect retort whenever the FA tried to claim its complete authority over English football.

At least the situation was not as volatile as in Ireland, where Sunday sport occasionally provoked violence. The *Sporting Chronicle*, for example, reported in May 1905 that on their way to a Sunday game a gaelic football team had been forced to seek overnight shelter after being pelted with stones by angry Protestants.

In England the opposition confined itself mainly to letters and deputations focused on Good Friday matches, which had become increasingly popular since the turn of the century. Until then there had been few League matches at Easter simply because the season finished before then, but as the League expanded and the seasons lengthened Good Friday fixtures became commonplace. In the 1903–04 season there were only four League matches on Good Friday (though in the North non-League games were numerous). By 1914 there were only six First Division clubs *not* playing on Good Friday and the practice had spread to the South (there were no games on Good Friday or Christmas in either Scotland or Ireland).

In 1909, in response to this trend, the FA received letters from ninety-four branches of the Church of England Men's Society, demanding that action be taken to stop games being staged on Good Fridays. But the FA could only confirm its 1899 ruling; that while it would never encourage games on Good Friday, at the same time it was up to the clubs and players to make their own choice.

The C.E.M.S. tried again in 1911, sending a deputation to December's Council meeting, the one where Mr Simmons tried to get a clearer ruling on Sunday footballers. Again the FA declined to take further action, on the grounds that public opinion did not call for it.

There the matter remained for a decade, as Britain became preoccupied by more pressing matters than football on the Sabbath. Certainly there were no objections to British soldiers playing football against the Germans in no man's land over Christmas, 1914.

After the Great War, however, opposition was renewed as leagues began to operate again, invariably with full or almost full league programmes on both Christmas Day and Good Friday.

Flint magistrates were the first to ban Sunday football in their borough, after complaints that games were being held at the same time as services in nearby churches, and in January 1922 the FA received a letter from the Imperial Sunday Alliance and Sunday Lay Movement. This asked for the FA's co-operation in their attempt to persuade London County Council to reduce the numbers of Sunday games being played in public parks.

Of course the FA could do no such thing – the players were not affiliated to the FA. The Sectreary replied accordingly, adding that it was not FA practice to interfere with the action of other groups.

The religious lobby did not give up. A year later the United Council for Sunday Protection urged again for concerted action to influence the LCC and this time the FA made a token gesture by writing to the Clerk of the Council. Reminding the LCC of FA regulations on Sundays, Good Fridays and Christmas, Frederick Wall wrote, 'We are of the opinion that there are greater opportunities now than at any previous period for playing organized football during the week.'

In this at least Sir Frederick did have a point. Most workers had an afternoon off during the week, and apparently many of the Sunday footballers were men who already played on Wednesday afternoons.

Not surprisingly, however, his letter had no effect whatsoever. Why should the LCC prevent its population from using public facilities on a Sunday? Demand for pitches rose every year as the number of teams and leagues increased and the old image of the unruly Sunday pub game faded.

Yet when Sir Arthur Glyn tried to put the case for Sunday football in November 1922, in a speech at Epsom, he was lambasted by *Athletic News*, which called his views 'ill-considered and extraordinary'. Sir Arthur had asked, were all players babies, or could they not decide for themselves when they were going to play? The FA, he said, had quite enough to do without dictating Sunday football and he recommended that Sunday clubs form their own association instead of suffering a lot of humbug.

The reaction of *Athletic News* was hardly unexpected, in view of the fact that it so often acted as the mouthpiece of the authorities, but it is worth noting that a couple of years later the newspaper rather contradicted itself by commenting that 'it is distinctly unfortunate that E. H. (Eric) Liddell, the Scottish sprint champion, has scruples which will prevent him racing on the Sabbath'.

Liddell, as portrayed in the film account of the 1924 Olympics, *Chariots of Fire*, refused to enter his specialist event because the first heats were on a Sunday (although the Olympic Committee knew this and entered him for other events weeks in advance, rather than at the last moment, as suggested in the film). If Liddell's decision not to run was 'unfortunate', surely it was equally unfortunate not to recognize those footballers who chose to participate on a Sunday.

Nevertheless, problems among Football League clubs were comparatively few. Christmas and Good Friday fixtures were now well established, although certain clubs were still prohibited by their landlords from playing at home on those days. A rare concession was at Highbury, where Arsenal chairman Sir Henry Norris managed to persuade the Ecclesiastical Commissioners to drop their ban in 1925.

On one occasion, however, such restrictions brought about a dispute between neighbours Stoke City and Port Vale which had to be settled by the Football League's Management Committee in May 1923. Stoke were not permitted to use the Victoria Ground on either Good Friday or Christmas, and by pure coincidence they had been scheduled to play Southampton on both those days during the 1922–23 season. Southampton had the same restrictions at the Dell, which meant that on Christmas Day Stoke borrowed Port Vale's ground.

But Vale resented the fact that while the game on Christmas Day had raised only £500 in match receipts, on Boxing Day Stoke's home game at the Victoria Ground produced £3000. Why should Vale's own Boxing Day programme suffer on Stoke's behalf? The League settled the issue by agreeing to organize the fixtures so that every season each club alternated with home games on Boxing Day and Easter Monday.

Meanwhile the religious lobby had not quite given up hope of stopping all fixtures on Good Friday and Christmas. In March 1925 the chairman of the C.E.M.S. council, the Bishop of Swansea and Brecon, wrote a long and considered letter to *The Times* in which he appealed to the FA and all big clubs to reconsider staging games on Good Friday.

'There is undoubtedly, among all classes, a growing sense of the incongruity of the modern manner of observing the day which we profess to commemorate our Redeemer's death for us', wrote the Bishop. Organized football in country towns had already been widely discontinued, 'but the big clubs of the Football League are among the chief offenders'.

'It is the commercial consideration of the 'gate' which seems to govern their practice in this matter . . . No one would desire to deprive working people of a single hour of the scant opportunity for recreation which comes to them – least of all would the members of the society which I represent, the vast majority of whom are men of the working class.'

But football matches, together with cinemas, golf competitions and other forms of amusement were 'grotesquely inappropriate' for Good Friday, claimed the Bishop, and it was unfair for those deeply religious men who played either amateur or professional football to have to opt out of games organized by their clubs under 'the tyranny of modern practice.'

Since the Nonconformist church had proved so successful during the last twenty years in reviving the observance of Good Friday, the Bishop earnestly pleaded with the FA to lend its support to the 'restoration of Good Friday to its legitimate uses as a day of solemn remembrance of the Crucified'. He realized it was too late to change the fixtures for the current season, but might 1926–27 be different?

From the FA and the Football League the answer was still in the negative, but in other sports the C.E.M.S. appeal found considerable support, at least in the South Western regions around the Bishop's diocese. The Devon Rugby Football Union, plus seventy out of eighty-six Welsh rugby union clubs, all banned games on Good Friday, while there was definite support for a ban on Good Friday entertainments and sport in one Welsh seaside resort and a West Country city. In the North one industrial town had ordered its cinemas to close for the day.

That was not enough for the Bishop, who wrote to The Times again a year later to criticize football for putting money before all else, to the detriment of such a splendid game. 'As long as we still profess to be a Christian country, we cannot defend the custom of treating this special day as nothing more or less than an ordinary Bank Holiday.'

On this occasion The Times joined in the pleading with an editorial comment of its own. Football really was the 'worst culprit' when it came to disrupting this solemn day. 'Games which command large crowds force themselves on the public attention and have an obvious air of unseemliness', said The Times. Large clubs must of course make profits, it allowed, but other profit-making organizations (such as shops) were prevented by law or custom from operating on Good Friday and it was only 'the tyranny of the turnstiles' which dictated the football clubs' actions. 'The meaning of Good Friday', said The Times disdainfully, 'is understood by all but the culpably thoughtless.'

If that were true, there were many thousands of such culpably thoughtless people, all eager to watch holiday football at one of the season's most crucial and exciting stages.

A year later on Good Friday 1928 The Times renewed its attack, the leader comment directing its wrath once again at the promoters rather than the patrons. Fixtures were organized for profit rather than to shock religious sentiment, said The Times, so the best way to reduce the number of games was for the public to boycott them.

In his third letter on the subject, the Bishop of Swansea and Brecon noted that in South Africa a draft ordinance had been introduced 'to secure better observance'. If legislation in Britain was not possible then perhaps there could be an appeal for 'voluntary surrender', he suggested.

Adding his voice to the campaign, and indicating further its concentration in the South West, the Bishop of Worcester wrote, also in a letter to The Times, that Good Friday should be a day of 'quiet hallowing hush'. He called on readers 'to forget for a while our passion for speed'.

Only to a very small extent did these appeals have an effect on League clubs. That season eight First and six Second Division clubs did not play on Good Friday, although this was only a few more than the average season.

By the mid-1930s there were actually more League matches on Good Friday than ever before, and church leaders were becoming more outspoken on the issue.

One instance in 1932 is particularly noteworthy for the local passion it aroused. The Dean of Battle, Reverend W. W. Youard of East Sussex, had asked Battle Wednesday FC to cancel its Good Friday match, but his appeal was rejected in a manner which shocked the Bishop of Chichester and was reported to have caused a split in the small town. Wednesday's secretary Mr A. Hutchinson had claimed that although Good Friday was no doubt a day of religious observance, like Christmas, it really did not differ from any other public holiday.

'We are little surprised', wrote the Bishop in his Diocesan Gazette, 'at the lack of knowledge, as well as lack of feeling . . .' Good Friday was not, he emphasized, a day of festivity, nor was it a day for gate money.

The club's decision to go against the Dean caused a special meeting to be held, in which an aptly-named prominent resident called Mr W. Forargue condemned Battle Wednesday. Even the club's president threatened to resign in protest, while The Dean himself resolved not to become a vice-president, as Wednesday had originally hoped he might.

Here, surely, was a dispute of quintessential English eccentricity, with the centuries-old conflict between religion and secularism being invoked, if not in the name of sport certainly in the name of local pride. On one side stood the Dean, on the other a determined football secretary.

On this occasion the church won and Mr Hutchinson, the secretary, and his son, the club treasurer, were forced to resign. It was not a question of Good Friday, said Hutchinson Junior afterwards, but a case of refusing to accept dictation from people who had no interest in the club.

Few clubs experienced such direct conflict, however. Most continued as it suited them without any pressure to do otherwise, certainly not from the FA or Football League. Yet at the same time the FA remained forever vigilant in the matter of Sunday football. In 1929 for example they fined Sutton FC £50 for fielding in an amateur cup tie two players who were ineligible because both had taken part in Sunday football. Two years later a warning was issued. 'Playing football on Sundays appears to be increasing. The special attention of Associations and clubs is called to this fact and to the necessity of their taking all necessary steps to deal with any breaches of the rule (25).'

This intransigence continued until the outbreak of World War Two, although it is difficult to assess how much of the FA's opposition to Sunday football was merely playing to the gallery. The rules were certainly relaxed during the war, when football provided a much-needed break for hard-pressed industrial workers, and in 1944 as politicians and academics sat down to formulate the shape and form of post-war Britain, among the various sub-committees set up to consider aspects of education, health and other major areas of planning was one appointed by the FA to study the future of Sunday football. Surely the FA would not revive its pre-war stance in the face of government recommendations for change?

As it reported to the War Emergency Committee in February 1944, the FA sub-committee had decided that Sunday football, although varying in popularity around the country, would undoubtedly continue after the war and that players who had participated in Sunday games should not necessarily be excluded from FA recognition, particularly where special circumstances applied.

The sub-committee felt that collecting gate money on Sundays was still 'taboo' (as well as illegal), while it was divided on the question of whether the FA's jurisdiction should be widened to encompass Sunday clubs and leagues.

Compared with the forward-thinking ideas of other committees involved with education, town and country planning, economic theory, social insurance and suchlike, which were inspired by the Beveridge Report of 1942 and culminated in the welfare state provisions of the Attlee government after 1945, the sub-committee's further views on Sunday football seemed rather timid and deferential.

In October 1944 the sub-committee decided to suggest to the FA Council that County Associations should work closely with ministers of religion to encourage the organization of clubs and competitions among church-going youths. Recommendations from the C.E.M.S. were also considered. These were that no professionals should play on a Sunday, only friendly games be played and not those which might attract large crowds, and that additional work by club staffs should be avoided.

With these provisos in mind the sub-committee thus decided to recommend that the FA completely revise its rules on Sunday football. The major change called for was to delete that part of Rule 25 which stated that any person who had taken part in Sunday football could not be recognized by the FA. In addition there should be added another clause, suggested the committee, allowing for matches under FA jurisdiction to be played on Sundays if that was the only time teams could play, as long as no gate money was taken and no nearby church services were affected.

But this was too much for the FA Council, meeting soon after the war. While they were prepared to allow the war-time relaxation of the rules to continue until further discussion, the Council could not accept Sunday games played under their jurisdiction and would not recognize former Sunday players.

Despite the apparently obvious need to harness and help nurture the expanding body of clubs, officials and organizations, especially in the midst of an unprecedented boom in all major sports, still the FA would not relent. Yet other national sporting organizations, notably rugby and cricket, recognized Sunday games without any apparent sufferings.

Meanwhile the situation allowed that while affiliated FA members would commit an offence by playing on Sundays, any disorganized or indisciplined body of men could indulge in a travesty of the game without fear or hindrance. What was to stop these unaffiliated Sunday teams from paying illegal expenses to their players, or even adapting the FA rules to suit themselves? The reticence of the FA seemed entirely inconsistent with its desire to act as guardians of the game. Not surprisingly there was much disagreement within the Council, with a particularly outspoken debate almost splitting the members in 1946.

But it was not until February 1955, almost exactly fifty years after the first rules on Sunday football had been formulated, that cracks finally appeared in the FA's wall of prejudice.

The FA agreed to put forward a proposal to delete the clause relating to former Sunday players. At the time there were possibly as many as 300,000 people involved in Sunday football, 50,000 of whom came under the aegis of the recently formed National Sunday Football Association, whose President was the former Labour Prime Minister Clement Attlee.

The proposal was adopted. It was, wrote James Walvin in *The People's Game* (London: Allen Lane, 1975), 'the first effective breach in the seventeenth century restrictions governing sports on the Sabbath'. At last a Sunday footballer could become a member of the FA, and even if the FA had still not officially recognized Sunday football, it had at least implied that there would be no punishment for anyone taking part.

It took another five years for the last barrier to fall, but even then there was still a sense in which Sunday football was held to be an aberration. 'Sunday football is a social problem of modern times', wrote J. R. Witty in 1959 (in Caxton's four volume work *Association Football*).

Not a healthy pursuit or a boon to the footballing nation . . . but a 'social problem'.

After months of discussion the FA Council made the final decision on 27 May 1960. All previous restrictions were to be dropped and Sunday football was officially recognized.

This meant the possibility of 41,000 registered Sunday players in sixteen leagues, plus all the officials, applying to join the FA, and there were thousands of others outside the National Sunday Football Association who might also wish to take up their new status. Not surprisingly, chaos reigned for the first year or so while County Associations and committees met to iron out the relationship.

Sunday clubs were still prohibited by law from charging any gate money, but a poll in 1961 indicated that a sixty-one per cent majority of clubs accepted this restriction gladly. Opponents said that it was hypocritical of the FA to let teams play but not take money.

The Lords Day Observance Society of course opposed the FA's decision, while many charities were delighted with the results borne by attractive fund-raising Sunday games. Otherwise the rest of the footballing nation carried on regardless. Sunday football held nothing for them . . . or did it?

Britain was one of only a few countries where first class football was not held on Sundays. Yugoslavia divided its programme over the whole weekend, Austria, Hungary and Belgium had most games on a Saturday, while the West German Bundesliga was moving from Sundays to Saturdays. Italian and Spanish football had always been concentrated on Sundays, as is the case in most of Eastern Europe and Latin America.

In Britain however, Sunday sport was catching on. The John Player Sunday League popularized Sunday cricket from 1967 onwards, while Rugby League made its first tentative moves towards Sunday games in the same year, before switching all its games officially in 1977. In France there were race meetings on Sundays, while in the United States Sunday sport was widely accepted.

But in the decade after the FA's decision in 1960 only one professional Sunday match in England was sanctioned, a Southern League game between Wisbech Town and Dunstable Town on 19 March 1967. To circumvent the 1780 Sunday Observance Act entry was by programme only, and overall the experiment was a great success. The attendance of 1372 was three times larger than for the previous Saturday home game.

Ten days later Lord Willis presented a 'Sunday Sport Bill' in the Houses of Parliament, but failed to obtain a second reading, and in May 1971 Nottingham Forest put forward a proposal at the Football League's AGM for Sunday League games. This too was unsuccessful.

The eventual breakthrough came not as a result of events in the football world but as a consequence of the fuel crisis, precipitated at the end of 1973 by war in the Middle East. Just before Christmas 1973 the FA asked the Home Office for dispensation to waive the 1780 Act during the oil shortages, which had led to a three-day working week (therefore many people were now working on Saturdays) and a ban on floodlighting (which prevented any mid-week fixtures).

The Lord's Day Observance Society had already lodged its objections in anticipation of such a request, but in any case the minister responsible for sport, Eldon Griffiths, refused to waive the law on the grounds that it would have required legislation. But there was nothing to stop clubs admitting the public by programme only, or even making people temporary one-day members of the host club.

The Football League was frustrated by this however, especially since the Government had prohibited clubs from using generators for floodlighting. The Bishop of Coventry, Dr Cuthbert Bardsley, was sympathetic. 'When one sees young people mooching around the streets on Sunday afternoons is it not better for them to watch a football match?'

The Bishop was, however, against professional games on a Sunday morning, which was the time chosen for the first ever senior game a week later, on 6 January 1974, a Cup tie between Cambridge United and Oldham Athletic. In the afternoon further ties were played at Bolton, Bradford City and Nottingham Forest, all in front of above-average crowds. A threatened demonstration at Bolton by the Lord's Day Observance Society did not materialize, but the Society did describe the Sunday experiment as the 'thin edge of a pernicious wedge'.

A fortnight later the Football League gave the go-ahead for Sunday League games, and although only a handful of clubs showed any interest, opposition was strong. Bob Lord, the controversial Burnley chairman, was against the idea, as was the well-known Welsh referee, Clive Thomas. He was reported as saying he would seriously consider resigning if Sunday games caught on – for family rather than religious reasons.

Many players were against Sunday football because it would mean sacrificing their traditional Saturday night out. The pools companies were obviously wary too, as were the television companies, worried about their popular Sunday afternoon coverage. Clubs also had to consider relations with their neighbours. 'Playing football and making profits on Sundays is wrong', said the Arsenal secretary Bob Wall. 'We will not disturb the peace and quiet of the neighbourhood of Highbury on that day.'

'If Sunday comes in', said Brian Clough, then manager of Brighton, 'I walk out.' Ironically his future club Nottingham Forest was then at the forefront of the pro-Sunday lobby, along with Coventry City and Bradford City.

The first League games on a Sunday took place on 20 January 1974.

There were twelve, none of them in the First Division, and with one exception all the gates were extremely encouraging. Two clubs doubled their average and three more came close. For Walsall it was their best gate for two seasons. A week later the Scottish FA followed suit with equal success, and the first ever Division One game on Sunday took place at Stoke soon after.

'The public seems to like them', noted a *Times* leader, adding with caution that Sunday games were still a novelty, however. Meanwhile for one player they were a matter of conscience. Swindon Town's nineteen-year-old goalkeeper Jimmy Allan withdrew from a Sunday game in deference to the wishes of his father, a member of the United Free Churches of Scotland.

The Bishop of Norwich was unhappy also. In a letter to *The Times* he suggested that Sunday football adversely affected the players' families, created social disruption because of the need for extra trains, police, staff and catering, and was therefore taking away from hundreds their day of rest, which everyone needed. It also took Christians away from church services.

The *News of the World* meanwhile did a poll of First Division clubs and found that all except Coventry City preferred Saturday games.

Nevertheless, the Sunday experiment had raised some important issues, the crucial one being that the Sunday Observance Act of 1780 was now more honoured in the breach than its observance. If clubs could get round the prohibition of charging admission money then what was the point of preserving the Act? The Labour MP for Dagenham called for repeal in the Commons in February 1974, but was defeated by sixteen votes.

For the next seven years there were no first class Sunday games. But in August 1980, as part of their charter, *Soccer–The Fight for Survival*, the League chairmen asked Hector Monro, the Minister for Sport, for a relaxation of the law in order to allow a maximum of six League games to be held each weekend on Fridays or Sundays.

They were rebuffed, and a couple of weeks later in November the FA firmly refused permission for Port Vale to hold their Cup-tie against Bradford City on a Sunday. For a while it seemed as if the situation before 1973 would prevail, with the curious possibility that an 'unholy alliance' against Sunday games would be formed between the pools promoters and the Lord's Day Observance Society. The FA also seemed as determined as ever on the matter.

Again *The Times*' letters page played host to the debate. The Bishop of Norwich joined in once more, with Lord Robertson, calling for a ban on all Sunday sport, not merely football.

In February 1981 however, the matter was finally resolved. A limited number of six League games per Sunday were to be allowed, and on February 15 the first official game (given that the 1974 games were contingency arrangements) took place at Darlington, although not before the Police Federation had voiced its opposition to the principle.

Observers noted carefully the attendance at the games. Darlington had their average gate trebled. Orient's gate was double the average on one Sunday, and forty per cent up on another, but a few weeks later Oldham Athletic actually had a lower than usual gate for their Sunday match against Cambridge.

There were more questions in the Commons. Could the Minister for Sport, Hector Monro, give his assurance that Sunday games would be the exception, asked the Tory John Carlisle. 'The best thing to do on a Sunday is to go to church. After that people can engage in lawful activity', said another Conservative, John Stokes. Labour's spokesman on sport, the former League referee Denis Howell, pointed out to the House that Sunday cricket, rugby, golf and athletics were all tolerated. So what was all the fuss about?

What indeed, for as the season wore on it soon became apparent that Sunday football was losing steam. There had been only twenty-nine games all season, and only one First Division match (at Forest almost inevitably). The League clubs, it would seem, had been very keen to have the option of Sunday fixtures, yet once they had it very few decided to exercise it. Sunday football was obviously not the panacea some had imagined.

Since then the issue has ceased to be contentious. The first British international to be held on a Sunday took place at Cardiff in June 1983, when Wales played Brazil – who could only manage to play then because of their tour schedule – and there was hardly a murmur. In 1984–85 a total of thirty-three Sunday games were scheduled, including those to be televised live. Crystal Palace led the way with four home games, with both Nottingham clubs having three each on a Sunday.

In common with so many topics of heated public debate the arguments have proved to be more fearsome than the reality. Football supporters have demonstrated that on Sundays (if not on other days) they can behave themselves just as well as Sunday cricket or rugby fans. Nor has it been proved that church attendance had been adversely affected. In short, Sunday football is now accepted and barely noticed, as attention has switched instead to the more controversial Sunday trading laws.

Opposition to Good Friday fixtures has all but died away also. The use of floodlighting enables clubs to arrange more midweek games, while lower attendances and higher unemployment have meant that a concentrated spell of games over the Easter period is now less attractive. Easter Monday is now a more popular day for holiday football, and although Good Friday games still attract healthy attendances, the fixture list is only a fraction of what it was between 1920 and 1960.

Christmas Day games have all but disappeared. From a complete League Programme on Christmas Day 1956 the number of games declined so rapidly that by 1963 there were no games at all (this period coincides exactly with the introduction of floodlighting at most grounds). Brentford tried to reverse the trend by rearranging their home game against Wimbledon to eleven o'clock on Christmas morning 1983. 'We hope to revive the old tradition of the husbands going to football on Christmas Day while the wives cook the turkey', said Eric White, one of the club officials.

Fortunately it was a lone voice. There were no letters to *The Times*.

10
'Please Sir, Can We Have Our Club Back?'

WHAT is the worst fate that could befall your favourite football club? For some supporters the answer might be relegation, or expulsion from the Football League, for others it may be FA Cup defeat at the hands of an amateur village team. But if your club was threatened with extinction, perhaps the very worst scenario one could conjure up is that of outsiders not only taking over the club but actually removing it from your area and transplanting it in a different location, far away.

If that seems a touch extreme then let us go back to 1964 and the Scottish town of Falkirk. Roughly comparable with Accrington or Leamington Spa in terms of size and population, Falkirk is midway between Glasgow and Edinburgh, a few miles South West of the Forth. Five minutes drive to the North is Stenhousemuir, to the East is Bo'Ness.

But although Falkirk has a catchment area of approximately 50,000 – less than any Football League club – by a quirk of history the town has two senior Scottish League teams, Falkirk and East Stirlingshire. Compared with Falkirk's, East Stirlingshire's following is small but certainly committed, as two brothers from Glasgow discovered in a twelve month court battle unique in the history of British football.

In the mid-1950s two brothers Jack and Charles Steedman built up a car dealership called Milngavie Motors, on the North West outreaches of Glasgow, and though successful in business their real passion was football. Both were 'fitba daft', as they say in Scotland.

Jack had played as a professional with several junior clubs before hanging up his boots at the age of twenty-five and together the brothers helped manage a junior team (in Scotland the term 'junior' refers to non-League status rather than the age of the players). But the Steedmans had higher ambitions and in June 1957 they read in the newspapers that East Stirlingshire, who had just finished bottom of the Scottish Second Division, were desperate for the injection of new funds and new ideas. Jack and Charles had both, and they were young and enthusiastic.

Formed in 1881 the 'Shire' had suffered a somewhat bleak history. Apart from winning the Second Division championship in 1932 success in senior competitions had eluded them. Forever in the shadow of neighbours Falkirk, whose much superior Brockville Park stadium is barely half a mile distant from their own Firs Park, Shire's lack of support and resources meant that promotion would always be a dubious honour. The club simply could not afford First Division football. Shire even lost their League membership once in the 1920s, and after a poor 1938–39 season (during which an attendance of only thirty-two was recorded for a League match against Leith), when the League resumed in 1946 Shire found themselves playing in the short-lived 'C' division.

When the Steedman brothers arrived at Firs Park the club was, despite its return to the Second Division in 1955, totally insolvent. An investment of £1040 bought them a fifty-one per cent stake in the club and of course two seats on the board of directors, but as the brothers wrote later, 'We were considered crazy because there were virtually no assets. The ground was rented on a year-to-year lease. The boundary wall was non-existent, there was no equipment and one signed player.'

With three weeks left until the 1957–58 season the Steedmans found the other five directors 'tired and dispirited with the fight for survival'. Gates had been under 200 and it was imperative that new and radical policies be adopted.

Over the course of the next five years the Steedmans took whatever course they deemed necessary, working tirelessly to rejuvenate the club's finances and the team, often with large injections of their own cash. Jack even played in one game himself during the early days when numbers were short. They promised to get East Stirlingshire into the First Division, and in 1963 kept to their word, despite having sold off much of the young talent for a healthy profit. Eddie McCreadie's sale to Chelsea was perhaps the best remembered deal.

But the brothers also believed that if the club stayed in Falkirk it really had no long term prospects of success. The Steedmans therefore considered a number of ideas. One was amalgamation with Falkirk FC, who were very keen, though not surprisingly the other Shire directors and supporters were not. Another idea was to move to the nearby boom town of Grangemouth, where a new stadium was being built. The supporters did not raise any objections this time, but the Grangemouth local authority could not give Shire sufficient guarantees.

Finally there was the new town of Cumbernauld, between Glasgow and Falkirk, but it transpired that the necessary facilities would not be available for some five years.

Nevertheless in the short term the Steedmans were successful at Firs Park. So secure seemed the club that in November 1963's report to the shareholders, shortly after promotion, the brothers wrote, 'It is most encouraging that when most other clubs are bemoaning their possible fate, when bankruptcy seems just round the corner, that we, the Shire, can report an increased profit due largely to more than doubled gate receipts.'

Without doubt the Steedmans treated the Shire as their personal property, and while the going was good no one questioned them, but as the 1963–64 season wore on their previous fears were confirmed; that, for all their efforts, Firs Park was never going to be able to sustain a First Division outfit. Accordingly, they revived their idea of moving the club, only this time their plan seemed so unusual and so controversial that if some contemporary accounts are to be believed, from heroes of Falkirk the Steedmans became almost overnight the most vilified men in town.

This sudden and completely unexpected turnaround began in April 1964, when East Stirlingshire were bottom of the First Division after just one season among the big clubs. Typical of their ambitious attitude, the Steedmans had taken a considerable risk by making the players full-time, and partly as a result of this, by February of that year the club was £2970 in debt and losing about £350 a week. The sale of a player weeks later staved off liquidation just in time.

Worse than this, worse than relegation was the response of the supporters. 'Our gates have been shocking', said Jack Steedman in April 1964, at the end of that disastrous season, although the average gate of 3230 would nowadays be little short of a miracle (Firs Park has a capacity of 12,000).

There had been only 550 for a home game against Motherwell and 3500 for a mid-week evening match against Rangers, the lowest League attendance ever to witness a Rangers fixture. Even the highest gate of 7500 for Celtic's all-ticket visit was composed of only some 1000 people from the Falkirk area.

'Do we try to exist in the Second Division and do our best not to win promotion?' the Steedmans asked the supporters. 'Do we pay the players a bonus for every game they lose?'

So it was that, in anticipation of these problems, even as the 1963–64 season began Jack and Charles began looking for yet another radical solution to the Shire's 'so-called' intractable problem. Unknown to the supporters, they were searching for a junior club to merge with East Stirlingshire, so that one club's potential could be enhanced by the Shire's League status. It was not a new idea, but it had certainly never been put into practice before.

The most promising club the Steedmans could find was Clydebank Juniors, conveniently situated a short distance from their Milngavie business. The Steedmans reckoned that with a concentrated population of 70,000 and a catchment area of 80,000 Clydebank was ripe for a

League club. Indeed it was the largest Scottish urban area without League representation. There had been a Clydebank team in the League, from 1914 to 1931, and although occasionally quite successful on the pitch, being promoted twice, the club had finally resigned and gone out of business.

But the 1960s were booming. Close to Clydebank was the new, sprawling housing estate of Drumchapel, and in the town itself were the enormous John Brown shipyards and the well-established Singer sewing machine and Goodyear tyre factories.

It was a complete contrast with Falkirk, where Firs Park sat in the middle of a declining industrial area. Furthermore, Clydebank Junior's nearest neighbours, Partick Thistle and Dumbarton, were several miles away and each had their own specific catchment areas. For a junior club average gates of around 400 were very promising, and Clydebank had one invaluable asset, the ownership of their ground, Kilbowie Park.

When first approached, however, the Clydebank officials were suspicious and unwilling to fall in with the Steedmans' plans. But there was a desire to bring first-class football back to the town and eventually, after much persuasion, they were convinced that the merger was the best means of achieving that.

But surely East Stirlingshire's supporters would never allow the club to be taken away from them? As football enthusiasts the Steedmans must have known how much anger their plan would arouse.

'As far as the emotional side was concerned we were totally in the wrong', Jack Steedman admitted twenty years afterwards. 'We knew at the time that it was wrong of us to deprive the handful of people immersed in the club of the right to watch the team on Saturday.' But, he insisted, it was only a handful of supporters, not even shareholders, and apart from these few, 'We were firmly of the opinion that no-one cared in Falkirk any more.'

The first stage of the plan went well. At a Firs Park board meeting on 8 April 1964 the Steedmans moved that in view of the club's deteriorating fortunes the merger with Clydebank should take place and the club move to Kilbowie Park, thirty miles away.

Both the other directors present agreed, reluctantly, because they knew how serious was the situation. For the last seven years the Steedmans had been making all the major decisions and without them it would be even harder to carry on. A fifth director, Bobby Corbett, was not at the meeting but as soon as he found out what the brothers were planning he resigned in anger. 'Clydebank could not support a football team in the palmy days of long ago', he said. 'I do not know how they can support one now.'

The following night the Steedmans attended the Clydebank AGM and gained approval for the second stage of their plan, which they announced at the next East Stirlingshire board meeting a week later.

The proposal was that seventy-four members of Clydebank would each receive ten newly-created shares in East Stirlingshire FC Ltd – those 740 extra shares to be issued at an Extraordinary General Meeting scheduled for April 24 – in return for which the company would take over Clydebank's assets. In short, East Stirlingshire would gain a ground valued at around £13,000, while Clydebank members were given the opportunity of being part of a League club. The company would then move to Clydebank and carry on its League career, probably under a new name. It was confirmed that there would be no objection from either the Scottish Football League or the Scottish FA.

Immediately the news broke in Falkirk the small band of supporters was shocked and angry that the Steedmans, the miracle workers, should even think of transporting their club in such a way. Shire's most distinguished follower, Provost John Maxwell said 'I myself would rather see the team go down to the Junior League than see it go to Clydebank. It will not be a Falkirk team anymore.' Others said they would prefer the club to fold completely. Significantly however, most of these outraged souls had not been regulars at Firs Park. In fact the Steedmans had never even seen the Provost.

Negotiations with Clydebank were in an advanced stage, according to the Steedmans, and so if there was going to be any opposition time was of the essence. The treasurer of the Supporters Club, backed unofficially by Shire lottery money, said, 'We must fight the move. The cost is no object.'

The following week saw a frantic succession of meetings. Aid was sought from the Scottish Federation of Supporters Clubs, for whom the Steedmans' action had important ramifications. The lottery had, after all, raised some £30,000 on behalf of the club over the previous six years, with no strings attached. Now their efforts seemed likely to be in vain – a warning to other supporters that they should obtain a guarantee that the same would not happen to their fund-raising.

When a public protest meeting was held in the town on April 21 therefore there was a distinct mood of defiance among the 200 present. In a stinging attack, Provost John Maxwell told the assembled, 'It is terrible that two people, because they hold the majority of the share capital, should be able to make a decision like this.'

Another view was that of William Muirhead, who wrote later in an open letter to Charles Steedman, 'Does he seriously expect fans to see the new team in Clydebank as their team? Either he thinks we are bigger fools or he is not as shrewd as we thought.'

After this stirring meeting the newly-formed Supporters Club committee sat until after midnight trying to find out how many shareholders they could muster in order to prevent the Steedmans carrying through their plan at the EGM with the necessary two-thirds majority.

It was a daunting task. The members' book was long out of date and the shareholders had been so apathetic that for years the hamper man, Willie Munro, had had to be called in to attend Annual General Meetings, just to make up the numbers. Even with a few enthusiastic supporters allowed in to express their views there were still so few attending that the meetings were generally held in one of Firs Park's small dressing rooms.

But gradually the supporters did find the slumbering shareholders, in appreciable numbers. One Shire man even gave up his job for a while in order to travel around the country looking for shareholders.

There is no doubt that the Steedmans were genuinely taken aback by this fervour. Suddenly everyone seemed to be a die-hard Shire supporter. Men and women who had probably not been to Firs Park for years professed their devotion. Shareholders who had long forgotten that piece of paper hidden away in a drawer dusted down their shares and prepared to join battle. If only, the Steedmans must have thought, if only these people had supported the club when they were in the First Division.

As they were soon to discover, however, not all the so-called forgotten shareholders were bona fide. There were allegations of forged signatures, and some of the names put forward turned out to belong to people no longer in this world. For example, most of the shares belonging to the Supporters Club had been passed over to it in trusteeship before the Second World War. Since then the Club had been disbanded, then revived, but with entirely different personnel.

The mounting opposition took its toll on the brothers. With public criticism and personal abuse ringing in their ears, on April 22 the brothers sent a letter to all the shareholders stating that they were open, after all, to any 'genuine and realistic offer'. This, surely, signalled the end of the threat to East Stirlingshire. The brothers were backing down.

According to the *Falkirk Herald*, whose editor was in broad sympathy with the supporters, various groups and individuals planned for a takeover. Corbett headed one faction, the Supporters Club offered to help, while another group of five businessmen led by a former director Bill Moffat also prepared to bid.

But their efforts were badly co-ordinated and despite reports of 'generous' offers being made for their shares, the Steedmans refused to accept any of them, even Moffat's group offer of 8s 6d for every 5s share. This refusal seemed very odd in view of the brothers' earlier insistence that the company was in dire financial straits. If it was so bad then surely such a good offer would have been snapped up. In fact, by April the financial situation was much improved, and would become more or less balanced by the end of May with the sale of a second player.

More importantly the Steedmans felt, rightly or wrongly, that none of the bidders were people of sufficient substance to make a go of the club. The offers had not been put in writing, they made no account of the fact that a couple of promising Shire players were wanted by other clubs for fees totalling £25,000, and the bidders gave no proof that they could guarantee the club's debt.

Finally, much of the money being offered was allegedly derived from the Shire lottery, and therefore it should not have been used for the purpose of buying shares.

What it boiled down to was the fact that the Steedmans were simply unwilling to throw away seven years' hard work by selling up to the wrong people. But these factors were not considered by the supporters, even long after the event. They believed there was a completely different reason why the Steedmans had turned down Moffat's 'generous' offer. They thought, wrongly as it transpired, that the brothers had made a crucial mistake in their calculations.

Briefly, it was said, the Steedmans had assumed that their fifty-one per cent shareholding would give them a majority vote at any shareholders' meeting, which of course it did so long as the meetings were so sparsely attended. In reality, however, the company articles provided for a wholly different voting system, specifically designed to stop large shareholders like themselves from gaining an unfair advantage over the rest.

Article 30 of the company stated that members could vote as follows:
– one vote for each of their first ten shares
– one vote for each of their next five shares up to a total of 100 shares
– one vote for each of their next ten shares thereafter.

It was said repeatedly in subsequent hearings that the Steedman's actions thereafter were taken in order to rectify this situation, which they had apparently only discovered to their great horror *after* suggesting the move.

In fact, the Steedmans now say that they discovered the weighted voting system in January or February 1964, a few months *before* they planned the merger. Until that point for sure they had never seen a copy of the company's articles of association, and none appeared to exist in Falkirk. In the end they had to go to the Registrar in Edinburgh to read, among others, article 30. True, the discovery in early 1964 had been a great shock to them – technically they did not control the club after all – but they still believed, as Jack said, 'There was no shareholder interested or alive to frustrate any move we wanted to make, despite the weighted voting.'

They discussed the matter with their solicitor just in case, but decided to press on.

At the time of the merger plan, in April, the Steedmans owned between them approximately 4180 of the total 8000 shares, giving them an estimated 456 votes. In normal circumstances this would have been easily sufficient to outvote the rest of the shareholders. But because of the feverish activities of the supporters' committee, to the brothers' considerable consternation they were no longer assured of an easy passage. Reports suggested that the supporters had somehow gathered around 714 votes pledged in opposition to the merger plan, although undoubtedly many of the proxy votes they had gathered were bogus.

Certainly the Steedmans could not allow the April 24 EGM to proceed. So, it was suggested afterwards, they put their own shares up for sale simply in order to divert people's attention from the cancellation of the meeting, and also to win time while they replanned their strategy. The Steedmans probably never intended to sell the shares at all, it was said. Opponents also alleged that on the very same day the brothers put up the shares for offer, they also cancelled the EGM.

In fact the Steedmans had decided in the absence of a serious offer from any other group in Falkirk that as directors of the company they should do their utmost to safeguard its future, which they believed meant moving the club to Clydebank. If the supporters were going to wield their highly suspect block of votes to prevent this plan going ahead, then they too would have to increase their own supporting vote.

The Steedmans' new plan was as follows. Instead of calling an EGM in order to authorize the creation of new shares so that Clydebank's assets could be bought, the brothers would simply transfer some of their own existing shares to Clydebank members. Because of the voting system they calculated that by transferring ten shares each to seventy-four Clydebank people, thus creating 740 new votes in their favour, they could defeat any future opposition by the Falkirk-based supporters.

Ironically this change of plan ran contrary to the brothers' previous intentions. At the Clydebank AGM they had offered the members only one vote each per ten shares, since, as Jack Steedman said later in court, 'We decided that they shouldn't be handed the company on a plate and we decided that they should only have seventy-four votes.' Now they were planning to give the Clydebank members 740 votes and thus technically jeopardize their own control. Nevertheless, it was a very neat solution altogether; no EGM would be necessary and voting control, in the short term at least, was assured.

The next stage was actually to transfer the shares. According to the company's Article 13, all shares for sale had to be offered first of all to the directors. By this time, however, the two Falkirk based men had faded into the background and the Steedmans were joined on the board by a friend and neighbour of theirs, John Breckenridge, who was a former East Stirlingshire player, and two Clydebank officials, James Heggie and James Walker. The actual transfer of shares took place on 5 May 1964 and it was the alleged method of this transaction which ultimately was to decide the fate of East Stirlingshire.

What could the Falkirk-based supporters do now?

The new board had still not rearranged the EGM. It had changed the team's name to E.S. Clydebank (although the company's name remained unchanged since this was the name registered at the Scottish Football League) and the offices had been transferred from Firs Park to the Steedman's offices at Milngavie Motors.

Hardest of all for the supporters to stomach must have been the arrival on May 14 of a team of workmen to strip down the standing enclosure at Firs Park, in order to convey it to Clydebank. After the roof they started dismantling the rickety floodlights and the goalposts. East Stirlingshire Football Club was being torn away from under the supporters' very noses, and yet they were apparently helpless to stop it.

They were not the only Scottish supporters to be desperate at that time however, because while the Steedmans were orchestrating the move to Clydebank, Glasgow Rangers had formulated a radical and controversial plan to restructure the Scottish League by creating two divisions of sixteen clubs each. The plan entailed expelling five of the worst supported and least successful League clubs. Rangers picked out Berwick Rangers, Albion Rovers, Brechin City, Stranraer and Stenhousemuir, and at an Ibrox meeting grateful representatives of the remaining clubs voted in favour of the plan.

It was internecine stuff, with the little clubs scrabbling for approval and unity within the League shattered by Rangers' proposal. On May 26 however, the Rangers move was defeated in the courts, largely thanks to the efforts of a Stenhousemuir supporter called Robert Turpie, who was also a solicitor in Glasgow.

But the plan did have some bearing on East Stirlingshire's predicament. As the Supporters Club wrote in a letter to every senior Scottish club, it was grossly unjust that five clubs be axed while E.S. Clydebank gained an easy passage into the League. Sadly, only four clubs bothered to reply to the letter. It really did look as if the Shire were alone.

Meanwhile the East Stirlingshire players were pretty confused themselves, although they backed the move because it promised to bring them a rise in wages. One was sold, three asked for transfers and seven were given free transfers, so having been full-timers the season before they had to sign on the dole.

It was now the end of May, and time was running out for the supporters. Then, finally, the board called the long-awaited EGM for June 9 at Milngavie Motors.

Two bus-loads of Shire fans made the journey to Glasgow, but instead of the hostile exchange everyone anticipated the two-hour meeting was surprisingly orderly, with the Steedmans formally announcing the merger plan and the supporters heckling to little effect.

For all their enthusiasm it was apparent that the Supporters Club committee did not know where to turn. They did not even appear to consider the possibility of retaining a team at Firs Park to compete in the local junior league, as did neighbours Bo'Ness, also a former League club. This was despite the help offered by the Steedmans to start off a new junior club. For the fans it was all or nothing.

One man who had been to the public meetings sensed this, and at the next gathering back in Falkirk he stood up to suggest the formation of a Shareholders Protection Association. Shareholders, he said, would carry much greater weight in law than supporters.

This man was a former chairman of East Stirlingshire and a well-known magistrate, independent councillor and campaigner in Falkirk. In the early stages of the Steedman's action he had been reluctant to get involved, believing in many ways that the brothers did have a valid argument. Maybe there was no room for two senior clubs in Falkirk.

For years his only involvement with the club had been his ownership of a small piece of land next to Firs Park, which the Shire rented, but seeing the desperation of the supporters he at last threw himself into the struggle. His name was James Middlemass, and with him as a figurehead the newly formed S.P.A. prepared to take the dispute into the courts.

Working closely with Middlemass and the S.P.A. was another campaigner, fresh from a battle in the courts to save his own club's skin, Robert Turpie. From then on the whole complexion of the dispute changed. It had started as a quarrel between two directors and a hard-core of twenty enthusiasts. Both sides had worked closely with each other for seven years and were well acquainted, but with the entry of the S.P.A. into the question, and especially the legal acumen of Turpie, suddenly the Steedmans found themselves confronting relative strangers. Their only contact with Middlemass up to that point had been over matters concerning the rented land.

One of the S.P.A's most crucial tasks was to gather up a definite list of shareholders and sort out the real from the bogus proxies. This the Association managed, but there was a long battle ahead, and by the time the next season approached in August it looked thoroughly defeated.

Meanwhile the Steedmans had been busy consolidating their position in Clydebank while bidding sad farewells to Falkirk. They thanked the *Falkirk Herald* for its past coverage of the club's activities and offered to lay on free buses for all the Falkirk-based fans who might wish to see E.S. Clydebank play at Kilbowie Park.

But the brothers' most urgent requirement was to prevent the S.P.A. blocking the move at a late stage. If this had happened, they were informed, it would almost certainly lead to the club being expelled from the Scottish League. E.S. Clydebank had to play its games at Kilbowie Park, as registered with the authorities. To make matters more urgent, it was no secret that with an odd number of clubs in the Second Division at that time the Scottish League might well have used the dispute as an excuse to get rid of one and make the numbers even.

To make their position doubly sure therefore, the Steedmans decided to transfer a further 670 shares in blocks of ten to another sixty-seven individuals. Again however, this transfer was to be the root cause of their downfall. What the Steedmans did this time was to go around their family and all the staff at Milngavie Motors handing out a series of forms.

The forms included a transfer of shares, an undated form of proxy (so that the Steedmans could vote in their place without prior consultation) and documents which ensured that the recipients could retransfer the shares back only to the Steedmans. No money changed hands. No individual refused. So, perhaps without ever having seen the Shire play, perhaps without ever having attended a football match, these people became shareholders of East Stirlingshire Football Club Ltd.

There was no attempt to conceal the fact that this was merely a ploy to frustrate the S.P.A. If Middlemass and his committee were going to go all out to find long-forgotten shareholders then the Steedmans were going to retaliate by creating new shareholders in Clydebank. 'The reason we did it was obvious. We told everyone', said Jack Steedman. 'It was to frustrate the wishes of the alleged majority.'

Meanwhile on July 16 the S.P.A. tried to force a confrontation with the Steedmans by raising an action in Glasgow Sheriff Court, but it was unsuccessful. A second attempt did succeed however, and as a result a second EGM was called for August 6, just two days before the start of the season.

The timing was crucial. If the S.P.A. could not get the Shire back to Firs Park it would do all it could to prevent E.S. Clydebank kicking off on Saturday at Kilbowie. No kick-off meant no more League membership.

In order to defeat the Steedmans, even at this late stage, the S.P.A. had to prevent the 142 new shareholders in Clydebank and Milngavie from voting at the EGM. With that in mind Middlemass and seven other shareholders went to the Edinburgh Court of Session and obtained from Lord Cameron an 'interim interdict' preventing the 142 votes being cast. The basis for Lord Cameron's decision was that because the S.P.A. was in the process of seeking a Court ruling to determine whether the transfer of shares was valid or not, while a judgement was pending those votes should not be used. The Steedmans were given seven days to reply.

That was two days before the EGM and four days before the start of the season. Would the Falkirk men kill off E.S. Clydebank before the team had even kicked a ball in anger?

Thursday August 6 came, the day of the EGM. Retribution was in sight. But no! If the 142 shareholders could not vote, replied the Steedman's counsel, then nor could the Falkirk-based shareholders. If the club was returned to Falkirk it would have disastrous consequences for the company, argued the Steedmans, and the company was, after all, their responsibility. In addition, the Scottish League would expel the club if Saturday's game scheduled for Kilbowie Park was played elsewhere, and the club would still have to pay the usual £300 guarantee to the visitors.

Now Lord Hunter was in the chair, and he too granted an interim interdict, but this time in favour of the Steedmans, to stop the S.P.A. from voting at the EGM. It would be wiser, said Lord Hunter, if the meeting did not proceed while certain matters were still sub judice.

Deadlock!

The EGM lasted ten minutes, long enough for the bus-loads of shareholders to hear the Messenger-at-Arms read out the interim interdicts. Middlemass then took the S.P.A. over to a nearby hall to explain to the bemused what had happened.

Later that night he and his adversaries expressed their regret, genuinely, that from then on the matter would have to be decided in the courts, because despite it all Jimmy Middlemass had a lot of admiration for the Steedman brothers. They too respected him. But it was the people of Clydebank who were the happiest thirty-six hours later as E.S. Clydebank kicked off their first-ever fixture at Kilbowie Park, a League Cup match against the Shire's old neighbours, Stenhousemuir.

Imagine the gloom that hung over a deserted Firs Park on that first day of the season – the terraces empty, the offices cleared away, the enclosure a mere skeleton of steelwork, the pitch uncared for, while almost exactly the same team which had played there only a few months before (all of the players did eventually sign for the new club) were now playing in new colours, on a neat pitch surrounded by lively, expectant faces.

The arrival of League football at Clydebank was a great success, with an estimated 6000 crowd turning up to see the first game, an exciting 2-2 draw. Considering that on the same day both Rangers and Celtic were playing at home and there was a bus strike, such an attendance was indeed remarkable.

It was also a relief for the Steedmans, for whom the previous five months had paid a heavy toll in strain and worry. This had affected both their business and their families. At least now they could begin to enjoy their football again . . . if only for a while.

As Firs Park gathered dust and weeds, Kilbowie Park bloomed. Gates, not surprisingly, fell to an average of around 1500, but this was still healthy for the lower division. The club pools were bringing in a regular income and the team did very well to sustain second place in the Second Division until the New Year. The Steedmans, whatever could be said about their methods, had certainly been vindicated in their choice of location.

But not one Falkirk-based East Stirlingshire supporter took up the brothers' offer of a free bus ride over to Kilbowie Park. This was perhaps significant, since it was quite common for Rangers, Celtic and Hearts supporters also living in Falkirk to organize and pay for regular buses for much longer journeys.

Perhaps very few people did care, while the twenty or so supporters who had campaigned for the Shire refused to watch the team on principle. They knew that the prefix E.S. before the name Clydebank was only a formality – in fact it was often omitted completely in the newspapers.

While Kilbowie Park pulsated with a 14,900 crowd for a Scottish Cup replay against Hibernian, and large gates were recorded for friendly floodlit games against Sunderland and Ipswich, vandals broke windows in the forgotten stand at Firs Park and no-one in Falkirk dared mention anything about the lease with the owners, British Rail, in case they got ideas and decided to sell the ground. Yet the Steedmans were still prepared to hand over the lease to the supporters so they could start up a junior team. While there was hope of legal victory however, this offer was never accepted. It was still all or nothing.

As the year wore on the S.P.A. remained active, and when the company's AGM was called for 17 December 1964 in Clydebank, once again the Shire activists determined that the 142 new Clydebank shareholders should not be given the opportunity to cast a vote which might permanently isolate the football club from Falkirk.

Middlemass asked Lord Hunter for another interim interdict

therefore, and after a long discussion with the Steedmans it was finally agreed to postpone the AGM until February 1. This was to give the courts time to decide on the action Middlemass had raised, to seek a court declaration that the Steedmans and others had formed 'a fraudulent scheme to secure that East Stirlingshire take over the business of Clydebank Juniors and carry on business at Clydebank, contrary to the will of the majority of registered members of the club'.

The February date passed however, and as E.S. Clydebank lost their early season form and dropped out of the promotion race (they finished the season in fifth place), the courts finally came around to the action of 'James Middlemass and others against Charles Steedman and others' in March 1965. It was to be the moment of truth for East Stirlingshire Football Club. Literally, the question for the supporters was 'To be or not to be?' and Lord Hunter, sitting in judgement at the Court of Session in Edinburgh, was the only one who could decide.

But there was another fundamental question raised by the case, a question which aroused the interest of some of the top legal brains in Scotland. This was the issue of a company director's fiduciary duty.

Did a director have to put the commercial interests of his company second to the wishes and desires of the shareholders, in football or any other business? It was an important principle and one which had yet to be decided in the Scottish courts. Thus the fate of East Stirlingshire looked as if it may well become a test case. Certainly the Steedmans and their counsel were keen to fight the case on this issue.

On the footballing side the issues were well known. The S.P.A. had behind it a sense of tradition, an appeal to local sentiment which held that, however correct the economic arguments to the contrary, no man had the right to sacrifice the Shire for the benefit of some junior club thirty miles away. It was a heart-warming plea.

For their part the Steedmans had only to point out the enormous success of the transfer. The E.S. Clydebank record spoke for itself. Besides, it was all very well saying the supporters had rights, but it was the Steedmans who had poured money into the club and the people of Falkirk who had not responded. Beyond Falkirk footballing opinion probably favoured the Steedmans' argument, but it has to be said that amid the legal jargon which swamped every newspaper report it was, in truth, hard for outsiders to distinguish the real issues.

The crucial legal point was that Jack and Charles Steedman had to convince the court that the transfer of so many shares to 142 individuals was not, as alleged, achieved contrary to the company rules, and that the move to Clydebank itself was in the best interests of the company.

It promised to be one of the most compelling cases ever to involve professional football in the courts, and for eight days of complex legal debate, so it proved.

The court was packed with East Stirlingshire supporters, who behaved impeccably throughout as they listened to Robert Turpie and I. M. Robertson (later Lord Robertson), both of whom had successfully challenged the Rangers reorganization plan ten months before, now conduct the S.P.A's action against the Steedmans.

The defendants had an impressive legal counsel themselves, among them Donald Dewar, who twenty years later became Shadow Secretary of State for Scotland.

For eight days the Shire fans had their heads filled with references to interim interdicts, Articles 13 and 30, share transfers, directors' fiduciary responsibilities and a host of other technical company matters that seemed so distant from the essential problem – Shire fans wanted their beloved club back.

They listened as James Middlemass, the one-eyed doughty campaigner, gave evidence for four-and-a-half hours. He told the Court how under the Steedmans the club had enjoyed four good seasons, making a profit of £12,500, but one bad patch and the brothers simply lost heart. They were only interested in First Division football. Furthermore, he said, they wanted to bring the club closer to their own business, where they could keep a closer eye on it. (This was a bitter pill for the brothers to swallow, coming as it did from a man who had not attended a single AGM since the Steedmans had joined East Stirlingshire).

Clydebank officials such as James Heggie and James Walker were also questioned. Had they really known what they were doing? A couple of Milngavie Motors staff were called up, and the Court heard how a secretary had walked in one day and asked them to sign some papers without telling them why.

It was not revealed until later that one of those witnesses had been dismissed from the business for dishonesty. Yet on this evidence stood the allegation that so many responsible people in a thriving business had simply signed forms without questioning the content. 'What kind of quality of employee do you think we have?' asked Jack Steedman afterwards.

Then the Steedmans told their story. It took a day and a half.

For sure they had rescued the club and poured their own resources into it, and they were appalled that the supporters seemed more worried about their own convenience than the survival of the club as an entity.

But why had they kept the shareholders in the dark for so long? Jack Steedman said that they could not delay on the deal by waiting for shareholders. They would have lost the opportunity and would thus have failed as directors to get the best for the company. Falkirk, he said, was just not the right setting. 'You need black tenements for football supporters, not delightful houses like Grangemouth (where he had thought of moving the club before) . . . the more bad housing in a district, the better it is.' It was a dubious analysis, and potentially insulting to inhabitants of Clydebank as well as unfeeling towards tenement dwellers in Falkirk. (Ironically the black tenements around Kilbowie Park were soon after swept away and built over with modern council homes.)

Charles Steedman told the Court that if the transfer of shares had saved the company then surely it must have been proper. But had the company needed saving? Two transfer fees had made the financial position quite acceptable by May 1964.

So the questioning, the recapping, the recording and the evaluation went on. Would fiduciary duty win over sentiment? Would the lawyers win their place in the law books? Would the judge believe that the Steedmans really went through the correct motions to transfer the shares to 142 people? The brothers and the Shire faithful had to wait another six weeks until May 7 for Lord Hunter to weigh up the evidence and finally announce his verdict.

It was a tense moment for the bus-loads of supporters who had made the journey to Edinburgh, but it was worth it. To the complete and utter amazement of Jack and Charles Steedman, and a few lawyers too, Lord Hunter found in favour of Middlemass and the S.P.A.

In Hunter's judgement the transfer of shares had indeed been contrary to the company's articles and was therefore invalid, although Lord Hunter was not prepared to say, as the S.P.A. had claimed, that there had been a fraudulent scheme to take over Clydebank Juniors. But his verdict was enough to save the club.

'Never in our wildest dreams did we think the move would be frustrated on a technicality', said Jack Steedman, recalling the decision 'The judge just did not believe that we went though the motions of transferring the shares properly.'

One man who may have helped the brothers with his evidence, since he had gone through each legal step with them, was their solicitor. But he opted not to stand in the witness box. The Steedmans might also have helped their case by bringing out into the open the whole business of forged and false proxies, as collected by the supporters. But against the advice of their counsel the brothers insisted on not raising the issue. It would have meant putting individual supporters into trouble, and they were unwilling to penalize the men who had done so much for the Shire in the past.

So the result was clear and the Steedmans were ordered to pay costs, which at around £7000 were quite considerable for 1965. They were disappointed, but by no means bitter. They had, in their own words, played to win and they had to accept defeat. But they would never forget how certain members of the S.P.A. had professed their loyalty so much, yet done so little in the years before.

Immediately after Lord Hunter's judgement a jubilant James Middlemass announced that the long postponed AGM would be held at the Burgh Hall, Clydebank, on the following Thursday, May 13. He claimed expansively that his group could command a total of 900 votes, including proxies, in opposition to the Steedman's total of about half that amount. The Shire would be going home.

There was celebration all over Falkirk as Lord Hunters' judgement became known. Requests from around the country poured in for transcripts of it – the S.P.A. later printed it as a booklet – and the club prepared for a royal return. But before this could happen the long awaited AGM had a few matters still to resolve. James Middlemass took Charles Steedman's place as Chairman. John Reid sat in Jack Steedman's seat.

The Steedmans did attend. They were, after all, still directors, and when a vote was proposed as to whether the club should revert to its old name, its old team colours and its old ground, the brothers even tried at that late stage to halt a decision on the grounds that this was a matter to be decided by the board of directors only. Not surprisingly they were overruled.

Still Jack Steedman warned the assembled that their decision would finish the Shire. Charles spoke out, 'Sentiment itself does not pay wages.'

But these were their parting shots. E.S. Clydebank were finished. Four days later at the first meeting of the newly-elected board back at Firs Park, the Steedman brothers resigned and, for a short period, they were without a club. They were not even members of the original Clydebank Juniors.

After the meeting Jack and Charles went back with James Middlemass to his home, a few yards from Firs Park, where the three men drank tea and ate cake. There was no animosity left. Both sides knew that their own personal struggles were only just beginning. Middlemass might have helped steer the club back to Falkirk, but, as he soon discovered, the new board could not persuade the players to follow. John Arrol, the goalkeeper, said 'None of us are very keen to go back to Falkirk.'

Those men and boys the Shire were able to sign up after a series of trials had to train in borrowed kit, until the rest of the team's equipment was sent back from Kilbowie Park. New floodlights were hastily rigged up, broken glass was cleared from the pitch and a local boys club helped restore Firs Park by weeding the terraces. Clydebank helped matters by paying £6000 to the Shire for their old enclosure.

On June 18 there was another shock for the Steedmans – the Scottish Football League failed by just a few votes to admit a newly-constituted Clydebank FC to membership. Scottish football opinion was incredulous. Even though it is very rare for new clubs to be elected in Scotland, the Second Division had nineteen clubs, which meant each club had two free Saturdays every season, and yet here was the Scottish League turning down a proven outfit which in many ways had shown itself to be far more progressive and viable than most of the rest.

Thus Clydebank faced the following season in the Combined Reserve League and half the team, still registered with East Stirlingshire, decided that a place at the Shire was not such a bad prospect after all.

All that remained therefore was the long-awaited return to Firs Park, a League Cup-tie against nearby Alloa Athletic on 18 August 1965. Hundreds of joyous, flag-waving supporters and well-wishers lined the Falkirk streets as a procession left the new Shire social club, led by a local pipe band. At a pre-match luncheon, attended by representatives from Falkirk FC, Alloa, Stenhousemuir and Dumbarton, William Muirhead of the S.P.A. called the celebrations the 'supreme climax'.

An emotional James Middlemass said, 'It's a miracle, a miracle.' Later he described it as a fairy story come true. Outside there was even a local woman selling copies of the poem she had written entitled 'Victory for the Shire'. And victory there was, at least on that afternoon, as a crowd of 3000 saw East Stirlingshire beat Alloa with a single goal five minutes from the end. A victory dinner dance rounded off the celebrations a few hours later.

And they all lived happily ever after. Or did they?

When the euphoria eventually died down, had the months of struggle really been justified? For sure the club survived. Sometimes only just. But there have been some high spots, as for example in 1969 when Firs Park had its record gate of 11,500 for the visit of Hibernian in the Scottish Cup. In 1980 Shire even won promotion again to the new style Division One – Falkirk just beat them to the Championship by one point – and a year later the club celebrated its centenary. In addition, Firs Park was purchased from British Rail, a major step. And so what if Shire were relegated after only two seasons in the First Division; had they not proved that they could rise again?

But there have also been some very difficult times during which the club has struggled, often on gates of around 200. Middlemass, who soon gave way to younger men and now attends matches as an honorary president, is painfully torn between a barely-acknowledged acceptance that the Steedmans were probably right and his own deep-seated sense of justice.

His involvement with the S.P.A. campaign was certainly not the whimsical affair of an eccentric old Scottish politician, however. It was a serious, hard-fought matter. But no sooner had the club been saved than the shares went back into their dusty drawers and the so-called life-long supporters suddenly found themselves busy again on match days.

Shire supporters would argue that that is not the point. The Steedmans had wanted to prove that they could achieve success but they cynically used another town's club to prove it. Thus, one question was often asked. If the Steedmans thought Clydebank were such certainties for success, why then did they not leave East Stirlingshire completely and make a clean start at Kilbowie? Why get the Shire mixed up in it all?

'East Stirlingshire was simply a vehicle for them', says Middlemass in retrospect.

Jack Steedman says differently. 'If we had known beforehand that so many people cared, instead of moving the club we'd have asked the Shire fans for a donation to keep the club going. But we couldn't find enough people to talk to.'

So, presuming there would be no concerted opposition they saw Shire's status as the perfect way to bring first class football to Clydebank. 'We could never have established a senior team in Clydebank without East Stirlingshire. The members there wouldn't have been interested in us otherwise.'

For the Steedmans the story does have a happy ending. After a season in minor football, in 1966 Clydebank FC became fully-fledged members of the Scottish League in their own right. Their club lottery, organized by the first Commercial Manager ever appointed by a Scottish Football club, was by then producing twenty times the amount that had been raised at Firs Park. In their first season the Bankies finished just one place above the Shire, who were second bottom, but by 1976 they were promoted, and for one season in 1977–78 they even competed in the Premier Division. Since then, although fairly established in the First Division, Clydebank have suffered very badly from the depression around them; John Brown's is a quarter of its former size, both Singers and Goodyear closed down their factories and inevitably gates have fallen dramatically, often to less than 500.

It is not quite the great dream the Steedmans had planned for, and yet, in other ways the brothers have achieved the status they wanted.

Jack acts as managing director of Clydebank and is the active and respected treasurer on the Scottish League's management committee, while Kilbowie Park has a thriving social club and is now an all-seated ground. Jack's son Ian is the club secretary and of course Milngavie Motors prospers also.

There is no hostility between Clydebank and the Shire nowadays. Robert Turpie and the brothers are close friends and the court case if anything binds the parties together rather than divides them. It is still talked about.

'I always knew the Steedmans were good football men', says James Middlemass, which in Scotland is as high a compliment as the brothers are ever likely to wish for, and the closest to reconciliation at least from among the former members of the S.P.A.

Could the situation at East Stirlingshire in 1964 ever be repeated? Most certainly. It only requires the major shareholders to agree and the majority of supporters to stay at home on Saturday afternoons.

As Charles Steedman once said, 'Sentiment itself does not pay wages.'

11
Power to the People

$\boxed{\text{T}}$HE 1960–61 season was only a few weeks old when Jimmy O'Neill, Stoke City's Eire international goalkeeper, received a mysterious telegram asking him to ring a telephone number in a West Country town. O'Neill rang the number and a man asked if he would like to earn some money by making sure Stoke lost their home game against Norwich City on August 27.

The Stoke 'keeper asked for time to think it over and then reported the approach to his manager, Tony Waddington. On August 27 Stoke drew 1-1 with Norwich but O'Neill had a poor game and was very worried about the matter. The CID was informed and within hours the newspapers had reported the bribery attempt.

Few realized then that this was the beginning of a five-year trail which was to result in the exposure of the biggest ever conspiracy to affect British football; a plot so wide that although only twelve players were actually convicted and banned for life by the FA, there were possibly as many as a hundred footballers involved.

The problem, as always, was one of evidence. So many people knew that football matches were being fixed, but so few were prepared to name names or put their allegations in writing.

In Chapter Five we looked at some of the earlier attempts to arrange results, but whereas in the inter-war period there had been several convictions and disciplinary proceedings, between 1945 and 1960 there were only rumours. Occasionally, a controversial figure like Trevor Ford would spell out the reality.

'How often have you seen a club requiring a couple of points from the last match of the season winning by umpteen goals to one?' wrote Ford in his autobiography, first published in 1956. 'It happens time and time again, and you won't be far wrong if you reason that the viper of bribery had reared its ugly head again.'

With O'Neill's story in 1960 the public was given its first real glimpse of how deeply this 'viper' had bitten British football. Almost as soon as the bribery attempt was exposed a whole string of allegations followed, some in public, some in private letters to the Football League. Almost overnight, match fixing became a major problem.

The allegations fell into two, distinct categories. Firstly, there were alleged attempts to fix matches affecting promotion and relegation issues, such as we saw in Chapter Five. On 14 October 1960, for example, Glen Wilson, the manager of Exeter City, revealed in the *Daily Mail* how in April 1958 he had played for Brighton in two crucial Third Division South promotion matches against Watford, who were already destined to drop into the newly-created Fourth Division. Brighton won both games, played within four days of each other, after an alleged arrangement between the players; neither set of club officials were involved. 'This sort of thing happens all the time', Wilson told the *Mail*. Watford's captain in 1958, Johnny Meadows, also spoke to the *Mail*. 'We wouldn't have beaten them anyway', he said. In fact the League already had their suspicions about one of these games, having received a letter from the referee.

For one dramatic week in October 1960 the *Daily Mail* poured out a series of similar revelations about match fixing in contemporary football, the result of extensive investigations by four reporters; Michael Borissow, Bernard Jordan, Harold Pendlebury and Robert Greaves. But the *Mail*'s survey confirmed that there was a second, far more widespread cause of match fixing, and that was betting, almost certainly the motive behind the alleged approach to O'Neill.

It is on this sad and sordid topic that we conclude our history of 20th Century soccer scandal.

According to the *Mail* 'the majority of players' staked their winning bonuses on the result of games. Despite this being against FA rules the players would put money on their opponents to win, thereby either gaining a bonus for winning or a similar return from a bookmaker for losing. It was a well-established form of insurance, but it was only possible because at that time one could bet on the result of a single match.

The most popular form of betting on football was called Fixed Odds betting. It had begun in the 1920s but only really took off during the soccer boom of the late 1940s. Conducted mainly by the large bookmakers, it had an annual turnover at its peak in the early 1960s of nearly half-a-million pounds – a fraction of the income from pools but a viable business nevertheless. As for the pools, coupons were issued for Fixed Odds, or bookmakers might alternatively have their own separate lists with the odds 'borrowed' or based on the printed coupons. William Hill's led the field in Fixed Odds betting, and of the pools companies only Littlewoods became seriously involved.

It is important to note that until May 1961, when on-street betting shops were made legal (Henry VIII had outlawed them because they took men away from archery practice), all betting was conducted either illegally on the streets or via the telephone or post with bookmakers' offices. In addition, because of the Ready Money Betting

Act of 1920, no one was allowed to bet with cash. Thus pools money had to be sent in the week after the coupon had applied, and Fixed Odds bets had to be 'on account'. At the end of the week the bookmaker would settle this account accordingly.

Fixed Odds betting did have other restrictions. In order to bet on just one match the punter had to know his bookmaker very well, and stakes were generally kept to a maximum of around £5-10, although the average was below ten shillings. The odds were fixed according to current form and League placings, and were usually around 5-2 for a typical match. If one could be sure of the result – and who better to influence it than a goalkeeper, such as O'Neill – by placing several bets on one game the potential winnings were high indeed. With a national network of middlemen placing the same bets the profits could be enormous, and very difficult to trace.

For even higher returns, the odds for three away wins commanded odds of around 14-1, rising to as high as perhaps 50-1 for three draws. Fixing a match to end in a draw was much harder, however, because it required the co-operation of players from both teams. As a result, bookmakers and the authorities deemed these three match Fixed Odds bets to be fairly safe from corruption. Surely there was no-one who could 'fix' the results of three separate matches. Or was there?

Alerted by O'Neill's story, from September 1960 onwards the Football League and the newspapers sought out the 'fixers', and in the process discovered a betting ring larger and more influential than they had ever imagined possible. Yet for at least three years no disciplinary or police action was taken and the newspaper articles served only as pieces in a large and mainly incomplete jigsaw.

In the wake of the O'Neill incident came the stories of three players who were each at the end of their careers and maybe felt they had little to lose and perhaps, from cheque-book journalism, much to gain.

On October 9 the former Welsh international, Swansea and Manchester City wing half Roy Paul revealed sensationally in the People, 'I was paid to lose matches . . . I've been a soccer wide-boy. I've cashed in where angels feared to tread.' Paul's former Manchester City colleagues were outraged by his further claim that several of them had shared his illicit pay-out.

One totally unexpected confession came from the former Celtic and Scotland centre-half, Bobby Evans, who was then finishing his career at Chelsea. Evans admitted that he had once, in a foolish moment, tried unsuccessfully to bribe an Everton player. He had never made any bets himself and had never been involved with any match fixing before. Luckily, for this one uncharacteristic lapse the Scottish player was not punished.

John Higgins, whose career at Bolton had just finished prematurely at the age of twenty-seven, claimed that he had been approached to fix a game, against Manchester City. A man offered Higgins £200 to lose, before the game, then at half-time when the score was 1-1 he doubled the offer. Higgins refused the bribe and Bolton won 3-1.

It soon transpired that the approaches to Higgins and O'Neill had allegedly been made separately by two players who were not only then at the same club but who also lived in the same house and had both played with the Liverpool clubs during the late 1950s. The newspapers revealed their names, the Football League knew their names, but neither was punished through lack of evidence.

The man who spoke to O'Neill on the telephone said in the *Daily Mail* that the Stoke goalkeeper had completely misunderstood the nature of their conversation. He had made no improper suggestions at all, and he added, 'I have never had a bet on a football match in my life. I don't even understand Fixed Odds betting.'

Higgins claimed that he was approached after a casual conversation in Manchester's Continental Club, a favourite haunt for players. He had treated the offer as a joke until the player actually approached him at the ground.

Several of the other players allegedly involved also had Manchester or Liverpool connections, a link which became more significant as the conspiracy was unravelled.

Jimmy O'Neill told the League all he knew, giving the names of two more former and current players whom he thought were involved. But for some reason, perhaps because the newspaper publicity made it impractical, the League rejected a suggestion by the Leicester chairman Len Shipman that O'Neill be used as a decoy to catch one of the 'fixers'. Such a ploy had worked many years before in similar cases (see Chapter One). Instead, as Alan Hardaker wrote in his autobiography, some of the guilty men escaped 'because the Law and the League could not get the evidence to nail them. Their names are on file at Lytham, but I hope those files never see the light of day again.' Having seen those files I can confirm that among those suspected were figures of considerable note within the football world. Had they been investigated in 1960, how different the next five years might have been.

Instead, over the course of the 1960–61 season the League accumulated an assortment of allegations and suspicions against some twenty clubs and individual players, many of whom were said to be in debt to bookmakers. But how serious was this secret information held by the League? Did it really amount to the kind of widespread corruption suggested by the *Daily Mail*?

One letter in League hands alleged that a West Ham player had received £1000 to lose matches on three separate occasions. One of West Ham's matches, which resulted in a surprise 5-3 win for Newcastle at Upton Park on 20 February 1960, had actually triggered off sufficient suspicion for the League to start monitoring various match scores. Apparently the game, together with Grimsby's surprise win at Brentford on the same day, had attracted heavy Fixed Odds betting (as monitored by the bookmakers collating their coupons).

The West Ham match was perhaps the one referred to in Alan Hardaker's autobiography, where the League secretary recalled how one First Division director was so embarrassed by his team's lack of effort as they conceded five goals at home that he had been forced to leave the ground at half-time.

Also in February 1960, but only revealed in October (when 'frank confessions' seemed to be all in vogue) Bury's South African-born winger, Johnny Hubbard, claimed to have been offered the astonishing sum of £3000 in order to fix a game against Barnsley. This was more than a year's wages for a top player, and even if not exaggerated (or indeed wholly concocted) to suit the requirements of popular journalism, the sum might well have been a false carrot dangled to lure Hubbard. If the player had fixed a game with such a sum in mind he would have almost certainly been paid less, in the full knowledge that he could hardly complain openly. The offer, said Hubbard, came from a Scottish First Division player whom he would not name.

Another tip-off for the League came from a club director after Arsenal's surprise 5-2 win against Manchester United on 23 April 1960. Arsenal were then suffering a run of poor form, while United had been unbeaten in their previous five games. Three other matches that day were suspected; Swansea v Derby (score 1-2), Bolton v Chelsea (2-0) and Nottingham Forest v Newcastle (3-0). Crewe's performances had also been suspect and the following week the League sent three officials to watch closely their match against Northampton. This followed allegations made by five Oldham players following their game against Crewe.

Publicly, after consultation with the FA, the League dismissed the letters they had received as untrue. But the MP for Stoke South, Mr Ellis Smith, announced that if the League did not make their own full enquiry he would raise the matter in the House of Commons.

The *Manchester Evening News* reported on October 12 that Alan Hardaker appeared 'more shy and evasive than ever'. In his autobiography Hardaker admitted that '. . . even if only half of the information fed to me was true, it still meant football was sick'.

After inviting certain players to answer the allegations, and having sent their findings to the Director of Public Prosecutions on 17 October

1960, the League and FA were advised by lawyers not to start any proceedings since there was insufficient evidence. For this we cannot blame the football authorities.

Yet it is true that Alan Hardaker did try to persuade his Management Committee to set up its own full investigation, only for some of the members to reply that they simply could not and would not believe there was any substance in the newspaper reports. As a result, despite demands for an enquiry from men like Matt Busby, manager of Manchester United, the League did not take the matter further. In retrospect this seems inexcusable. Would the likes of Charles Sutcliffe have been so apparently complacent?

For sure the Football League and the *Daily Mail* knew far more than they were legally able to reveal in October 1960, but that accepted, what the *Mail* did print was enough to put all British football under a cloud of suspicion, and in the public eye it was still enough to make the League's apparent inaction a mystery.

In brief, these are some of the allegations reported by the four *Mail* investigators.

They found that the famous referee, Arthur Ellis, had once been offered £35 to fix a game. They found that three players were so deeply in debt to bookmakers that they were forced to repay them by taking orders to fix certain matches. One of them was allegedly told, 'Your side have got to lose on Saturday. It's up to you to fix the game.' But although the player then gave away a penalty his side still won, and so the bookmakers pressed him harder. As the *Mail* reported on October 11, 'When a footballer runs on the field with the aim of fixing a game, his own bet is probably no more than £20 to win £30. But by throwing the game he may win £3000 for his Fixed Odds gambler contacts who have staked £2000.'

The unwritten rule of the 'bent' footballer was to make his efforts seem genuine. 'So the give-away penalty, the suicide pass, the crafty own goal, the fake injury and the hospital pass become the tactics of the bought footballer.'

According to the *Mail* the centre of all this corruption was Manchester, 'home of soccer Fixed Odds gambling', where players gathered in cafes and night-clubs to arrange matches, sometimes with betting agents.

But was all this unexpected controversy a direct symptom of the other ills in British football, or was it merely down to the machinations of a few dishonest players and bookmakers?

The year 1960 was crucial in the players' campaign to achieve their long-standing aim of abolishing the maximum wage. In Chapter Eight we saw the first shots fired, in the Sunderland case, and they ended in legal embarrassment for the FA. Could this experience have inhibited its efforts to pursue the match fixers?

Then in Autumn 1960, under Jimmy Hill's leadership, the Professional Footballers' Association threatened to strike in January 1961 unless certain demands were met, including abolition of the maximum wage. By December 1960 it was clear that the League would finally bow to this demand, thus ending the stormy sixty-year history of this controversial ruling.

So greater rewards were on the players' horizons – although higher wages would not come quickly and for some not at all – and it could be argued that the match fixers were exposed at the worst possible time for the players' cause.

Jimmy Hill was also worried about the growing number of players 'selling' their confessions, starting with Roy Paul in the *People* less than a fortnight after the O'Neill story broke. He advised players not to make such confessions, and warned them about newspaper methods and the increasing use of private investigators. PFA secretary Cliff Lloyd suggested an amnesty for all players who had taken part in fixing attempts, a call echoed by the *Daily Mail*'s J. L. Manning. 'It was important,' wrote Manning, 'that players be given the chance to discuss bribery attempts without fear of retribution.'

But there was no amnesty, and by the end of the 1960–61 season the spate of allegations and confessions seemed to have died away so completely that the public could have been forgiven for believing that the newspaper stories were either false or that the publicity had scared the fixers sufficiently to put an end to their corrupt practices.

In fact the real problem was only just beginning.

In October 1961 the League reopened its dossier of secret information, this time after being alerted by bookmakers who were suspicious of heavy betting on two particular League matches.

Commanding Fixed Odds of 10-1 as a double bet, these matches had taken place on 21 October 1961, and both resulted in surprising away wins; Tranmere Rovers at York and Bradford City at Mansfield. Previously, both Tranmere and Bradford had only won one away game each, while both York and Mansfield had good home records. To add to their suspicion, the bookmakers noted that many of the bets, especially in Yorkshire, had been placed in the same surname or from several new clients.

A Mansfield man had also written to the League to voice his own suspicions. He claimed that the game he saw was full of strange decisions, including the inexplicable disallowance of a Mansfield equalizer.

So the bookmakers collected their information and discovered that twelve individuals in particular had placed Fixed Odds bets on these games with some twenty different gambling concerns. The first step, announced the following Tuesday, was to withhold the winnings. The second was for Littlewoods, unknown to the public, to lend Alan Hardaker the services of two security investigators, both former policemen. These men then travelled the country to interview the twelve punters.

Their confidential report, dated November 14, revealed the following. Firstly, all twelve had seen the newspaper reports and were aware that a fix was suspected, but none of them seemed at all perturbed by the enquiry. One man in London said that he had merely acted on the advice of an uncle in the North. Another was an army sergeant who had unwittingly allowed his name to be used by other punters, so that they could send more than one coupon each. One of the men investigated was said to have been a compulsive gambler who simply used a whole ring of friends' and relatives' names to put on coupons.

These people, concluded the investigators, were mostly innocent. Their cheques had been stopped and once the story of a suspected fix was revealed none of them claimed any winnings. Only one of the twelve wanted to pursue his claim with the bookmaking firm of Ladbrokes. His name was Jimmy Gauld and he was a thirty-two-year-old Scottish footballer with Mansfield Town, whose career was in jeopardy after breaking a leg.

Having questioned Gauld, the two investigators reported to the League, 'Although Gauld is an astute individual, there was no evidence at all to connect him with the alleged fixing of the matches.'

How wrong they were. Had they dug a little deeper they might have discovered that Jimmy Gauld used to play for Everton. His team-mates at one stage were Jimmy O'Neill, now with Stoke, and also the man who allegedly offered O'Neill a bribe in August 1960. But no connection was made and the investigation proved nothing except that the large bookmakers were aware of the problem and were determined to guarantee the integrity of their Fixed Odds operation. However suspicious those two match results had been, in the absence of any further evidence or proof no one could do more.

Or could they? As Alan Hardaker admitted four years later, he actually interviewed Gauld at the League's headquarters on 29 November 1961, a few weeks after the Littlewoods investigation. 'Although Gauld denied any knowledge of anything wrong, apart from the fact that he had to admit that he was taking part in Fixed Odds betting, the final impression was that he was not telling the truth.'

Hardaker was quite right, but even though he handed his findings over to Lancashire County Police still no concrete evidence was found, and we now know that games continued to be fixed after November 1961, and that perhaps the most important consequence of the League's fruitless investigation was that the fixers became richer and bolder, if not any cleverer.

And so to 1963 – a year marked by the rise of the Beatles and Martin Luther King, the exposure of the Profumo scandal, the Great Train Robbery and the assassination of President Kennedy. For professional footballers it was also a crucial year, in which George Eastham took his club, Newcastle United, the FA and the Football League to court in a mainly successful bid to end the long-imposed 'retain and transfer' system.

Having abolished the maximum wage in 1961, with Eastham's partial victory players could at least look forward to greater, though hardly total, freedom from what was commonly termed as 'slavery' to their clubs. But Eastham's case was not the only one to bring soccer into the dock in 1963.

Unknown to them, the beginning of the end for the fixers appeared to come on 7 April 1963, in the form of a short, barely noticeable article tucked into the bottom of page eleven of the *People* newspaper. Apparently bookmakers were bemoaning the fact that on the day before they had been obliged to pay out a total of £100,000 to punters who had placed bets on a Fixed Odds double. The two matches concerned were Derby Country's home match against Scunthorpe, which Derby won 6-2, and Stockport's 4-1 victory at home to Hartlepools. Neither result was a surprise; Scunthorpe were only just above Derby in the Second Division, while Hartlepools were firmly rooted at the bottom of the Fourth.

Yet with odds of 6-4 on two home wins the betting had been heavy enough during the week to suggest that a syndicate was in operation, and by Friday morning bookmakers were desperately trying to lay the bets off – that is, spread their liabilities to other bookmakers. By late Friday it became impossible to place any bet on this particular double.

One of the bookmakers was particularly angry, but not because he had lost a lot of money. Jack Pointer of Norwich had refused to take big bets for some time because he had fallen prey to 'betting coups' in the past. 'There is likely to be such a stink this time that the Football League will have to investigate', said Pointer.

Alan Hardaker's reaction was typically dour. 'The truth of the matter is that the bookies are nowhere near as smart as they like to think. If they choose to include matches in which even a four-year-old can pick the winner on their Fixed Odds coupons, that is their look-out.'

In fact some of the bookmakers were not so dumb. They well knew that matches had been fixed and made bets themselves. But even if, in private, Hardaker knew Pointer was right, he and millions of others had only three weeks to wait for the *People* to reveal the first of a truly shattering series of articles which would expose, at last, the real conspiracy.

'SOCCER BRIBE SENSATION' read the headline, and so it was. Esmond Million, the twenty-five-year-old Bristol Rovers goalkeeper, confessed to the *People* that on the previous Saturday he had deliberately allowed his opponents to score two goals in Rovers' away match at Bradford Park Avenue.

According to Million he was telephoned before the game by a go-between, who said that a friend wanted Bradford to win the game. Million was in debt at the time, having been transferred from Middlesbrough the previous summer without being able to sell his bungalow on Teeside. So when the caller offered him £300 to throw the match, Million accepted. On the day before the game he was handed £50 by the go-between in Doncaster and was told to return the money if Bradford lost.

On Saturday the game went badly for Bradford, and the fixers, as Rovers comfortably built up a two goal lead. Million was forced therefore into making two obvious errors. First he let a back pass slip through his fingers, then he missed a cross, both mistakes resulting in goals for Bradford's young striker Kevin Hector. But after the equaliser Million had no further chances to let in another goal and so the game ended in a 2-2 draw. The fix had failed.

Anger with Million in the Rovers' dressing room afterwards fermented into rumour and suspicion during the following week. By Friday the facts were known and the Rovers manager Bert Tann called the players together in the board room at Eastville, where he bluntly accused Million of taking a bribe.

'I have never felt so small in my life', Million told the *People*. He confessed his guilt, was immediately suspended by the club, and now no one was talking to him.

'It looked so easy', he was reported as saying, 'I thought I'd be £300 better off without having to do anything for it. But it didn't work out that way. Now I face the sack and I haven't even got the money.'

Ironically, three days after the game Million's bungalow in Middlesbrough was sold and his money worries were solved, but his was not the only sad tale. Also suspended by Rovers was their inside forward, twenty-six-year-old Keith Williams, who, it was revealed a week later, was approached by Million to help him fix the game. Together they shared the £50 advance.

But Million made the mistake of trying to involve another Rovers player, full back Gwyn Jones, who refused the bribe and confronted

Million twice during the Bradford game. 'I hope you are not trying to throw it Es', Jones warned him.

Williams also turned out to be a reluctant fixer. When first approached by Million he refused the offer, but on returning home he found his wife had tried to commit suicide by taking an overdose of aspirin. She was depressed about their financial difficulties. So Williams accepted Million's offer, but when it came to the actual game he had yet another change of heart on the pitch and decided to put all his efforts into winning. In fact it was his pass that led to Rovers' first goal, and the press generally praised his overall performance.

The immediate reaction of bookmakers and the Football League to the People story was cautious. They had read enough lurid confessions in Sunday papers to sense that even this one might have been dressed up to suit the 'Frank, Fearless and Free' style of the People.

As to the actual bribe, the first reaction was that perhaps a rich and fanatical Bradford supporter had offered the money in a desperate attempt to keep his club from relegation to the Fourth Division. This was quite feasible. It was near the end of the season and Bradford and Bristol Rovers were both fighting to avoid twenty-first place (Bradford did eventually go down).

To add credence to this theory, the bookmakers pointed out that there had been no heavy betting on the game nor any noticeable pairing of it with another result. Partly as a consequence of the October 1961 scare, at the request of the League the bookmakers had virtually eliminated all betting on single games and were now only accepting Fixed Odds bets on doubles. It was a relatively simple task therefore to determine that few doubles bets had included the Rovers v Bradford fixture. (It was later discovered that the match had in fact been part of a four match plan by the syndicate.)

One thing was certain. Neither Rovers nor Bradford had anything to do with the fix. The Yorkshire club was naturally stunned to discover how it had managed to draw, while public-spirited Rovers, in exposing the two mens' behaviour, had at a stroke deprived themselves of key players at a crucial period of the season.

Although they survived in the Third Division Rovers were also quick to point out that Million and Williams had cost a total of £10,000. The League offered them no compensation, nor would it help Rovers by allowing them to sign new players after the deadline. Might it have been, therefore, that other clubs knew of guilty players within their midsts but said nothing publicly for fear of weakening their teams?

A week after the People's first revelation, on May 5 the newspaper shocked the footballing world a second time by revealing who Million's contact in Doncaster had been. He was Brian Phillips, the thirty-two-year-old Mansfield Town centre half, who made his confession only hours before playing an excellent part in Mansfield's home match against Gillingham. Phillips and Million had been team-mates at Middlesbrough between 1956 and 1960.

The *People*'s article came as great personal shock to Phillips, who later told the police, 'I was so depressed at the time I nearly committed suicide. . . I have not slept for three weeks.' But Phillips really was only a go-between, acting, he said, for a syndicate of professional gamblers.

For the time being the most important consequence of these admissions was that in July 1963 Million, Williams and Phillips found themselves in Doncaster magistrates court, where all three were found guilty under the Prevention of Corruption Act of being party to an attempt to fix the Rovers v Bradford game.

All three, it was said in court, were of previous good conduct but were in financial trouble. They were fined the maximum of £50 each, with costs, and three weeks later, as expected, received the ultimate penalty from the FA, permanent bans from football and football management.

'These are isolated cases', announced the FA after its decision. 'The amount of bribery in existence is negligible compared with the great mass of football being played, which is free from any taint of corruption.' This was quite true, but there still remained a strong suspicion that neither the FA nor the Football League was doing enough to stamp out corruption. In the House of Commons, for example, the Labour MP for Barnsley, Roy Mason, badgered the Government to take action on bribery in football. 'The Attorney General ought to be taking an interest. This is a national matter'. said Mason. He also said that the problem was too important to be dealt with solely by private commissions at the FA and Football League.

Alan Hardaker's response was defensive. 'Nothing new has been said that we have not either suspected or investigated, and the Management Committee are entitled to resent anyone suggesting that this sort of thing is rife unless they come forward with concrete evidence in support of their allegations.'

Whether it was rife or not was hardly the issue. Criticism of the League was founded upon the fact that while it had investigated without success, a Sunday newspaper had apparently tracked down some of the guilty men and obtained 'concrete evidence'. That confessions might possibly had been 'bought' was unfortunate, but at least it brought results. Of course the stories also added considerably to the *People*'s circulation.

The League did however, take one important step in May 1963, and that was to ban any further Fixed Odds bets on doubles. From then on the minimum number of matches linked to a single bet was to be three. The League had the power to do this because it held the copyright for fixtures included on Fixed Odds coupons (see Chapter Seven).

For the three banned footballers there was a sudden, and painful change in their lives. From being the centre of so much attention as professional sportsmen they now found themselves as outcasts.

'They might as well cut off my feet', said Williams to the *Daily Mail*. 'I expect I will finish up as a labourer.' This was the job Phillips had taken on since his suspension. Million had returned to Middlesbrough and became a bus driver.

These broken men had but one small consolation, and that was the generally recognized fact that they were not the real culprits. But Detective Chief-Superintendent Joe Smalley of the Nottinghamshire CID said that the police had still been unable to trace the mastermind, the mysterious 'Mr X' who was undoubtedly behind this betting ring. Little did Smalley realize then that once again it would be the *People* who would lead the police to their man, albeit in a most unorthodox way.

During the early 1960s the *People* enjoyed one of its most active and effective periods as a campaigning newspaper. Under the editorship of Sam Campbell it frequently exposed public scandals both at home and abroad, and was well equipped to give its reporters the secret identities and cash resources often needed to investigate difficult matters.

The *People* decided that the prerequisite for its investigation into soccer bribery was evidence so solid that they could print the names and addresses of the players involved, plus the details of the matches which had definitely been fixed. Thus one of the *People*'s most determined young reporters, Michael Gabbert, then aged twenty-seven, found himself embarking on a twelve-month investigation around the country with a ready-made kit for obtaining affadavits and a comprehensive list of solicitors. Backed up by a small team of freelance journalists, Gabbert also had with him one of the newspaper's football experts, Peter Campling. (Gabbert himself knew little about the contemporary football scene, although he had been offered a trial by Portsmouth when he was fifteen.)

Before the *People* could reveal who 'Mr X' was, another player had yet to be exposed.

After Million, Williams and Phillips came the turn of Ken Thomson of Hartlepools United. His confession was published in the *People* on 4 August 1963 and it showed that the Aberdeen-born centre-half had agreed to bet with the mysterious syndicate on his own team losing a game at Exeter in March of that year. His winnings amounted to £200. But, said Thomson, 'I took bribes, but I fooled the syndicate. I never had to "throw" a match because we were well beaten anyway.' (Hartlepools finished bottom of the League that year.)

In fact Thomson was eventually acquitted of having 'conspired to fix' the Exeter game, but although he claimed never to have played badly on purpose he was found guilty of the charge relating to two other Hartlepools games played in April 1963, against Stockport and Crewe. On the first game, which was linked with another game as a double, Thomson won £327. On the second, which was part of a four team accumulator bet, Thomson lost his £50 stake because two of the games ended in a draw. One of those was the match which Million tried to throw for Bristol Rovers. A week after the People had exposed that fixing attempt the police began to question Thomson.

Although it was barely recognized at the time a pattern of contacts between footballers was slowly emerging. Thomson's previous club had been Middlesbrough, where he was a team-mate of Esmond Million and Brian Phillips. A week later, on August 11, Thomson confessed in the People that it was Phillips who had first approached him.

Later articles revealed that Thomson had wanted to win the money to help finance his entry to Durham University's Bede College, where he was about to start a teacher's training course. But he never was allowed to coach schoolboy footballers, because on 2 September 1963, as a result of the People's articles, Thomson was banned for life by the FA.

After being told his fate by a commission in Sheffield Thomson said, 'I knew I was breaking the rule.' But he earnestly hoped that the FA might reconsider his ban in future years, and that he might win the pools to enable him to repay Hartlepools the £4000 fee they had paid Middlesbrough for his transfer. With that he went off to study, and he hoped, to forget the whole affair.

Returning to the People of August 11, apart from Thomson's admission the most important disclosure yet made was the announcement that the newspaper knew the identity of the 'shadowy' boss figure, the 'mastermind' behind the bribes ring.

He was named, at last, as Jimmy Gauld, the 'astute individual' who the League's investigators had apparently dismissed as innocent two years before and the man who Hardaker thought was lying but could not prove it.

Born in Aberdeen, after joining his local club Jimmy Gauld was first noticed while playing for Waterford, in Eire. Charlton brought him into League football at the age of twenty-four and in forty-seven games for the London club as an inside-forward Gauld scored the useful total of twenty-one goals. Everton showed an interest, and in October 1956 he went to Goodison Park for a fee of £10,500. This was a period when

Jimmy O'Neill was at Everton, together with the player alleged to have offered O'Neill a bribe in 1960. Also at Everton then, but only as a junior, was Keith Williams.

After a year at Goodison Park, during which he scored seven goals in twenty-three League appearances, Gauld went South to Plymouth. He continued to attract attention with twenty-five goals in sixty-four games, until in August 1959 he was transferred once more to Swindon Town, where he stayed just over a year, making forty-one appearances and scoring another fourteen goals.

It was at Swindon, as he claimed later, that Gauld first came into contact with match fixers. The connection began at the end of the 1959–60 season, when Tranmere Rovers needed at least one point to be safe from relegation to the Fourth Division. According to Gauld several Rovers players made an arrangement with three Mansfield Town men to win their game at Field Mill on April 30. Mansfield themselves were already certain to be relegated.

Gauld was told of the arrangement by a friend at Mansfield, who suggested that if Gauld could also get Swindon to lose their match against Port Vale on the same day – both sides were in mid-table – then a good double bet would be on.

The fix worked, Mansfield losing 2-0 (Tranmere stayed up) and Swindon losing 6-1. But Gauld and two other Swindon players won only £40 on the coup and the Mansfield men complained later that Tranmere's players had not paid them in the end. There was another problem when one Mansfield player, the West Indian winger Lindy Delaphena, suspected his team-mates of fixing the game and allegedly had to be paid off by the three guilty players.

All this was not admitted by Gauld until 1964, but the timing of the fix put it exactly at the period when the football authorities and pools companies were beginning to have their suspicions, especially about the four matches (see before) which took place a week earlier on 23 April 1960.

As Gauld told the *People* in 1964, 'Swindon were comfortably in the middle of the League with nothing to gain or lose, so it didn't seem such a terrible thing to do.' His winnings had been peanuts, he said, 'But it set me thinking . . .'

At that stage Gauld was only a beginner in a circle of 'fixers', at least one of whom was almost certainly a Scottish First Division player. But over the course of the 1960–61 season Gauld's career took some unexpected turns. After a season with Swindon he returned to Scotland with St Johnstone, where he might well have lost his growing influence had he not returned to England a few months later in November 1960. But after only three games with his new club Mansfield, in which he scored twice, Gauld suffered his worst-ever injury by breaking a leg in a game against Hartlepools on 28 December 1960, a game in which he also scored. For months his career hung in the balance. He was twenty-nine, a proven goalscorer in the lower divisions and Mansfield were near the foot of the Fourth Division.

So while Gauld waited for his leg to heal he developed his betting syndicate. This was so successful, as he told the *People* in 1964, that despite the interest shown in his affairs by Littlewoods and the League in November 1961, at its peak the syndicate was earning around £1000 a week, although with the number of players involved those winnings did not stretch far. The professional gamblers, middlemen (who often placed the bets) and a few dishonest bookmakers made a great deal more in comparison.

Apart from his own extensive network of former team-mates, Gauld claimed that he was always being contacted by other players wanting to join him. 'In fact I was amazed by the number of players who were eager, not just willing, to get into the act.' Often there would be as many as three or four 'bent' players in one team, and at least a dozen, perhaps twenty teams were affected.

One of the conditions of involvement was that a player had to place a bet on the match he was helping to rig. That way he had a vested interest in making sure the result went as arranged. Winnings were shared out according to the size of each personal stake, but if one fix did not work, all the money was lost, and if any advance had been paid this had to be paid back. No one was simply paid a flat fee to throw a match and no one was ever told which other matches his stake money was on, so that he would know as little as possible. In fact several of the players had never even met Gauld or knew his role. They had always dealt with go-betweens.

Overall it was a good plan. By grouping together three, four or five games, the syndicate received better odds, and by using middlemen the system was reasonably well hidden. Only when enough unsuspecting bookmakers were badly stung was there any fuss, and on a couple of occasions when bookmakers did refuse to pay out winnings the players had little scope for complaint, although some apparently suspected that Gauld was cheating them.

There were other occasions when the syndicate was working so well that Gauld actually suggested the setting up of a kitty, out of which losing bets would be funded. This would throw bookmakers off their scent and give the illusion that they were just ordinary punters. The players rejected this idea, although at times the bets were losers anyway.

All this took place between early 1961 and April 1963; from the time

Gauld realized his footballing career was over to the date of the first revelations in the *People*. There appeared to be no doubt whatsoever that Gauld was the ring-leader. Brian Phillips told the *People*, 'Everything I did, I did on Gauld's instructions . . . Gauld was the mastermind behind the betting coups.'

Yet even though this was revealed in August 1963, Gauld's unmaking did not lead to an immediate round-up of guilty footballers. In fact, the *People*'s investigation had only just begun.

On August 18 a genuinely shocked public was faced with yet more details of the syndicate's affairs. It was revealed that the FA now had the names of nine players know to have thrown matches and that at last it publicly admitted the gravity of the situation.

'If the bribery is as widespread as is now alleged, then it is even more serious than we realized. There is no doubt there will be a further enquiry', said Denis Follows, Secretary of the FA.

The League announced that it was setting up an 'intelligence network' of players, trainers, officials and managers, while the bookmakers decided to team up and create an early warning system which would warn of heavy betting on certain games. Apparently the vast majority of Fixed Odds bets were still less than 10 shillings, so with extra vigilance and co-ordination a syndicate might easily be spotted at work.

A week later, on 25 August 1963 the *People* wound up Round One of its campaign against soccer bribery for that year, but not before Gabbert and Campling had made their own personal recommendations.

They accused the FA and Football League's measures of not being sweeping enough, especially the decision that for the coming 1963–64 season the minimum recommended Fixed Odds bet would be on three matches. (The League only had copyright powers to influence those bookmakers who issued coupons. The many smaller bookmakers who might just chalk their football selections onto a board were beyond its scope.)

The *People*'s investigation had shown that Gauld's syndicate often betted on as many as five games. Three of these would be fixed, the other two would be 'bankers', that is, the results fairly predictable. But the three fixed games would rarely go against known form – the fixing would merely make sure of the result – and so they too aroused minimum suspicion.

Alan Hardaker's response to the *People* had so far been incomprehensible. He told the newspaper, 'There is no bribery in football. It is unthinkable.' On a later date he said, 'If you can produce a man who can successfully fix three matches, then I'll hail him as a bit of a wonder.'

As Gabbert wrote, Mr Hardaker had only to meet Jimmy Gauld of Mansfield to find such a miracle worker. What Gabbert did not know was that Hardaker had indeed met Gauld before, in 1961, but that neither he nor the police had been able to prove anything against him.

After April 1963, however, Gauld was again under police suspicion, not only because of the *People* but also because his name had been mentioned in the hearings of Million, Williams and Phillips at Doncaster Magistrates court.

The result of this suspicion was that in the autumn of 1963, while those three players and Ken Thomson adjusted to life without football, Jimmy Gauld was fined a token £60 at Rochdale magistrates for offering bribes to footballers. A ban by the FA, even if it had been considered then, could not hurt Gauld because his career was finished anyway, and instead of being punished further, Jimmy Gauld actually received his last ever payment from football in November 1963. He was paid £500 from the PFA's insurance fund for injured players.

To add to this irony, when Gauld was again approached by the League to give further evidence the former player still refused. This time however the reason was not Gauld's fear of being caught – the *People* had already exposed him. Instead, Jimmy Gauld had found a new way of making money, and an already complex affair was about to take its most twisted, and many said most unsavoury turn.

To put it bluntly, Gauld began to work for the *People*.

As Michael Gabbert recalled it, the *People* had first come across Gauld after being tipped off by a Mansfield player. Gauld admitted his involvement straight away and showed the reporters a drawer full of betting slips, letters and coupons. From then on he was given a straight choice.

He would almost certainly not escape conviction whatever happened, but if he was to co-operate with the newspaper and help to obtain evidence against other players involved, at least he would guarantee himself some extra money.

According to Gabbert, Gauld did not hestitate to accept this stooge's role, despite warnings of the possible consequences. Gabbert said that Gauld seemed positively to enjoy his role over the next few months, during which he deliberately sought out his former accomplices.

But if Gauld's role was always open to question, perhaps the most controversial part of the *People*'s continuing investigation was the actual method by which Gauld obtained evidence. In the majority of cases, accompanied by Gabbert and Campling, Gauld would contrive to have chance meetings with the players involved. Often this meant hours of waiting around, with many near misses drawing out the process over the space of months.

One example of how these three operated came in Leeds. Gauld was sent out from the Queen's Hotel to make a search of all the pubs and bars in the city centre, until he found his old Swindon team-mate Jack Fountain, who was then back in his native Leeds but playing for York City. Gauld took Fountain to his car where a tape recorder had been hidden, and engaged him in conversation. Gabbert was watching them all the time. Then Fountain and Gauld parted and Gauld brought the tape over to Gabbert. It was later used in evidence at Mansfield Magistrates Court.

'We used Gauld to trap the others in the most cynical way', Gabbert recalled. 'He knew he was selling his friends down the river.'

On other occasions Gabbert himself had to use Gauld's own evidence as a means of persuading the guilty players to confess. With one player they had insufficient evidence so Gabbert used bluff. He went to the player's front door, and without introducing himself Gabbert asked him that while he knew the player had only made a few hundred pounds on throwing a particular game, did the player realize that some of the bookies had made over £10,000 on the bet? Not knowing that the man at his door was a reporter the player immediately became angry at this discovery and thereby gave himself away.

By the spring of 1964, largely thanks to Gauld, the *People* had definite evidence and confessions from another seven players and the names of at least a dozen others known to be involved. But Gabbert felt he could not always trust Gauld. He knew the former player was in a difficult and perhaps dangerous position, and the reporter was always nervous in case a rival newspaper caught the scent of the story and went to press first. As soon as was legally possible therefore, on 12 April 1964, the *People* launched Round Two of its report on bribery. This time the articles were to be so truly momentous that on the Sunday of issue, copies of the paper were reputedly changing hands in Glasgow for £5 each.

The simple reason was this. Previously, none of the players named and suspended had national reputations and all were from the lower divisions. The *People* of April 12 added a sudden, and totally unexpected dimension to the story.

Billed as 'a shattering exposure' the *People* called it 'THE BIGGEST SPORTS SCANDAL OF THE CENTURY'.

In fact the story was very similar to that of Million, Williams and Phillips, but with one major difference. This time the *People* named three First Division players, each at the height of their careers. To add to the furore, two of them were England internationals. From that day on the public referred to the entire bribery affair of the 1960s as 'the Swan, Kay and Layne scandal' simply because these three were the most famous players involved. Yet in many ways their connection had been only marginal.

Of the three First Division players named by the *People*, the closest to Gauld was David 'Bronco' Layne, one of the most prolific scorers in post-war football. He began his career with Rotherham in 1957 but made his name at Swindon Town, where he became an acquaintance of Gauld. At Bradford City from 1960–62 Layne broke the club's scoring record with forty-four goals in just sixty-three games, and he was soon scoring at a similar rate in the First Division, after Sheffield Wednesday bought him for £16,000 in June 1962. In seventy-four games for Wednesday he scored a further fifty-two times, making his overall career record only slightly less consistent than that of his contemporary Jimmy Greaves (though better than Liverpool's Roger Hunt and even marginally better than Ian Rush's League record, at least as it stood until the end of the 1983–84 season).

Named with Layne in the *People* was his Sheffield Wednesday team-mate, the England defender Peter Swan; a tall, lithe centre half, once a coal miner who had been a regular at Hillsborough since 1958. Capped first in 1960, after nineteen consecutive appearances (many alongside Bobby Robson, later manager of England) Swan seemed destined to play in the 1962 World Cup. Sadly illness spoiled his chances in Chile and with the arrival of Alf Ramsey as manager the popular Swan dropped out of the international reckoning.

Tony Kay, the third of the exposed trio, was a former team-mate of Layne and Swan's. In December 1962 the red haired wing half had become the most expensive player in Britain when Everton bought him from Wednesday for £60,000, and eleven months before the *People's* article Kay had won his first full England cap against Switzerland. At Wednesday, wrote the club's historian Keith Farnsworth, 'Kay contributed the energy, flamboyance and fire; he had the arrogance, the hardness of tackle, and the drive which lifted his colleagues . . .'

Swan, Kay and Layne's involvement in the bribery ring was confined to just one match, the only First Division match known definitely to have been rigged by Gauld's syndicate. (Although Layne had played in the suspected Mansfield v Bradford City game in October 1961 but was not implicated.)

As the *People* declared:

'December 1st 1962 – soccer fans, and all who cherish the good name of British sport, should all write that date in bold, black letters. It was the Day of Infamy for British football . . . (on which the) ugly cancer of corruption spread its evil growth right up to the highest strata of soccer.'

The game that Swan, Kay and Layne were alleged to have thrown was Sheffield Wednesday's away match at Ipswich. Ipswich won 2-0, and the biggest irony of all was that the *People*, in its report of the game, made Tony Kay the best Wednesday player with eight marks out of ten. Swan and Layne's performances ranked equal to over half the other players.

The story began, as the *People* explained, 'innocently enough'. Layne went to an evening match at Mansfield and got into conversation with Gauld, who later brought up the subject of betting and persuaded Layne to have a go at contacting two other Wednesday players with a view to fixing a game. Gauld said later that he did this because he thought no one would ever suspect a First Division game of being rigged.

Each of the trio staked £50 for their bets and Gauld then arranged with his contacts for Lincoln to lose at home to Brentford and York to lose at Oldham. As was usual, none of the players were ever told which were the other games Gauld had fixed.

The three match bet worked but some of the bookmakers were suspicious and refused to pay out in full, so Gauld's winnings were about £1000 less than they should have been. As a result the Wednesday trio received only £100 on top of their stake money.

Layne was absolutely distraught when Gabbert confronted him on the matter and he soon confessed. He told the *People* that during half-time at the Ipswich match his manager had torn him off a strip for playing badly. 'After that, I give you my word, I really did play my best', said Layne. He also swore that that had been the only match he had thrown.

'When I think back – why, when I was a kid I used to pray every night that one day I would play for Sheffield Wednesday . . . I suppose that's all over now.'

Swan later admitted his guilt also. But he claimed, as Ken Thomson had a year before, that he had not deliberately played badly. 'It was money for jam', he told the *People*. 'As it turned out I didn't have to do anything to lose the match. Ipswich got an early goal and that was that.' But he realized the seriousness of his situation. 'What's going to happen to us now? This could mean the end of football for all of us.'

From that week until the final court case in January 1965 the glittering careers of Swan, Kay and Layne would be held agonisingly in the balance. They were suspended on full pay by their clubs but they played no football and knew that life bans might result.

On the Monday evening after the news had broken Wednesday had a home game against Tottenham. At half time a hushed crowd heard Wednesday's secretary Eric Taylor's announcement in which he asked the supporters to 'bear with the club in this most tragic affair'. It was an emotional night at Hillsborough, alleviated only by two goals from Layne's stand-in, Derek Wilkinson. Like Bristol Rovers a year before, the club had lost two key players through no fault of their own.

More revelations followed the week after, and, to add to the torment of Swan, Kay and Layne, the new exposures only emphasized how compared with Gauld's other contacts their own involvement had been merely peripheral.

On 19 April 1964 the *People* named six more players in 'shattering disclosures'.

The best-known was Dick Beattie, the St Mirren and former Celtic and Scottish Under-23 goalkeeper who had also played for Portsmouth and Peterborough. He was described by Gabbert as the worst offender in the ring. 'He was an artist at deliberately letting in goals while appearing to have unluckily missed making a miraculous save.'

Indeed so good was Beattie at this that Peterborough had decided to buy him after he performed apparently heroically in their 3-0 defeat of Portsmouth. But that game had been fixed and Beattie soon started doing the same at Peterborough. In one rigged game, against QPR, the score was 1-1 with only a few minutes left, so Beattie contrived to throw the ball straight at a QPR player, who scored. 'It was a very near thing', Beattie remembered, 'and there was a hell of a row about it in the dressing room afterwards.'

But Beattie made one crucial error off the pitch. As if to demonstrate that Gauld's ring was hardly a slick gang of professional swindlers, Beattie once sent a registered letter to Gauld addressed 'Care of Mansfield Town'. He put his own address on the back. This envelope and a subsequent tape-recording of Beattie's voice, made by Gauld, formed the evidence used by Gabbert to persuade him to confess.

The other five players named by the *People* were: Walter Bingley, a full-back and former team-mate of Gauld's at Swindon. He also played for Bolton, Sheffield Wednesday, York and at the time of the *People*'s article, Halifax Town.

Jackie Fountain, a wing-half and another former Swindon player who started at Sheffield United. He was now with York City.

Ron Howells, also a wing-half, who had played at Portsmouth with Dick Beattie. He also appeared for Wolves, Scunthorpe and now Walsall.

Bert Linnecor, a utility player who began with Birmingham but was now near the end of a long career with Lincoln.

Peter Wragg, an inside-forward who played with four Yorkshire clubs, Rotherham, Sheffield United, York and now Bradford City, where he was the captain.

Although Bingley, Linnecor and Wragg were not subsequently

prosecuted, the fact that their names were listed in the *People* was a serious blow to their reputations. But these five were merely the unlucky ones, almost randomly caught out on the strength of Gauld's evidence. Howells, for example, said that there had been three or four others involved when he was at Scunthorpe, and there was no way of knowing if Gauld might have been trying to shelter certain other players.

It was also true that few of the named players knew of the others' involvement. Gauld had always kept the identity of his contacts at each club a secret from the others, and it was revealed that there were several players who knew of the ring's activities and independently placed bets accordingly, but did not actually participate or help throw matches. One Southampton player in this position told the *People*, 'The only thing I was sorry about was that they didn't let me in on it.'

On April 26 Gabbert changed his angle slightly. That week the *People* printed the story of how five Mansfield players had allegedly clubbed together to bribe Hartlepools in a vital Fourth Division promotion match.

Mansfield were fighting for fourth place with Gillingham, whereas Hartlepools were firmly rooted at the foot of the division. Gabbert claimed that the five Mansfield players, one of whom later became a manager, had arranged to 'secure' the match on their way up to the North East.

Their contact at Hartlepools was Ken Thomson, and although the game began badly for Mansfield, who were soon 2-0 down, they fought their way back and in the end won 4-3. After the whistle, claimed Gabbert, one of the Mansfield players ran over, ostensibly to shake hands with a Hartlepools player but really in order to place £10 in his hand. Subsequently the *People* named four of the five Hartlepools players allegedly involved, and one of the Mansfield men, Sammy Chapman, was suspended by his club.

Armed with confessions from some of the men involved, the *People* called this exposure 'the worst shock of all'. Yet as we have seen in previous chapters, if we are to believe the claims of several players this kind of end-of-season arrangement was apparently quite common, and would certainly not have shocked people in the game as much as the betting ring articles. Inevitably the *People* demanded that Mansfield should be sent down from the Third Division, but as we saw in the Enoch West case, even if corruption was proven demotion would have been unfair to all the honest players at the club.

After this latest disclosure the League conducted its own enquiry into the affair but found much of the *People*'s evidence to be questionable. One of the players mentioned in the article as playing cards on the team coach, for example, was known never to play. The match also went contrary to expectations. Hartlepools had taken the lead, and one of the players accused of being involved in the arrangement actually scored twice. But later he allegedly told the People, 'Plenty of clubs get together on promotion and relegation, don't they?'

So although the People claimed to have confessions, the club denied everything, and apart from Chapman's suspension no further action was taken. However, three men's careers in League football did end prematurely while three others played on, some with great succcess.

Meanwhile Jimmy Gauld had told the People all he was going to tell, and so his part in the investigation came to an end. For services rendered over the course of the previous seven months, during which he worked almost full time in the People's pay, Gauld received £7000 plus a few expenses. By the standard of the day it was hardly a vast amount, considering the extensive publicity and coverage gained by the newspaper as a result of Gauld's activities – not to mention increased sales of 300,000 more copies every week – but to outsiders it appeared to be a fortune, and proof alone that Gauld cared only for money.

On Saturday, 2 May 1964 Gauld's involvement with football, such as it was, also came to an end. In his absence an FA commission in Sheffield debarred him permanently from football or football management.

The following day the People printed some of his parting words. For the previous three weeks Gauld had been hiding out in Paris, but he was now ready to speak to the police, whom he had avoided as long as he was in the pay of the newspaper.

'If I could get a year's imprisonment and have the whole thing forgotten I would go inside gladly', said Gauld. 'I wouldn't even ask to see my wife and kids first. I've always reckoned that I am a bit of a hard man, but the strain of waiting and not knowing has proved too much for me. I'm a nervous wreck.

'I know there will be a lot of people gunning for me. Players who say I've ratted on them . . . the newspapers . . . the bookmakers, to say nothing of the police . . . but I want to get it all over with once and for all. Then I can forget about it and start to build a new life for the wife and kids.'

For one of Gauld's contacts however, it was too late. Joe Hancock, one of the bookmakers involved in the syndicate, was so frightened of prosecution that a few days before Gauld's statement he drowned himself.

On Monday May 4 Jimmy Gauld was interviewed by two Detective Superintendents of the CID, who had already received all the evidence accumulated by the People. A month later the papers went to the

Director of Public Prosecutions, and from that moment there can hardly have been a footballer or supporter in the land who was not waiting with bated breath to see who would be summonsed and what punishment might befall the guilty.

That most of the named players were guilty seemed indisputable. They had, after all, been the subject of one of the most blatant trials by newspaper ever witnessed in this country.

Indeed this, and other issues arising from the affair aroused several perplexing questions, and Roy Mason, MP for Barnsley, asked most of them. Continually pressing the Government and particularly the Attorney General to take action on football bribery, Mason twice criticized the police for 'the ineffectiveness of their piecemeal investigations'. He also pressed the Home Secretary on whether Fixed Odds betting was socially desirable. Did it make bribery much easier? The Government fended off his questions, except to say in one instance that they did not feel that raising the number of matches for a Fixed Odds bet above the minimum of three would be 'appropriate or effective' in dealing with the problem.

But Mason did not give up, and he was joined in the House by Stoke's MP Ellis Smith, who urged the Home Office to pursue the investigations, particularly in view of the forthcoming 1966 World Cup. The scandal, he told the House, had 'cast a black cloud of suspicion over the whole sport'.

Mason added, pointedly, that the bribery ring could have been 'unearthed and cleared up twelve months ago' had it not been for 'the rapid and dangerous growth of cheque-book journalism . . . (which) is discouraging key witnesses from giving evidence to the police . . .'

In theory this criticism of the People's methods was quite valid. The newspaper had after all paid a man to withhold evidence from the police.

In practice the People had no choice but to operate in the way it did. Alan Hardaker and the League had apparently shown themselves to be incapable of finding the evidence needed to expose men like Gauld. Even accepting the fact that none of the Management Committee were trained detectives it is still hard to believe that so many suspects, Gauld included, managed to evade conviction for so long, especially before the People's first disclosures in April 1963. Indeed Hardaker played the whole affair down so much in public that he seemed to treat the allegations almost contemptuously, which of course in reality he did not, while in private he went so far as to ask for legal advice on the possibility of banning the People's reporters from every football ground in the League.

Hardaker's main objection to the People's investigation was almost certainly that it threatened to destroy football's already shaky reputation. Even in 1964 violence was beoming a worrying feature of the game, both on and off the pitch. Gates were dropping and the entertainment value of soccer was in frequent question, whilst players were at the same time enjoying the highest level of wages and freedom ever known in League history. Adverse publicity in the run-up to the World Cup was the last thing English football needed.

Nor did the People relent. Even as the proceedings against Gauld and nine others began at Mansfield Magistrates court in September 1964, Gabbert launched a third series of revelations on September 13.

This time the starting-off point was alleged drug-taking at Goodison Park, home of the League champions Everton. Unknown to the directors, alleged the People, pep-pills had been in regular use among the Everton players. One, the former goalkeeper Albert Dunlop, had become an addict and after losing his place in the team had tried to commit suicide. Dunlop recalled in the People being so deeply in a stupor during one game that after the final whistle he stayed on the pitch and dived at the feet of a St John's Ambulance man.

The series of articles also contained a strong element of bribery. On September 20 and 27 Dunlop claimed in the People that Everton players had contributed to a bribes kitty in order to win important games in the weeks before winning the championship. Again the device used for extracting confessions was a hidden tape-recorder, with Dunlop playing the same part as Gauld.

One bribery attempt was dismissed by the man alleged to have made it as 'just a joke'. But Everton were furious at the allegations, conducted their own enquiry and soon after issued statements denying everything (these statements came from an Everton director we first met in Chapter Seven as the legal officer of the PPA, Mr E. Holland Hughes).

Michael Gabbert was not therefore the most popular man in English football circles. Indeed he claims that after the last series of articles a private detective was assigned to tail him for three months in an attempt to find some irregularities in his own personal and professional life.

Tony Kay reported the People to the Press Council, but he failed to get any satisfaction. The Council's statement in July 1965 said, 'The payment of informers, the tape-recording of conversations and the setting of traps are unsavoury methods of getting information. But their use is justified it it is the only way in which the fraudulent and scandalous can be unmasked; and they are indeed methods which are used by the police in the detection of crime.'

Further support for the People came from Francis Williams. Writing in the New Statesman in May 1964, Williams stressed the legal risks taken by the newspaper in naming so many players. 'The prospect of staggering legal damages' was, he wrote, 'appalling'. Yet despite the exposures, and in vindication of Gabbert's approach, the *People* received only one writ and that was for a matter unconnected with the main allegations. Having gone through their 'trial by newspaper' the players could have taken libel action, but none of them did.

Unpleasant though its methods had been, was the *People* also justified in withholding evidence from the police until it first went to print with the story? Williams considered that it was arguable whether the police would have acted so assiduously if those first revelations had not been printed and thus the public's anger aroused.

So, he concluded, the *People* was worthy of praise for acting in the best traditions of a campaigning newspaper, a role which he suggested other papers might also adopt to their advantage. The *People*'s 'sensational prose style, tailored to a mass audience, should not disguise the hard, careful work it puts into investigating'.

To his credit Alan Hardaker also praised the role of the *People*. In his autobiography, written thirteen years later, he wrote, 'The Sunday newspaper dug its considerable teeth into the matter, and although they used methods which raised many a righteous eyebrow, I do not think they could have done the job any other way. It is impossible to handle muck without getting your hands a little dirty.'

More praise came from the *Daily Sketch*. 'By revealing the whole story . . . the *People* newspaper had performed a valuable service to British football.'

But had Gabbert revealed the whole story?

In common with many others he believes otherwise. As Roy Mason warned the House of Commons, 'Only a third of this iceberg has reared its head.' Alan Hardaker reckoned that for every player caught there were another twenty who escaped conviction owing to a lack of evidence. Gabbert estimated that about a hundred players were involved, and that in addition to Gauld's mainly Northern syndicate there was another just as big operating in the South and South Wales. None of this second group was ever convicted.

In addition, as the tapes gathered by Gauld revealed at Mansfield Magistrates court – where after some debate they were ruled as admissible evidence, one of the first times this ever happened – it was not only players who were involved. One of Gauld's contacts had been offered an £80 bribe by a club director. Other information showed that a club trainer was also implicated.

But what of the ten players now enduring the critical attention of the nation?

After the committal proceedings in Mansfield all ten were sent to trial at Nottingham assizes, where again the *People*'s methods were strongly challenged. But in answer to a comment that the *People* was 'the nastiest and most caddish of newspapers' Mr Justice Lawton replied that whether or not that was true, 'Rather a lot of British people seem to like it, don't they?' Counsel for the defence said that the jury was being asked to substitute real justice with a trial by a newspaper, while Gabbert defended his use of tapes by saying they were a trap into which only the guilty could fall.

Gauld was described as 'an unpleasant rogue' and the 'spider in the centre of the web'. But there was sympathy for those only involved marginally. Peter Swan, for example, had never even seen or spoken to Gauld until they were together at Mansfield Magistrates Court. At the Nottingham trial Justice Lawton said, 'For £100 Kay has finished what is probably one of the greatest careers in football. He is virtually finished in this country, and I am told in any other.' He would now have to leave his Everton club house and give up his part-time jobs as a steward and an amateur coach. 'He was tempted once, and fell', said the judge.

Considering that Million and Willians had received only small fines for their part in the bribes ring, Peter Swan, Tony Kay and David Layne suffered heavy punishments. Each were given four months imprisonment.

Three players received six month sentences; Sammy Chapman, formerly of Mansfield and Portsmouth, Ron Howells, and Ken Thomson, who had already started his teacher's training course.

Dick Beattie's sentence was nine months, Brian Phillips and Jack Fountain received fifteen months and finally, the ringleader, Jimmy Gauld was sent to gaol for four years and ordered to pay £5000 costs.

Before sentencing him Judge Lawton told Gauld, 'Your crime has been great. It is my duty to pass a sentence on you to make it clear to all evil-minded people in all branches of sport that this type of activity is a crime and a serious crime ... You are responsible for the ruin of footballers of the distinction of Kay and Swan and you have ruined the life of an intelligent man like Thomson.'

But Lawson's judgement was not the end of this sad and sordid affair. As Swan, Kay and Layne played together for Thorp Arch Open Prison football team, to the delight of the soccer-mad governor, the FA was preparing to deal with the players on their release. No one expected clemency, but of all the ten, Swan, Kay and Layne were the only ones still in their prime with a potentially lucrative career in the balance.

All three were banned for life within days of their leaving prison, as were Beattie, Fountain, Chapman and Howells. Gauld, Thomson and Phillips were already banned. There were pleas for consideration from as high up as the House of Lords, where Lord Willis asked the Government to intercede on the players' behalf. Since the World Cup was so near, he suggested, was it not a good thing 'to show some clemency, declare an amnesty, and give these young men a chance to fight their way back to the profession they adorned so long?'

It was a valid point. If a judge had seen fit to punish these men with prison sentences, was that not enough? They served their terms, and like any other individuals leaving prison had a right to rehabilitate themselves. But now the FA was barring them from the one profession which above all offered them a chance to reform. For sure not all of the ten wished to return to football; some were too old and wanted to start new lives. But for those who did wish to go back to the game, either as a player or coach – even if it was only to train youngsters – the FA's ban was a bitter pill to swallow after months in prison. However guilty they were, never let it be forgotten that to these men football was the only way of life they knew, and now they were barred even from a Sunday afternoon kickaround with a local pub side.

'I never cried so much in my life', said Tony Kay, remembering the moment he was told of his ban.

'The FA had to do something', said Peter Swan long after these events, 'but we never thought they'd stop us playing football.' He and David Layne hoped to carry on playing in perhaps another country, and there was a chance to go over to the States where soccer was not entirely affiliated to the world body, FIFA.

But this never happened, and for the stars of 1964, 1965 signalled the beginning of a life forever tinged with sadness and regret. Peter Swan drifted from job to job, recognized wherever he went. His wife received abusive telephone calls and his children were baited at school. But he never lost hope that one day the authorities would relent, and so every year he put himself through the same training routines he had followed as a player. He trained regularly with David Layne, and occasionally went to watch his beloved Sheffield Wednesday, but from the terraces only.

Tony Kay stayed in Liverpool after his release from prison, and for a short while became a bookmaker, ironically. His life, he told journalist Arthur Hopcraft in 1967, was 'just going round in circles. Getting nowhere'. But he also still trained regularly, and using a different name played in casual matches, always keeping an eye out for men with cameras.

In 1966, the year that Swan and Kay might possibly have been part of an England squad preparing for the World Cup, there were further attempts to persuade the FA to relent.

The most conspicuous was a letter to *The Times*, signed by E.

Holland Hughes, Joe Mercer, Matt Busby, Denis Compton, Ted Dexter, Lord Willis, Malcolm Musgrove (Chairman of the PFA), Cliff Lloyd and Eric Moonman MP. It was argued once more that although the players had all been properly punished, 'We do feel however that the time has come for review.' There was, said the letter, a very different degree of guilt in all the cases. Some of the players had been 'quite clearly duped and misled by stronger and more vicious personalities'.

The FA was urged 'to give at least some of these young men some hope that they will be permitted, perhaps on terms of probation, to re-enter their profession before it is too late for them to do so'.

This plea was focused primarily on the cases of Swan, Kay and Layne. Almost everyone seemed to have forgotten about Esmond Million and Keith Williams, both banned for life for offences no greater than those of the more famous trio.

Not until 1968 did the FA review the bans, but in the end they concluded that although in future mandatory life suspensions could be changed to *sine die* bans, this change of rule was not retrospective. And so the former players grew older, and their hopes receded even further.

Three years passed, three seasons more were lost to them. Then in 1971 there was an unexpected glimmer of hope. The FA Council amended its rules to allow banned players the right of appeal after seven years. But would the players win their appeals?

Brian Phillips, now aged forty, was the first to try. On 7 September 1971 he faced an FA commission in Leicester, and he was successful. Eight years of pain and frustration were over. Too old to play Phillips might have been, but he still craved involvement with the game, and within eleven years he had achieved the cherished dream of every manager in the country. In 1982, as manager of the Notts Alliance amateurs, Rainworth Miners Welfare, Brian Phillips led his team out at Wembley for the Final of the FA Vase, in front of 12,500 fans. We need hardly guess the powerful emotions he experienced that day . . . back in the fold!

Peter Swan shared some proud moments too. Having successfully appealed against his ban on 19 June 1972, together with David Layne he returned to Hillsborough at the age of thirty-five. 'To say I am relieved is putting it mildly', said Swan at the time. 'The shackles have been taken off at last. I can already feel the grass growing under my feet. I cannot wait to get back.'

The Wednesday directors welcomed both players back, while manager Derek Dooley pledged to give them every chance to re-establish themselves. But even Dooley was surprised at how well Swan re-adjusted after his eight-year lay off. As Gerry Harrison wrote in The Times, 'The 1972 version of Swan is exactly the same as the 1964 edition – the same slim, gangling movements, the same close-marking and aerial supremacy, the same brief shorts, with the shirt won outside and the same hairstyle.'

Tears of joy were shed when Swan was told he would play in Wednesday's opening match of the season against Fulham, in which 23,000 fans gave him a welcome he will always remember. A few weeks later Dooley offered Swan a year's contract, which he signed without reading the details. He was prepared to play for nothing.

David Layne was thirty-three when he went back to Hillsborough, but an injury delayed his comeback and after a few reserve games he went to Hereford, where he made four further appearances without success.

Had Layne kept on playing between 1964 and 1972, and carried on scoring at the same rate as between 1958–64, even allowing for some loss of form and injuries he would have almost certainly scored a career total of between 290 and 340 League goals, more than goalscoring legends like Nat Lofthouse and Charlie Buchan and not far behind Jimmy Greaves. Such was the measure of the player destroyed by Gauld's betting ring.

Peter Swan did not score once in his 273 games for Sheffield Wednesday. He had to wait until he joined Bury for the 1973–74 season for his two and only League goals. By then he was thirty-seven and after thirty-five games for Bury he turned to non-League football, still keen to make up for the lost years.

For Peter Swan the proudest moment came in 1975. As player-manager of Northern Premier League side Matlock Town he won an FA Challenge Trophy winners medal after leading his side to a 4-0 victory over Scarborough at Wembley. His last previous appearance at Wembley had been twenty-three years earlier in May 1962, for England in a 3-1 win over Switzerland.

From Matlock, Swan moved to Worksop, then Buxton and back to Matlock again, where he became a life member. His physique hardly changed at all over the years, and at the age of forty-eight he was still playing occcasional charity games.

Sammy Chapman's playing career was already over by 1964, but as soon as his ban was lifted he too returned to the game, first with Peterborough and Crewe and most recently as a coach with Wolverhampton Wanderers. In common with Phillips and Swan, Chapman has sons who have also gone into the game, both as juniors with Wolves.

Of the other men caught up in this, the biggest, and in many ways the saddest scandal ever to affect British football, Esmond Million eventually emigrated to Canada, where he became active in professional ice hockey; Tony Kay emigrated to Spain and had no further involvement in football, and Ken Thomson, the man who wanted money to finance his studies, died prematurely of a heart attack on a golf course in the North East.

Michael Gabbert, the young journalist in charge of the *People*'s investigation, did not stay with the newspaper for long. After winning the Hannen Swaffer Award for Reporter of the Year in 1964 Gabbert moved to the *People*'s rival newspaper, *News of the World*, where he made his mark soon after by investigating drug abuse among pop stars such as the Beatles and Rolling Stones. He was most recently editor of the *Sunday Independent* newspaper in Plymouth.

Gabbert's co-reporter in the years 1963–64, Peter Campling, continued as a football correspondent, finishing his career at the *Sun* in 1984.

Jimmy Gauld slipped into obscurity remarkably soon after his trial, neither sought after nor seen by his nine fellow defendants. He never appealed against his lifetime ban, and curiously his name was seldom heard whenever the betting scandal was mentioned thereafter. That burden still belongs to Swan, Kay and Layne, the three big stars who had furthest to fall.

But we should not remember only the men who stood in the dock.

In the final article on football corruption, in January 1965, the *People*'s editor Sam Campbell bitterly attacked the League and the FA for not pursuing their investigations soon enough or hard enough, even after they had been given the names of all those allegedly involved. He berated the League for not even sending a representative to the two court hearings in Mansfield and Nottingham. Neither had the League nor the FA asked his newspaper for the secret tapes connected with Gauld or the Everton drugs and bribery case.

In short, Campbell was asking the public to consider why these scandals had gone on for so long, why some of them may well continue, and why so many guilty men were allowed to go unpunished? The League always claimed a lack of evidence, but how assiduously did it seek out that evidence?

Not surprisingly we cannot answer these questions faithfully. We too suffer from a lack of evidence. But the very fact that Campbell's concluding comments should have posed such questions implied that if Swan, Kay, Layne and the others were guilty then perhaps the very game of football itself was also guilty, of improperly guarding the interests of the vast majority of its followers and participants. As one First Division manager once remarked, however tenuous or apparently far-fetched some of the allegations concerning corruption seemed to be, if they were not investigated fully no-one would know if they were true or not. He was one of several men who asked the League to clarify the situation, but it never did.

Several footballers of the succeeding generation have since said that the prison sentences and life bans of 1963–65 shocked the profession so deeply that there was very little chance of such corruption continuing. Other commentators have added that however tragic the fate of the convicted players, and however thoughtful the intentions of those who sought to end their bans, as Arthur Hopcraft wrote in 1968, 'A court conviction on a charge of fixing football is not just a nasty blotch on the wall, but a jagged hole in the fabric. Two or three more like that and the whole structure falls in rubble.'

Clearly the FA had to act as it did, and hope that those players who had been involved but escaped punishment would be deterred from repeating their crimes thereafter. Many of them enjoyed successful and long careers while the likes of Swan, Kay and Layne were in disgrace.

That was partly the result of chance, partly a problem of finding evidence. But if bribery in British football was suspected again, would the current administrators of the game be seen to be more effective than those in the early 1960s? And would clubs behave as Bristol Rovers did, putting the good of the game before their own, vital demands?

We can only hope that they would, having learnt the lesson of their predecessors.

Jimmy Gauld's betting ring may now be just a part of footballing history, but if we conclude that only those players who went into the dock were the blameworthy ones, we lose entirely the significance of the People's investigation.

12
Could it Happen Now?

IN the introduction to this book I wrote that *Soccer in the Dock* was first and foremost a history of one small, but important aspect of British football. There is one final question which goes beyond that brief and has to be tackled, if not answered entirely, before we allow soccer out of the dock.

Is there any bribery or match rigging in British football today?

Firstly, as far as corruption involving betting is concerned it is highly unlikely, simply because the betting system which prevailed in Jimmy Gauld's era no longer exists. In fact Fixed Odds betting more or less collapsed in 1964, not as a result of the bribery scandal but as a direct consequence of government taxation. Once the Fixed Odds bet became subject to a tax of twenty-five per cent it no longer attracted the vast number of punters it enjoyed during its peak in the late 1950s and early 1960s. When the tax subsequently rose to thirty-three per cent and then forty per cent, Fixed Odds disappeared completely.

In the 1970s a new form of betting on football emerged, called Individual Odds betting, in which each match in a group – with a minimum of three in a group – was given separate odds, similar to race horses. The only individual games one can now bet on are cup games and internationals. (Individual Odds are still, however, often erroneously referred to as Fixed Odds.)

Technically it would still be possible to rig matches in order to win these modern bets. But, the only real chance of making a large winning would be to place a large stake, and with players' wages so much higher nowadays the relative demands of a 'bent' footballer would be high enough to make such a gamble comparatively unprofitable.

There are other obstacles. When Gauld's ring was in operation, British betting shops were in their infancy and undergoing several teething problems. Nowadays, with modern communications and greater awareness it is a simple and quick process for any outlet to contact a central office with full details of any suspicious or unusually high bets.

It is just possible that a betting coup could be perpetrated once, perhaps by rigging a cup game, but thereafter it could be easily prevented. With betting on football now only two to three per cent of bookmakers' total business, and the average stake on an Individual

Odds bet being £2.50, the large scale wager soon raises alarm bells.

But the betting ring of 1960–63 was very much an isolated case within the greater context of football corruption. By far the most persistent form of match rigging has been tied up with promotion and relegation issues. Does this second form of bribery still occur?

In the course of this book we have come across several comments from former professionals, the gist of which is, 'It happens all the time.' Even bearing in mind the fact that footballers have often made apparently shocking comments in exchange for newspaper fees, we should consider that if indeed it was common for teams to get together to arrange end of season matches between 1900 and 1965, why should it be any different today? After all, there is now considerably more money at stake, the advantages and disadvantages of promotion and relegation are probably even greater now in such terms as gate receipts, wages and television coverage, and above all, human nature is human nature.

The short answer is, we do know that attempts have been made to rig games, but we have no concrete proof that any matches have actually been fixed successfully. We must simply be aware that these things happened in the past and they could happen again.

The long answer is that the best means of detecting such corruption – the football grapevine – is a more sophisticated network than it has ever been before. Extended newspaper, radio and television coverage gives the press, public and fellow footballers a degree of intimacy with the game that was unthinkable before 1965.

Furthermore, the fate of those footballers caught up in the betting ring in 1964 had an enormous impact on the profession. A lifetime ban from the FA was one risk, but a prison sentence was another, wholly new element. Before 1964 not one footballer had ever been gaoled during his career for attempting to rig a match. Thus when the Wolves player Bernard Shaw told the *Daily Mirror* in 1977 that he had been approached with a view to throwing a game he said, 'They picked the wrong man coming to me. They forgot I was brought up in Sheffield round the corner from Tony Kay.'

Shaw's reaction was one of several quoted in what the *Mirror* billed as 'the most explosive soccer story of the decade', in which various allegations concerning attempts to rig matches were made.

The story first saw the light of day in the *Sunday People* (where else?) on 17 September 1972, a few months after it was alleged that a middleman had approached a Wolves player in the hope of making sure Leeds would win their last match of the 1971–72 season. Had Leeds beaten Wolves in that game they could have won the Double, but instead the Wolves team were so upset by the approach, and allegedly several others during the game, that they played with extra determination and beat Leeds 2-1. Despite numerous statements in the *People*, a Football League enquiry and a reference to the Director of Public Prosecutions, no further action was taken.

Five years later and a few weeks after the former Leeds manager Don Revie had gone to the Middle East, having left his position as England manager under controversial circumstances, the *Mirror* re-opened the case on 6 September 1977. In addition to the allegations concerning the Wolves match the *Mirror* revealed others going back to 1962, all related to alleged attempts to fix the results of important games. Don Revie issued a writ for libel against the newspaper, and although this was not pursued he was successful in a High Court action to invalidate a ten year ban imposed upon him by the FA.

It was all a far cry from the days of Billy Meredith and Barney Travers, and a very different outcome from that of Enoch West's four year legal battle to clear his name. After the Manchester United v Liverpool scandal in 1915 *Athletic News* said this: 'We have no hesitation in saying that 99 games out of every 100 games are honest contests.'

I have no hesitation in saying that 999 games out of 1000 are honest contests. Yet purely on the consistent pattern of evidence we have seen in this book, it would be naive to believe that match rigging has not happened since 1965, or that it will not happen again.

Equally, we would be wrong for this realization to cloud our overall appreciation and love for the game. Just because a few apples are likely to turn out rotten does not mean we should avoid eating the fruit ever again.

Never let it be forgotten either that despite all the scandals, the headlines, the broken men and the shattered illusions; despite all the times that soccer has found itself in the dock, the game still survives, loved and played by honest people and watched over by caring supporters.

For that reason alone we ignore some of the events in this book at our peril.

Bibliography

BOOKS

Appleton, Arthur	Hotbed of Soccer (London: Rupert Hart-Davis 1960)
Creek F. N. S.	A History of the Corinthians F.C. (London: Longmans, Green and Co. 1933)
Fabian A. H. and Green G. (eds)	Association Football (London: Caxton 1960)
Farnsworth, Keith	Wednesday! (Sheffield City Libraries 1982)
Football Association	Yearly handbooks and minutes
Ford, Trevor	I Lead the Attack (London: Stanley Paul 1956)
Golesworthy, M.	Encyclopedia of Association Football (London: Robert Hale 1956–76)
Grayson, Edward	Sport and the Law (Sunday Telegraph 1978) Corinthian-Casuals and Cricketers (Ian Harrap at the Pallant Press 1983)
Green, G.	History of the F.A. (London: Naldrett Press 1953)
Hardaker, Alan	Hardaker of the League (London: Pelham 1977)
Harding, John	Football Wizard: the story of Billy Meredith (Breedon 1985)
Hill, Jimmy	Striking for Soccer (London: Peter Davies 1961)
Hopcraft, Arthur	The Football Man (London: Collins 1968)
Hugman, Barry	Rothmans Football League Players Records 1946 –81 (Rothmans 1981)
Mason, Tony	Association Football and English Society 1863–1915 (Eastbourne: Harvester 1980)
McMillan, Alan	Showing in Black and White Only (East Stirlingshire F.C. 1981)
Rollin, J., Williams, T. and Dunk, P. (eds)	Rothmans Football Yearbook (London: Queen Anne Press 1970–85)
Soar, Phil	The Hamlyn A–Z of British Football Records (London: Hamlyn 1981)
Sharpe Ivan	40 Years in Football (London: 1952)
Sutcliffe, C. E.	Story of the Football League (Preston 1938)
Thornton, Eric	Meredith to Mercer – and the Cup (London: Robert Hale 1969)
Turner, Dennis	A History of Fulham 1879–1979 (Fulham 1979)
Wagg Stephen	The Football World (Brighton: Harvester Press 1984)
Wall, Sir F. W.	Fifty Years in Football (London: Cassell 1935)
Walvin, James	The People's Game (London: Allen Lane 1975)
Ward, Andrew	Manchester City Story (Breedon Books 1984)

NEWSPAPERS AND PERIODICALS

Athletic News
Burnley Gazette
Bury Guardian
Clydebank Press
Daily Dispatch
Daily Express
Daily Mail
Daily Mirror
Daily Sketch
Falkirk Herald
Football Gazette and Telegraph (South Shields)
Football Monthly
Glasgow Herald
Leicester Evening Mail
Leicester Mercury
Manchester Evening Chronicle
Manchester Evening News
Midland Daily Telegraph
New Statesman
News Chronicle
News of the World
North Eastern Daily Gazette
Sporting Chronicle
Sporting Life
Sports Argus (Birmingham)
Sunday Chronicle
Sunday Dispatch
Sunday People
Sunderland Echo
The Times
Time Out
Western Independent
Western Mail
Yorkshire Evening Post

8/5